Sexua
offen
the c
and t

Th
ing ra
disor
challe

De
will b
on se

Sam:

Anne

Sexual Offences

Law and Context

Samantha Pegg and Anne Davies

Routledge
Taylor & Francis Group

LONDON AND NEW YORK

First published 2016
by Routledge
2 Park Square, Milton Park, Abingdon, Oxon, OX14 4RN

and by Routledge
711 Third Avenue, New York, NY 10017

Routledge is an imprint of the Taylor & Francis Group, an informa business

British Library Cataloguing in Publication Data
A catalogue record for this book is available from the British Library

Library of Congress Cataloging-in-Publication Data
Pegg, Samantha, author.
  Sexual offences : law and context / Samantha Pegg and Anne Davies.
    pages cm
  Includes bibliographical references and index.
  ISBN 978-1-138-80606-1 (hbk) — ISBN 978-1-138-80607-8 (pbk) —
ISBN 978-1-315-75185-6 (ebk)   1. Sex crimes—Great Britain.   I. Davies,
Anne, 1947– author.   II. Title.
  KD7975.P44 2016
  345.42'0253—dc23
  2015031457

ISBN: 978-1-138-80606-1 (hbk)
ISBN: 978-1-138-80607-8 (pbk)
ISBN: 978-1-315-75185-6 (ebk)

Typeset in Times New Roman
by Apex CoVantage, LLC

Printed and bound by CPI Group (UK) Ltd, Croydon, CR0 4YY

Contents

Table of Cases

Table of Legislation

Introduction

This is a textbook on sexual offences and offending for students of law, history and criminology and for those of other disciplines interested in how the sexual offences of England and Wales have developed and been shaped by contemporary concerns regarding offending behaviour. There has perhaps never been a more pertinent time to be exploring sexual offences and offending. In recent years the proliferation of prosecutions for child abuse images, historic child sexual abuse, criminal justice responses to rape, the sexual abuse of children through grooming and the sentencing and managing of sexual offenders in the community has generated significant concern. These are matters that have not just occupied the substantive law but society as a whole, with policy and practice placed under the media and academic gaze.

We suggest that these considerations of the efficacy of our law and its systems need to be considered in their fullest context. We cannot accept claims of faulty law or legal systems or improvements to the same if we do not consider the history of the law in this area. The historical backdrop to offences and how they have been presented and shaped by media attention have too often been subsidiary issues to studies of sexual offending. This text then looks to these perspectives to drive our understanding of sexual offences both deeper and forward.

The Book

The aim of this textbook is to give all interested parties an accessible and current analysis of sexual offences and offending. By taking in a broad range of disciplines we aim to contextualize the law, but this entails brevity and we only strive to give context to those studying the subject and direction to those who intend to address those areas discussed in further detail. As such the book seeks to put the law in context, but does not claim to be the ultimate authority; we hope students will draw upon the text as a primer for further research. Equally we do not expect our readers to be experts in jurisprudence or the law and the concepts introduced will be explained as plainly as possible. Footnotes are provided for further research and in order to update the reader – as we indicate, the law moves apace in this area.

Chapters 1 and 2 principally provide the context for the later discussions of the law. Chapter 1 looks to rationales for legal intervention into sexual matters, including reasons for legal intervention, the statistical realities of sexual offending and how moral panics have shaped legal policy. Chapter 2 considers those protected and criminalized by the law we will be addressing in the later chapters – the female, the male and the child. By addressing the historically gender-specific nature of the law this chapter examines the relevance of being female and male to the law and the relevance of the child as victim and offender, establishing a context that is central to properly understanding our current legal framework.

We then provide a linear focus on sexual offences from Chapters 3 to 6. Although we seek, as far as possible, to move sequentially through the Sexual Offences Act 2003 (SOA 2003) some offences do not fall within the ambit of the SOA 2003 – for example sadomasochism is not dealt with in the SOA 2003 as a specific sexual offence and most prostitution and pornography offences are found in other Acts – and these areas are addressed at Chapters 7 and 8. Chapter 9 touches upon the international aspects of issues raised in the preceding chapters including the broadening of our law to capture 'sex tourists'. Chapter 10 addresses how we seek to protect the public from identified sexual offenders. The final chapter brings together some of the major benefits and criticisms of the offences that have been considered to ask where we should go from here.

Criminal Offences

For those unfamiliar with criminal law here follows a short introduction to the substantive law. There are subtleties to this that we do not have the space to detail here, notably the intricacies of *mens rea* and the place of general defences for relieving criminal liability.

When we speak of the substantive law in the following chapters we mean the written law, so both statutory law and common law. This is separate from procedural rules, such as rules of evidence, or the criminal justice system in which the law operates.

For the majority of the offences discussed in this text the offences are set out in statute (Acts), although a few are common law offences – so created by the judiciary. Creating new statutory law or amending the same is quite a lengthy process. Typically an area identified for change is subject to a number of consultations, by both independent and governmental bodies. When changes to sexual offences are proposed interested parties such as Liberty, the International Union of Sex Workers, Rape Crisis, the National Association of Probation Officers, the National Society for the Prevention of Cruelty to Children and other stakeholders have a number of opportunities to respond to consultations. The Sexual Offences Act 2003 (SOA 2003) was preceded by a consultation paper *Setting the Boundaries* published in July 2000 which led to a public consultation where Government and non-Government groups (900 in all) responded to the consultation paper's 62 recommendations. The consultations were then drawn upon to produce the White Paper (a document produced by the Government setting out details of future policy) *Protecting the Public* (2002) to which interested parties once again responded. This culminated in the Sexual Offences Bill, which had to be passed by both houses of parliament and receive royal assent to become law as the SOA 2003. Part 1 of the SOA 2003 then sets out the sexual offences, Part 2 the requirements for monitoring and supervising sex offenders and Part 3 a number of general matters including jurisdiction and commencement.

The commonality to the statutory and common law offences discussed in this text is the requirement that a criminal act must have been committed and the offender must have the necessary fault element for that offence, if one is required. In law the prohibited act, consequence, omission or state of affairs is termed the *actus reus* and the fault element the *mens rea*. For example, for the offence of exposure discussed at Chapter 6 of this text a person commits an offence if he intentionally exposes his genitals, and intends that someone will see them and be caused alarm or distress. So the criminal act is the exposure of the genitals and the fault element the intention to expose and the intention that they will be seen and cause alarm or distress. The difficulty often lies in how it can be proved to the criminal standard (beyond reasonable doubt) what the defendant was thinking at the time of the act. If the defendant has not admitted to the requisite fault element then the jury may infer *mens rea* from the evidence of what actually happened, a rule enshrined in section 8 of the Criminal Justice Act 1967.

Case law interprets these offences where necessary, so it may fall to the judiciary to decide what is meant by the term "exposing" for example. These matters are decided on appeal. An appeal may, for example, be made on the ground that a trial judge has got the law wrong in his direction to the jury (a point of law) or against sentence. If the defendant appeals against a conviction from the Crown Court he can appeal on the grounds the conviction was unsafe and that may be on a point of law, fact or both.

Criminal offences are classified as summary, indictable or triable either way. Summary offences are less serious crimes and can only be tried in the Magistrates' Court without a jury. Indictable offences are more serious offences which can only be tried in the Crown Court with a judge and jury. Offences triable either way are (unsurprisingly) offences that can be tried in either the Magistrates' Court or the Crown Court, dependent upon their seriousness. Where an offence is triable either way, the magistrates decide whether it should be tried summarily or on indictment, although the accused may elect to be tried on indictment. The old distinction between felonies (serious offences) and misdemeanours (less serious offences) was abolished by the Criminal Justice Act 1967.

The Criminal Justice System

This text details the law of England and Wales and any references to "our" law must be read as a reference to that legal system. Ireland and Scotland do share and draw upon aspects of our legal system but are separate jurisdictions, with separate laws, courts and processes. Some sections of the SOA 2003 do extend into the United Kingdom and where this is the case the term UK is used to indicate this.

Our criminal justice system involves a number of important agencies, all of which play a part in deciding whether a sexual act can indeed be labelled a sexual offence. The police are of course central to our criminal justice system, recording and investigating reported offences. The police then present cases to the Crown Prosecution Service (CPS), who decide whether to take a case forward to the courts based on the evidence, the public interest and, overall, whether there is a realistic prospect of conviction. The CPS are then the gatekeepers to our criminal justice system and have been performing this role since they began operation in 1986. The importance of these bodies in shaping our conception of sexual offending should not be underestimated and Chapter 1 addresses this in some detail.

All cases the CPS remits for trial will begin in the Magistrates' Court and some, the summary offences, will end there. Others (indictable and some either way offences) may be committed for trial at the Crown Court where cases are heard by a judge and jury. This said, the majority of cases we discuss in later chapters are appeal cases, so cases that have reached either the Queen's Bench division of the High Court or, more commonly, the Court of Appeal (Criminal Division) or the Supreme Court (previously the House of Lords). These cases set precedent, i.e. law that must be applied (subject to exceptions) in the lower courts. The European Court of Human Rights also sets binding precedent for national cases and cases can be appealed to this court from our national courts if they involve a violation of the rights set out in the European Convention on Human Rights or its Protocols. More information about the structure of the courts is available at the Courts and Judiciary Tribunals website https://www.judiciary.gov.uk.

The accused person is referred to as the defendant or, if appealing against a decision, the appellant. The person offended against is usually referred to as the victim, although the term complainant is now often favoured over victim as it carries fewer problematic connotations. A case against the defendant is normally brought by the Crown. Although a prosecution can be started by a private individual, this is rare. The defendant will be represented by counsel, either a barrister or solicitor with rights of audience (the right to represent their clients in the higher courts). The complainant will not have their own counsel to represent their interests, the CPS instruct a barrister or solicitor who brings the case on behalf on the Crown and must prove the guilt of the defendant beyond reasonable doubt.

Keeping Up to Date

Law evolves rapidly – there are frequently legislative amendments, interpretations by the appeal courts, new initiatives by criminal justice agencies and pronouncements by the Government and other interested bodies that impact on how sexual offences are interpreted and pursued. Fortunately there are a number of websites and sources that can be easily accessed to follow these changes.

In terms of substantive law it is a matter of following amendments to the Acts and these, including the SOA 2003, are now remarkably easy to access through the internet at http://www.legislation.gov.uk. You may find it useful to make use of the Explanatory Notes for Acts mentioned in this text, as we have when relevant. These are remarkably helpful and often overlooked. For Acts post 1999 the responsible government department produces a commentary in plain English that can be easily accessed by clicking on the "Explanatory Notes" tab. Details of changes to the Act brought about by later pieces of legislation and changes that Act has made to other pieces of legislation are also available by clicking on "More Resources".

For case law, Lexis and Westlaw provide updates. Major changes will attract commentary from academics, which are also accessible on these sites and more widely. For governmental consultations on changes to the law, problems with existing offences and suggestions for change https://www.gov.uk is now the central repository and holds various reports, statistics and research documents that used to be scattered across different departments – some of which can still be accessed at http://www.nationalarchives.gov.uk.

The CPS http://www.cps.gov.uk are a good source of information and an important tool for understanding how these gatekeepers are making decisions about which incidences should be taken to court. Not only do they produce detailed guidance for Crown Prosecutors but guidance on how particular offences and victims should be approached.

For bodies producing independent reports outside the criminal justice system the Office for National Statistics http://www.ons.gov.uk is important for the reasons explored at Chapter 1. But other agencies such as the National Society for the Prevention of Cruelty to Children http://www.nspcc.org.uk and the Child Exploitation and Online Protection Centre https://www.ceop.police.uk and Victim Support https://www.victimsupport.org.uk also provide invaluable reports on the reality of offending.

Ad hoc reports are also produced by Governmental departments and a number of these are detailed at Chapter 1. Independent bodies are also often convened to investigate matters when particular issues arise and these are usually available from the website of the body commissioned to address the issue such as the Independent Inquiry into Child Sexual Abuse https://childsexualabuseinquiry.independent.gov.uk, the Independent Inquiry into Child Sexual Exploitation in Rotherham (1997–2013) http://www.rotherham.gov.uk/downloads/file/1407/independent_inquiry_cse_in_rotherham.

The media are also a useful source of information. Cases that do not go on to appeal are often only detailed in media reports, but as Chapter 1 makes clear, these should be treated with caution. This said, the respectable newspapers provide sound and timely discussions of offending behaviour through websites such as *The Guardian's* Criminal Justice resources http://www.theguardian.com/law/criminal-justice and the law pages of *The Times* http://www.thetimes.co.uk/tto/law.

This textbook aims to draw on all of these resources to help explain, evaluate and contextualize the law relating to sexual offences. The subject matter is sometimes challenging and can give rise to strong opinions, especially where the law appears to interfere with individual rights and freedoms. We have endeavoured to include a range of differing views, which we hope will encourage students to think further on some of these issues. We hope you find this book both interesting and informative.

Chapter 1

Social Responses and Criminalization

Introduction

The law relating to sexual offences is complex and sometimes inconsistent. It often reflects a desire to protect the vulnerable, but at other times seems to reflect a particular moral view. In later chapters of this book we consider the legitimacy of sexual offences, of state intervention into private lives, the removal of individual liberty and how the state chooses to punish those who transgress the law. In order to understand why (and whether) the state has (or should have) this right we need to briefly consider the purpose of the law and why we choose to regulate sexual behaviour.

In regulating sexual activity the law intrudes in private sexual relations. Where there is no consent to sexual activity this is not usually a contentious intrusion (although as Chapter 3 considers, consent is by no means straightforward) but for other private sexual activities such as consensual sexual activity with a relative, sexual activity with an animal or between children we need to think about whether interference can be justified.

Law does not operate in a vacuum and the 'what' and 'why' of regulation is driven by our perceptions of dangerousness; both in terms of what may be injurious to wider society and to individuals. Our responses to criminal justice policy have become increasingly important with Governmental policy increasingly called upon to respond swiftly to contemporary concerns. These concerns are shaped by our understanding of what activities pose a threat and the media plays an important role here. Most of us gain our knowledge of crime statistics, victimization, sentencing etc., from media sources and these, in turn, draw upon official sources, some more accurately than others. The reliability of these sources and how they present offending behavior needs to be carefully considered.

This chapter seeks to provide context and resources for considering the sexual offences set out in the following chapters. Of course, as the following discusses, sexuality and appropriate sexual behaviours are subject to social shifts and the law often finds it difficult to keep pace with societal norms.

What is Law?

Jurisprudence is the study of law, its theoretical underpinning, its institutions and systems. The philosophy of law is a branch of jurisprudence that seeks to answer questions such as what law is and how and whether laws can be justified. This is not of course a book about jurisprudence and we can only touch on the subject briefly, but it is important to have a basic understanding of these concepts.

So to take the central questions first; what is the law? What behaviour should amount to a criminal offence? You may think these are simple questions with straightforward answers, but the answer is dependent upon your school of thought. For example, at the more esoteric end of reasoning is natural law, which dictates that standards governing human behaviour derive from nature – both the nature of human beings and the nature of the world. Here the law is understood to be a rational but ethereal thing, easily divined, say natural lawyers, from principles universally understood to be moral and right. Consequently acts such as murder and rape are inherently understood to be immoral and wrong regardless of whether they are criminalized under state law. These principles extend into every area of regulation, as the philosopher John Locke wrote:

> The state of nature has a law of nature to govern it, which obliges every one: and reason, which is that law, teaches all mankind, who will but consult it, that being all equal and independent, no one ought to harm another in his life, health, liberty, or possessions . . .[1]

Locke was concerned with the legitimacy of state authority and the rights of the people to grant (and take away) state power. But natural law has endured with proponents such as John Finnis[2] refining and updating the concept. This said, the content of natural law is less than clear, relying on an inherent sense of knowing what is inherently right and wrong without recourse to state law.

In a similar vein, Lord Devlin suggested the law's role is to promote and enforce a public morality. In a series of debates prompted by the Report of the Departmental Committee on Homosexual Offences and Prostitution (also known as the Wolfenden Report 1957)[3] Lord Devlin argued:

> Societies disintegrate from within more frequently than they are broken up by external pressures. There is disintegration when no common morality is observed and history shows that the loosening of moral bonds is often the first stage of disintegration, so that society is justified in taking the same steps to preserve its moral code as it does to preserve its government . . . the suppression of vice is as much the law's business as the suppression of subversive activities.[4]

To Lord Devlin social cohesion was all and the law a valuable tool for suppressing unacceptable behaviour and enforcing moral norms. Despite the fact this position is somewhat dated, we will see many sexual offences are justifiable almost solely on the grounds of immorality. The power of the state to limit autonomy for its citizens' own good, also known as state or legal paternalism, has attracted many detractors, including Locke and Immanuel Kant.[5] Despite paternalism having something of a bad name due to its linguistic roots in patriarchalism (the power of the monarch over his or her subjects), it does justify interference most would find acceptable. For example, we have an age of consent below which children cannot legally consent to sexual activity, a concept generally accepted in society.

Where natural and moral lawyers suggest certain values transcend state law, legal positivism suggests law is, quite simply, socially constructed. Proponents such as Hans Kelsen[6] and H.L.A. Hart[7] sought to divorce law from morality and the legal positivist looks to the legitimacy of the law, whether it has been enacted by a legislator, jurist or other authority granted the power of law making, and is unconcerned with the moral legitimacy of that law. This is an attractive theory, making law easy to identify (it is what is 'on the books') and is subject to evolution through time, culture and moral shifts. However, detractors have argued an acceptance of 'pure law' gives legitimacy to laws of regimes we would argue are morally abhorrent – such as slavery (which was legal in most of the British Empire until 1833) and the acts of Nazi Germany. For example, the Nuremberg laws of 1935 in Nazi Germany excluded German Jews from citizenship and prohibited them from marrying or having sexual relationships with non-Jews. These laws laid the foundation for subsequent legislation that denied Jews basic human rights, culminating in the Holocaust.

How then do we find a more socially acceptable definition of law? Perhaps we should turn to Utilitarianism, the philosophy that sought to define the law by legitimizing legal principles for the benefit of the majority. Jeremy Bentham posited the true goal of society ought to be the greatest happiness of the greatest number and argued no action is wrong in itself; its evil arises from its consequences and there can be no justification in prohibiting an act unlikely to produce harm. This idea was developed and modified by John Stuart Mill, in his essay *On Liberty* (1859), who argued that there are limits to the right of a state to interfere in the life and conduct of a citizen and his/her own good, either physical or moral is not a good enough reason to interfere – liberty is the important thing – the only purpose for which power can be rightly exercised over any member of society, against his or her will, is to prevent harm to others. Our law continues to be heavily influenced by utilitarian principles, as *Setting the Boundaries* (the consultation paper on sexual offences published in 2000) confirmed:

> Our other key guiding principle was that the criminal law should not intrude unnecessarily into the private lives of adults. Applying the principle of harm means that most consensual activity between adults in private should be their own affair, and not that of the criminal law.[8]

Despite this statement of utilitarian principle the law quite rigorously governs private sexual activity, an issue explored in the following chapters.

Utilitarianism then looks to limit state interference with activities adjudged immoral or socially unacceptable but that do not cause harm to others. This of course raises the question of what we mean by harm. If we accept harm can be more than physical and can involve social disintegration or moral degradation then it starts to look like the state can rightfully criminalize marginal and private activities that impinge on social welfare – an argument we see forcefully expressed by Lord Templeman in *Brown* (1993).[9] In *Brown* a group of homosexual men had engaged in consensual sadomasochism, including activities such as whipping, branding and piercing genitalia. None of the participants suffered injuries requiring medical treatment but the injuries amounted to bodily harm for the purposes of the Offences Against the Person Act 1861. On appeal and addressing whether it was correct for the law to intervene in cases where physical harm has been consensually inflicted, Lords Templeman, Jauncey and Lowry agreed that sadomasochism posed a threat to society that justified legal intervention.

Returning to our earlier question of how we can find a socially acceptable definition of the law we could perhaps accept the legal positivist argument that law is that which is enacted or articulated by those bodies we have given legitimacy to. The sociological view of the law supports this and further advocates that these resultant legal principles cannot be viewed in a vacuum – as an entity separate from the society they set out to regulate. The passage below is from an early attempt by Timasheff (1937), which seeks to prompt sociological investigations of the law and explains why we need to think more broadly about how the law interacts with society:

> In general, legal norms actually determine human behaviour in society: the triumph of law is the rule, its defeat in a concrete case an exception. Why is this so? What is the force of law? How does law determine human behaviour in society? What are the conditions for the efficacy or non-efficacy of legal norms- in other words, of adjusting or not adjusting human behaviour to the particular social patterns of behaviour forming law?[10]

As this extract suggests, we need to think about law in context; indeed this is the crux of this text. Here Timasheff has questioned whether the narrow and inward focus of jurisprudence is sufficient to fully understand how law operates in society. He makes an important point, one we take up ourselves in our discussions regarding changes (or a lack thereof) in behaviour. He has not been the only critic of jurisprudence. Feminist critiques of the law are also a form of sociological analysis and, in their most simplistic form, view law as an exercise of power by a stronger section of society over a weaker one. The unsatisfactory regulation of offences such as rape are often seen as indicative of patriarchal agendas that enforce and protect male rather than female interests.

What the law is is perhaps not as important as what it does, what it should do and the impact it has on society. What then is the function of the law, what is its purpose? Should it dictate behaviour or reflect and reinforce our existing values? In the field of sexuality this question becomes very important – remember we are talking about the state regulating bodily autonomy, in many cases what you can do, consensually, in the private realm.

Justifying Regulation

Sexual offences occupy an interesting position in our legal system. Though criminal offences, they are elevated to a special category of offence that may result in lengthy sentences and invasive forms of community management. The consequences for both offenders and complainants can be serious and long lasting – and the law has to strike a balance between protecting bodily integrity and preserving individual autonomy.

Any study of the criminal law will reveal that our legal system is one that preferences autonomy over state interference as our system is prohibitory, forbidding certain acts, omissions (in limited circumstances) states of affairs, circumstances and consequences. It does so in the knowledge that we can make choices about what we do and the consequences this will have – in short that we have free will. Consequently any prohibited acts coupled with a criminal state of mind can be rightfully criminalized and, as part of the same rationale, we have the right to choose not to engage in those prohibited behaviours. This is easier to understand and defend when we speak of offences such as causing grievous bodily harm, murder or criminal damage where the criminal act is usually nonconsensual and reverberates through the public realm. But when we are dealing with bodily integrity the principle of autonomy becomes contested. While there might be a measure of agreement about the central core of criminal offences, such as offences committed against young children, the issue of whether conduct on the margins should be criminal involves balancing a number of competing considerations and interests. Not only does the law seek to promote free will but to prevent others from intruding upon it, or engaging in activities construed as damaging to wider society. It is here the difficulties in regulation become evident; by setting boundaries to sexual behaviour the law is not only seeking to protect our autonomy but to restrict it.

So what are sexual offences and where do we find them? The easy answer is sexual offences are crimes within the Sexual Offences Act 2003 (SOA 2003), but this definition would exclude a number of important offences found in other pieces of legislation and the common law. The SOA 2003 also tells us nothing about how we have decided which offences should be classified as sexual. Indeed there is no single defining factor we can point to in labelling offences as sexual. Of course such offences typically have a sexual element – but even this is contentious, overlooking the violence of offences such as rape and assault by penetration where sexual gratification may be a mere side effect. In the light of this, rape has been increasingly discussed as a violent offence in international humanitarian law and many believe recasting rape as an offence of violence in national law would more truly capture its nature and that by continuing to classify such offences as sexual we are privileging the sexual element. A lack of consent is also central to many of these offences, transforming otherwise legal behaviour into a sexual offence, but an absence of consent is not always essential for the commission of an offence. Sexual activity between adults may be fully consensual but if, for example, those adults are closely related or engaged in sadomasochism resulting in injury then consent does not negate liability.

How then can we justify the criminalization and condemnation of sexual activity? To find the answer we must turn to the function of the law. Unfortunately there is no single governing function; rather there are a number of rationales for why we choose to prohibit or regulate certain acts. As *Setting the Boundaries* (2000) recognized, the need for prohibition can be justified on a number of grounds:

> . . . the criminal law should not intrude unnecessarily into the private life of adults. Applying the principle of harm means that most consensual activity

between adults in private should be their own affair, and not that of the criminal law. But the criminal law has a vital role to play where sexual activity is not consensual, or where society decides that children and other very vulnerable people require protection and should not be able to consent. It is quite proper to argue in such situations that an adult's right to exercise sexual autonomy in their private life is not absolute, and society may properly apply standards through the criminal law which are intended to protect the family as an institution as well as individuals from abuse.[11]

Legal intervention may be warranted but any interference with private and family life must be in accordance with the law and necessary in a democratic society. For example in *Dudgeon v United Kingdom* (1981)[12] the European Court of Human Rights accepted that national authorities could fix an age for lawful consensual sexual activity to protect those who are vulnerable on account of their youth, but any outright prohibition on homosexual conduct was a disproportionate interference with the respect for private life. Article 8 of the European Convention on Human Rights protects the private life of individuals against interference by public authorities and it is the right most often cited in appeals against conviction for sexual offences. While Article 8 seeks to protect dignity and autonomy it is a qualified right and Article 8(2) adds that interference can be for the protection of (amongst other qualifying factors) health or morals. Private life is broadly defined here and includes sexual preferences and sexual activity, but also the autonomy of the state to protect its national norms. This means a wide margin of appreciation is afforded to the state as they "are, in principle, in a better position than the international court to give an opinion, not only on the 'exact content of the requirements of morals' in their country, but also on the necessity of a restriction intended to meet them."[13]

So what are these norms that require state protection? They can be classified in a number of ways.

Social norms

In any society there are acceptable forms of behaviour and these may stem from morality, religion or merely social convention. For example, we do not accept people should be able to display their genitalia to strangers on a public street – but it is both legally and socially acceptable when this is viewed (one would imagine discreetly!) in public by a consenting partner. Equally sexual intercourse outdoors is something that only usually becomes unacceptable when others can view it. As Chapter 2 will illustrate, conformity and social norms are fluid concepts and the law often fails to keep up with shifts in social standards. Consequently the jury is, as we shall see, a valuable brake on the substantive law, preventing accused persons being convicted of an offence the public no longer considers unacceptable. The legislature has imported this normative standard into the SOA 2003 by way of an objective test of what amounts to "sexual" and this is examined further at Chapter 3.[14] Social norms are also used as justification for a number of offences, most explicitly in such offences as outraging public decency and obscenity, and the case of *Brown* vividly illustrates the power of the judiciary to set boundaries that reverberate throughout society. As we will see, the decision in *Brown* was not solely based on moral concerns, but it is perhaps the most famous and contentious example of the Law Lords drawing a line between the normal and the abnormal in private consensual relationships. Less contentious offences founded upon maintaining normal sexual relationships (and contingent to normal social relationships) include sexual activity with a family member and sexual activity with an animal. These ideas of normal and abnormal are of course subject to change. For example, until 1875 the age of consent was 12 and until the enactment of the Criminal Justice and Public Order Act 1994 consensual anal sex between a man and a woman an offence.

Family values and the family unit

Family values mean a number of different things, from protecting the vulnerable from pornography, for example, to preserving the idea of an 'ideal' family unit – mother, father and child. 'Family values' is a term that has fallen out of favour in the modern day but can still be used to reflect the social and cultural values of a model of family favoured by some, usually social conservatives. For example the Married Couple's Allowance tax policy was introduced in April 2015 to (in part) encourage these family unions.

The family unit is something highly valued as a source of social stability and the protection of the same an important function of the law. Although the idea of a family as mother, father and child is obviously a rather outdated definition of what constitutes a family, its importance to some sections of society has been echoed in case law and the debates regarding same-sex marriage. Clearly the definition of what constitutes a family has changed, and this is something reflected in the modern familial sexual offences, where the question of who is a family member has been broadened to include non-blood relationships and homosexual relationships.

Morality

Morality can be viewed as something separate from social norms; for example you may omit to engage in sexual activity in public because you feel it is socially unacceptable not because you personally consider it immoral.

The enforcement of moral norms has also been used as a justification for interference with rights, not just sexual rights, but in the field of sexuality its effects are heightened. Offences such as sexual penetration of a corpse and intercourse with an animal are almost exclusively justified on the grounds of immorality. Morality is however a very difficult thing to delineate within a society – it shifts over time and between individuals. The law tends to broadly adopt the approach of Lord Devlin discussed above, reflecting the morality of the majority; for example, many may still consider same-sex relationships to be immoral, but the law does not now interfere in these relationships as this condemnation is not in line with the moral values of our society. This approach has the benefit of lending public support and legitimacy to the law but can lead to interference with the autonomy of the minority, such as those who wish to engage in sadomasochism or sex in public toilets.

The vulnerable

The principal goal of the SOA 2003 was to protect the vulnerable and this is a laudable function of the law. This said the vulnerable is a broad and changeable class of persons. They may include those vulnerable by virtue of age (children, the elderly), capacity (the intoxicated or those labouring under a disability) or by situation (those subject to duress such as trafficked persons or those under the care of another). The Act seeks to make provision for these people and consequently capacity to consent is dealt with in a number of different ways in the Act.

As vulnerability has no exact definition the substantive law has to tread very carefully to ensure those capable of consenting to sexual activity have the right to do so. In many cases this is a matter for the arbiter of fact in deciding whether true consent has been given. However in some areas the law is not as flexible. For example as children are seen as vulnerable, sexual activity between two consenting 15-year-olds is, *prima facie*, an offence. The police and CPS then also have an important role to play in ensuring charges are brought in the correct cases.

It is worth remembering that the criminalization of a number of sexual activities is defendable on a number of grounds. Pornography is perhaps the best example here. Despite the fact that most pornography is not illegal in itself, sexual images depicting children are widely regarded to be an affront to morality, family values and propagate further offending against a vulnerable group and so the law heavily regulates this area.

Regulation in Action: Statistics and Sources

Regardless of rationale, we generally accept the law has a right and a responsibility to protect society and this is enshrined in substantive law and accomplished by the criminal justice system. Although offences are crafted by the legislature and judiciary these only become active when law enforcement agencies investigate and charge offenders. This, in turn, relies upon those offences being reported to the authorities. This symbiotic relationship influences how we view sexual offences, but the media also has an important role to play. Most people gather information about the prevalence of criminal behaviour from these informal sources, making decisions about what activities or actors pose a threat and which offences are fit for purpose. The media has significant power in shaping policy.

Statistics

If the media is to be believed your chances of being a victim of a sexual offence are higher than they have ever been. As the *Independent* squealed in 2014 "Sex offenders account for almost half of the increase in people in jail, Chris Grayling suggests; The most recent police figures show a 17 per cent rise in numbers of reports of sex offences between 2012 and 2013."[15] The *Express* reported "Rapes at a high of 22,000 – BUT Real total COULD Be 147,000"[16] and things were no better for children as the *Telegraph* headlined "Sex attacks on children rise 16pc".[17] Sexual offending is not a new theme for the press; in 2009 the *Telegraph* had headlined "Fears for public safety as number of sex offenders increases by 47pc"[18] and *The*

Times in 2011 "Sex offences increase again despite overall fall in crime".[19] But how realistic are these disturbing headline statistics and what can they tell us about sexual offences and offending?

The number of sexual offences recorded by the police for 2012–13 showed a less startling 1 per cent increase in sexual offending compared with 2011–12. However by September 2013 there was a 17 per cent increase in these recorded offences and a further 20 per cent rise on the previous year by July 2014.[20] Why do we have these substantial rises that have so excited the press? Is it due to a vast increase in sexual offending? Common sense will tell you such a substantial increase in offending is unlikely. You would be right; often such considerable upturns are the result of pedestrian changes; changes to police recording of offences,[21] the result of new offences coming into force or even state initiatives to encourage reporting of offences can have a significant increase on reporting rates.[22] In this case the rise was undoubtedly caused by the publicity surrounding the Savile Inquiry (discussed at Chapter 5), which caused an increase in reports of both historic and modern abuse. This is now being referred to as the 'Yewtree effect' (named after Operation Yewtree, the police investigation into allegations of sexual abuse by disc jockey and television presenter Jimmy Savile and others) and has impacted upon the crime figures through the reports of historic offences but has also prompted victims of modern offences to come forward and encouraged compliance with recording standards for sexual offences by some police forces. In actuality these headline figures may then tell us more about the media and the politics of the day than rates of offending behaviour. Crime statistics are notoriously difficult to understand and contextualize. Firstly there is no such thing as crime statistics *per se*; there are statistics of crimes experienced, reported crimes, recorded crimes, prosecutions and sentencing but these individual sets of statistics do not provide a picture of how an offence plays out through the criminal justice system. Secondly the hidden (or dark) figure of crime, a term used by criminologists to illuminate the number of offences that go unreported, is, of course, hidden. The Crime Survey for England and Wales (the CSEW) goes some way to addressing this but is subject to the problems outlined below.

So what is the picture of sexual offending in England and Wales? For the (statistical) year-end 2013, 55,812 sexual offences were recorded by the police, a 9 per cent increase on the 51,252 recorded for 2012 – and this rise includes historic offences. For the year-end to March 2014 there was an increase once again, with police recorded offences rising to a total of 64,205 incidents across England and Wales, the highest recorded since 2002–03.[23] As we will see, recorded offences do not necessarily translate into prosecutions and in 2013–14 8,554 defendants were prosecuted for sexual offences (excluding rape). This is a small rise of 783 from 7,771 in 2012–13. These are of course recorded offences and the number of sexual offences committed is likely to be far higher. A failure to report, no-criming (some crimes are subsequently 'no-crimed' where the police judge that no crime actually took place) and cancelling of offences all impact upon these figures. In terms of the Crown Prosecution Service's (CPS) caseload sexual offence prosecutions (excluding rape) rose from 1 per cent of the caseload in 2012–13 to 1.2 per cent of the caseload in 2013–14.[24] Sexual offences against children have also seen a similar increase and this is also almost certainly attributable to a higher rate of reporting and a clearer prosecution policy on proceeding with child sex offences.

The 2013–14 statistics showed a rise of 4,371 defendants prosecuted with 76.5 per cent successful outcomes.[25] In 2013–14 for offences relating to child abuse images there was a rise of 1,436 prosecutions on the previous year, taking the total to 20,373.[26]

Rape is excluded from these statistics amidst concerns about the attrition rate (reported incidents that do not proceed to a successful prosecution), which has been a cause of concern for many years. There are numerous reasons offences may not result in conviction; the complainant may decide to take the case no further, the police or CPS may decide there is no case to answer, there may be insufficient evidence or the suspect may be acquitted. The rape prosecution to conviction ratio in 2013 was at 36 per cent, down from 41 per cent in 2012[27] but, this said, 61.9 per cent of those cases referred from the police were charged in the 2013–14 reporting period – the highest percentage ever recorded.[28] The number of rape offences recorded to the year-end 2014 was 20,745, an increase of 26 per cent on the previous year.[29]

Figures also suggest those most at risk of victimization are white females aged 25–59. This risk of victimization decreases with age and it is at its highest for those under 24. Females in the lowest income brackets were also more likely to be victimized as were those with disabilities or illnesses.[30] Males were more likely to be the offenders, although there has been a rise in men reporting victimization. This gendered reality is largely reflected in the coverage of sexual offences, but carries some disadvantages for atypical victims of sexual offences, discussed further at Chapter 2. Perpetrators were then more likely to be males with a large proportion of offenders aged under 24 (26 per cent). In direct contradiction with the stereotype of the dangerous stranger, the statistics continue to confirm you are most at risk of a serious sexual offence (such as rape) from a partner, although when the offence is a less serious sexual offence (such as exposure) strangers pose an equal risk.[31] Although men are disproportionately recorded and reported as the aggressors in these sexual offences, reports suggest this is a rather simplistic view. There are significant numbers of male victims; it was estimated in 2013 that 72,000 males were victims of sexual offences per year and around 12,000 of these offences would be serious sexual offences.[32] Yet Police Recorded Crime figures showed fewer than 3,000 offences of sexual assault or male rape in 2013–14. There is clearly a reticence to report, perhaps due to an assumption they are unlikely to be believed, a reticence that can only have been significantly higher in preceding years.

There have also been concerns about the over use of cautions for sexual offences.[33] It may be surprising to hear that for rape and child sexual abuse some offenders have merely received cautions. In 2011 1,500 offenders were cautioned after having admitted a sexual offence. Of these, 19 offenders were cautioned for rape, with 16 of these cautions given to offenders under the age of 18.[34] That the majority of cautions for rape were given to young offenders tells you something about the use of cautions that is not made explicit in the media reports. In many cases the sex may have been 'consensual' and although, strictly speaking, there will still have been a criminal offence, and this is discussed at Chapter 4, the more practical response may have been the use of a caution.

This reality of sexual offending will of course change year on year. We need only look to the upturn in reports of child sexual offences as a result of the Savile inquiry and Operation Yewtree to see how an episode can prompt a significant change in criminal statistics. What will not change is the use of crime figures to sell and perpetuate 'stories'. The media commonly fails to explain that an upturn in sexual offending may be a good thing – it may mean people feel more confident reporting incidents to the police, or the police and the CPS are taking more cases to court. These statistics then need to be closely interrogated and our attention needs to turn to where these statistics are coming from.

Interrogating sources

There are two main sources of crime statistics, the Crime Survey for England and Wales (previously the British Crime Survey), which surveys and records experience of crime and captures offences that may not have been reported to the police, and the Police Recorded Crime figures (PRC), which, unsurprisingly, chronicle crimes recorded by the police. The CSEW has the benefit of counting offences that are unreported and unrecorded in other official sources, taking into account the 'dark figure' of crime. It does have its limitations; it is restricted to crimes against those resident in households,[35] it only records victim accounts (these may not of course be crimes in the strict sense), respondents might be unwilling to reveal sexual victimization, particularly if they live with a perpetrator, and it covers only a sample of the population.[36] It also does not include those in institutions or children's homes/ local authorities who, as recent reports have demonstrated, may be at high risk of sexual exploitation.[37] The CSEW is then useful for tracking trends – not providing an accurate picture of the number of crimes committed. You may then consider the PRC to be the better indicator of crimes committed, but the accuracy of the PRC figures has also been questioned. Incidents can, of course, only be recorded as crimes if they are both reported and recorded as such. Offences may not be reported for a number of reasons; the victim may not realize a crime has been committed against them or they may be scared to report the offence for fear of retaliation as the offence may have been (as sexual offences often are) committed by someone known to them. The victim may be incapable of reporting the offence through age, disability or incapacity; for example the victim may be a young child or a baby. This said, it is police discretion in the recording of crimes that has caused the most consternation.[38] An internal report by Her Majesty's Inspectorate of Constabulary (HMIC) found "a wide variation in the quality of decision-making associated with the recording of crime" which had ". . . the potential to impact on the levels of recorded crime".[39] A 2014 report by HMIC made for stark reading, concluding over 80,000 crimes a year were going unrecorded and the under-recording rates for sexual offences stood at 26 per cent.[40] This may, in part, be attributable to police officers disbelieving complainants who do not present as an 'ideal victims' and is something a number of reports have highlighted.[41]

The practice of no-criming has also raised concerns – an incident recorded as a crime may later be revisited by police to assess whether there is a non-criminal explanation and, if this is the case, the crime is re-recorded as a no-crime. No-criming has raised particular concerns in the field of sexual offences with a Commons Committee voicing concerns some police officers have recorded sexual offences "by means of excessive recourse to 'no-criming' decisions and classified cases as 'crime-related incidents' (CRI), rather than recorded crimes".[42] The difficulty with no-criming in sexual offence cases is complainants will often withdraw allegations through pressure, embarrassment or fear. No-criming in rape cases has been particularly controversial since HMIC revealed a wide variation in this practice between forces.[43] For example, for the offence of rape:

> . . . in Lincolnshire, for example, 26% of all reported rapes were no-crimed in 2012–13 and 20% were no-crimed in 2011–12. This contrasts with Merseyside, where 4% reported rape crimes were no-crimed in 2012–13 and 9% were no-crimed in 2011–12.[44]

The police are now under pressure to remedy this practice and undoubtedly this will lead to a rise in recorded sexual offences in the future.

Increased public distrust in official statistics led the Home Office to pass responsibility for compiling crime statistics to the independent Office for National Statistics (ONS).[45] The ONS now draws on both the PRC and CSEW to provide a more complete picture of offences and offending, producing an annual report 'Crime Statistics – Focus on Violent Crime and Sexual Offences', and occasional reports on specific areas such as hate crime.[46] From 2008 the CPS have also produced an annual report on violence against women detailing a range of offences, CPS findings, responses and recommendations. Retitled the *Violence against Women and Girls Crime Report* in 2011, and feeding into the Home Office Policy, *Ending Violence Against Women and Girls in the UK*, the report is now more comprehensive. These reports are useful – bringing together statistics it may otherwise be difficult to find and giving a clear picture of issues the CPS consider current in the field of offending against women and girls. The title does rather mask the breadth of the report, which takes in rape, child abuse and pornography – offences that are not entirely female centric. The Ministry of Justice, Home Office and the Office for National Statistics have also begun to produce ad hoc reports bringing together these statistics and these provide a useful overview of trends.

Reports of prosecutions and sentencing activity are also produced by the Ministry of Justice. These are quarterly and a useful summary bulletin highlighting trends is also published alongside tables detailing information such as conviction and sentencing.[47] The March 2014 bulletin notes prosecutions for sexual offences have increased by 21 per cent compared with the previous 12 months. These figures can be difficult to interpret as similarly titled offences in these statistical breakdowns will include historic offences sentenced under previous legislation, for example sexual assaults will include indecent assaults.

To ensure sentencing is in line with governmental policy, is suitably transparent and can be resourced the Sentencing Council also publish reports and statistical breakdowns – although these are infrequent.[48]

Statistics then are plentiful but can often be misleading and should be treated with caution. As we have addressed, there is little clarity in these statistics without looking at the context – and what clarity there is is not ordinarily reflected in media reportage. Luckily governmental reports are often dutifully clear in this respect, spelling out the possible causes for any substantial rise or decrease in offending. The media is less careful and we need to be wary of headlines that present startling crime statistics without careful contextualization.

The Media and Moral Panics

With a small percentage increase in offences why are the public so convinced sexual offending is on the rise? The newspaper headlines featured earlier are a clue; crime statistics are often used as the basis of a headline or story without being placed in context. Not only does sex sell but also, as numerous theorists have demonstrated, crime stories are integral to the news media – and a convergence between the two is media gold.[49] Sexual offences are then often the currency used to attract readers to both new and old media. But how have they shaped our understandings of sexual offences and offenders?

Media representations of criminality are not terribly accurate. The media focuses on serious examples of criminality and gives minimal attention to pedestrian offences such as property crime, road traffic offences and low level assaults. This provides a skewed picture of offending, offering detailed and relentless coverage of statistically infrequent offences such as murder and sexual offending. This picture of offending is warped further by a media that hones in on offences committed by strangers, particularly when the victims of those offences are children.[50] The media also preferences ideal victims, those that will capture media sympathy such as children and the elderly.[51] Media reporting is then highly selective giving a false picture of criminality. The increased politicization of sexual offences also makes these offences currency for the print media to play out political bias. As crime news has increasingly been drawn upon by journalists to illustrate party political points and influence an electorate, the 'spin' put on a particular story has often been driven by issues believed capable of supporting or challenging party competence in managing crime.[52]

These media approaches are at their most heightened in the creation of a moral panic. If you are unfamiliar with the concept of a moral panic it is a term popularly associated with the work of the sociologist Stanley Cohen and his text, *Folk Devils and Moral Panics*. Cohen's thesis outlines the processes by which a diverse set of local incidents and actors come together to present a threat to social interests. Cohen expressed the main thrust of his theory in the opening passages of his thesis as:

> Societies appear to be subject, every now and then, to periods of moral panic. A condition, episode, person or group of persons emerges to become defined as a threat to societal values and interests. Its nature is presented in a stylised and stereotypical fashion by the mass media; the moral barricades are manned by editors, bishops, politicians and other right thinking people; socially accredited experts pronounce their diagnoses and solutions; ways of coping are evolved or (more often) resorted to; the condition then disappears, submerges or deteriorates and becomes more visible.[53]

For our purposes the paedophile panics of the late 1990s and 2000s have perhaps been the clearest illustrations of moral panics in the landscape of sexual offences and offending. Although, as Critcher has outlined, paedophilia was not a new concern at the turn of the twenty-first century, initially appearing in the media in the mid-1970s and appearing as a heightened concern linked to organized abuse in the 1980s and 1990s when 121 children from the county of Cleveland were taken into care after a false diagnosis of sexual abuse by social workers.[54] But it was the murder of 8-year-old Sarah Payne by Roy Whiting in 2000 that coalesced public concern around paedophilia and created a moral panic.[55] Sarah had been abducted and her body found in woods at the side of the road. Her abduction had attracted significant exposure and the discovery of her body detailed extensively in the media. Once the perpetrator had been identified as Whiting, an offender already known to the police, the media response was unrelenting and a campaign spearheaded by the *News of the World* demanded a shift in policy toward public access over privacy in the case of convicted sexual offenders named 'Sarah's Law'. It was later revealed by Silverman and Wilson that the newspaper had performed research that indicated "a strong campaign on the issues of paedophiles would play well among its four million readers".[56] The campaign had the required effect, with public outrage directed at the management of sexual offenders in the community. Despite sustained pressure from the *News of the World* the Government initially ruled out public access to a sexual offender database and instead reviewed the management of sexual offenders in the community. Although the SOA 2003 tightened up legislative provision by introducing Risk of Sexual Harm Orders, moral outrage continued to be directed toward this ostensibly dangerous, although not statistically prolific, group of offenders and the *News of the World* continued to push for Sarah's Law until pilot schemes were announced in 2007. The Child Sex Offenders Disclosure Scheme has now been rolled out, and is discussed at Chapter 10. The murders of schoolgirls Holly Wells and Jessica Chapman in 2002 by school caretaker Ian Huntley also fed into these same heightened concerns[57] leading to the Bichard Inquiry (2004) and the reform of vetting individuals working with children.

The paedophile panics demonstrate the ease with which the media can establish moral boundaries, creating a stereotype of child sexual offenders as male loners. Despite children being significantly more at risk from those known to them,[58] the media had focused on the stereotypical image of a dangerous male stranger as the principal threat to the vulnerable.[59] Occasionally cases will come to light that challenge this stereotype and the paradigm of the dangerous male sex offender has also been periodically challenged by the identification of female offenders. As novel examples one may expect such cases to prompt moral panic. However, despite campaign groups such as Kidscape and the National Society for the Prevention of Cruelty to Children (NSPCC) calling for greater public recognition of female sexual offending, the abuse perpetrated by women such as Myra Hindley, Rose West and Vanessa George has had little real impact on our perception of typical sexual offenders.[60] Incidences of female sexual offending are thought to be low. Estimates range from 5 per cent to 20 per cent and such a small (or at least less visible) group of offenders are unlikely to dislodge the dominant constructions of men as the perpetrators of sexual offences and women and children as victims ingrained in social discourse and reflected in the media.

While concerns regarding paedophilia have periodically resurfaced, there had been nothing to match the Payne panic until the Savile Inquiry sharply focussed public attention upon institutional abuse in 2012. The failure of official agencies to protect the innocent has occupied press reports and ignited public ire and is discussed further at Chapters 4 and 5. A failure to identify and take action against child sexual abuse by agencies of the state has also become a more heightened concern in recent years. Street grooming provides a recent example, prompting a number of inquiries and drawing public attention to the dangers posed to vulnerable children.[61] The coverage of, for example, the Rochdale grooming 'gangs' identified that various agencies were at fault, but the media largely focussed on the fact the offenders were of Asian or British Asian heritage. Latterly the failure of social services and the police and CPS to intervene in known cases of exploitation became notable, but did not supersede the issue of race in the public mind. By demonizing a particular community the media oversimplified the complicated issue of child sexual exploitation linking it with race in the public mind.

It is not just moral panic that creates public tension with the criminal justice system, as those uncontextualized statistics earlier demonstrated. The importance of the media in propelling an issue into the public realm cannot be underestimated; but we should not assume the 'right' issue has been identified by the media. The media is concerned with capturing an audience, not telling statistical truths.

Conclusion

What does this short review of the purpose of the law, its functions, criminal statistics and media presentation of these statistics tell us? Firstly, there is no grand theory to justify criminalization; acts can be prohibited on a number of grounds – from the protection of morality to the protection of vulnerable individuals or the wellbeing of society. Whether the law should intervene and, if it should, how invasive that intervention should be is predicated upon how dangerous or widespread a behaviour is believed to be. This, in turn, is influenced by media reports and official responses to those reports.

Secondly, statistics are difficult, both to gather and interpret. Sexual offences are such a private matter that we can never get a true estimation of the scale of the problem. Statistics can provide snapshots of how the criminal justice system is dealing with offences as a whole, but under-reporting of offences and the attrition rate prevent many offences from reaching the courts.

Finally, the reality of offending is probably very distant from what the media presents. This is a significant worry as the concerns of the general public are often instrumental in bringing about legislative change.

The statistics do support that those socially considered to be under threat from sexual offences, women and children, are typically the groups in need of greatest protection. What is less well understood is the source of that threat, with offenders and offending behaviour rather simplistically rendered in the media. While our law strives to be gender neutral these statistical realities buttressed by social conventions means gender and age continues to be a significant issue for our legal system.

Notes

1 J. Locke *Second Treatise of Civil Government* (ed. Thomas Hollis) London: A. Millar et al (1764) (first published 1690) Chapter 2 sec.6.

2 J. Finnis N*atural Law and Natural Rights* Oxford: Oxford University Press (1997).

3 HMSO *Report of the Committee on Homosexual Offences and Prostitution* London: Her Majesty's Stationery Office (1957).

4 P. Devlin *The Enforcement of Morals* Oxford: Oxford University Press (1959).
5 I. Kant *The Grounding for the Metaphysics of Morals* Indianapolis: Hackett Publishing Company (1981).
6 H. Kelsen *Pure Theory of Law* (trans. M. Knight) Berkeley: University of California Press (1967).
7 H.L.A. Hart *The Concept of Law* (3rd edn) Oxford: Oxford University Press (2012).
8 Home Office *Setting the Boundaries: Reforming the Law on Sex Offences* London: Home Office (2000).
9 *R. v Brown* [1994] 1 AC 212.
10 N.S. Timasheff 'What Is "Sociology of Law"?' *American Journal of Sociology* (September 1937) 43 (2) pp. 225–235.
11 *Setting the Boundaries*, para 0.7.
12 (1981) 4 EHRR 149.
13 *Stubing v Germany* (2012) 55 EHRR 24.
14 Sexual Offences Act 2003 s78.
15 Independent.co.uk July 10, 2014.
16 October 17, 2014.
17 January 13, 2014.
18 *The Daily Telegraph* October 26, 2009.
19 *The Times* January 21, 2011.
20 Office for National Statistics *Chapter 1: Overview of Violent Crime and Sexual Offences 2012/13 and 2013/14* London: ONS. Accessible at http://www.ons.gov.uk/ons/dcp171776_352364.pdf.
21 For example, the counting rules (the counting and recording of offence) were revised to take account of the National Crime Recording Standard in 2002 to bring about consistence and provide a greater victim focus. These were revised again in 2010.
22 For example Project Guardian, an initiative by the British Transport police, Transport for London, Metropolitan Police and the City of London Police, sought to highlight unwanted sexual behaviour on public transport, which resulted in a 26 per cent increase in reporting of offences on the railway since its launch in 2013. Accessible at http://www.btp.police.uk/latest_news/local_news_london_underground/16_arrests_project_guardian.aspx.
23 Office of National Statistics *Crime Statistics, Focus on Violent Crime and Sexual Offences, 2013/14 Release, Chapter 1: Violent Crime and Sexual Offences – Overview* London: ONS (Feb 2015). Accessible at http://www.ons.gov.uk/ons/dcp171776_394474.pdf.
24 CPS *Violence Against Women and Girls Crime Report* London: CPS (July 2014). Accessible at http://www.cps.gov.uk/publications/docs/cps_vawg_report_2014.pdf p56.
25 Ibid. p. 66.
26 Ibid. p. 78.
27 Ibid. p. 48.
28 Ibid. p. 44.
29 *Focus on Violent Crime and Sexual Offences, 2013/14* p. 15.
30 Ministry of Justice, Home Office & the Office for National Statistics *An Overview of Sexual Offending in England and Wales Ministry of Justice, Home Office & the Office for National Statistics* London: Ministry of Justice (2013). Accessible at https://www.gov.uk/government/uploads/system/uploads/attachment_data/file/214970/sexual-offending-overview-jan-2013.pdf pp. 13–18.
31 Ibid. p. 16.
32 Ministry of Justice, Home Office & the Office for National Statistics *An Overview of Sexual Offending in England and Wales.*

33 Including concern from the BBC who received the figures through a Freedom of Information request sent to various police forces and found "more than 1,000 cautions have been issued in the past five years for sexual offences, including rape": see *BBC* May 8, 2015 http://www.bbc.co.uk/news/uk-england-22335575 and *BBC* January 1, 2015 http://www.bbc.co.uk/news/uk-england-30550868. For media reports see 'Hundreds of sex offenders escape with cautions' *The Telegraph* April 23, 2013; 'Anger as hundreds of sex offenders are let off with a caution' *The Express* January 11, 2013; 'Revealed: How police issue cautions for child sex offences committed by teachers, doctors and carers' *MailOnline* July 4, 2013; 'Revealed: 14 child rapists were punished with police CAUTIONS last year' *Mirror* May 21, 2015.

34 Ministry of Justice, Home Office & the Office for National Statistics *An Overview of Sexual Offending in England and Wales* p. 8.

35 Victimless crimes do not form part of the survey, nor do homicide or crimes against those not within a 'household' such as homeless persons.

36 Around 37,500 households took part in the 2013–14 survey.

37 The Crime Survey for England and Wales has also only recently included children aged 10–16 in their surveys and these children have to have parental consent.

38 This is a perennial problem and one discussed in its contemporary context in Cambridge Department of Criminal Science *Sexual Offences* London: MacMillan (1957) Appendix One.

39 HMIC *The Crime Scene: A Review of Police Crime and Incident Reports* (2012) London: HMIC. Accessible at http://www.justiceinspectorates.gov.uk/hmic/media/review-police-crime-incident-reports-20120125.pdf.

40 HMIC *Crime-recording: Making the Victim Count. The Final Report of an Inspection of Crime Data Integrity in Police Forces in England and Wales* London: HMIC (2014).

41 Independent Police Complaints Commission *Commissioner's Report IPCC Independent Investigation into the Metropolitan Police Service's Inquiry into Allegations against John Worboys* (2010). Accessible at http://www.ipcc.gov.uk/sites/default/files/Documents/investigation_commissioner_reports/worboys_commissioners_report.pdf; *Independent Police Complaints Commission 'Commissioner's Report IPCC Independent Investigation into the Metropolitan Police Service's Inquiry into Allegations Against Kirk Reid* (2010). Accessible at http://www.ipcc.gov.uk/sites/default/files/Documents/investigation_commissioner_reports/kirkreidcommissionersreport.pdf.

42 Public Administration Select Committee *Caught Red-handed: Why We Can't Count on Police Recorded Crime Statistics*, Thirteenth Report. London: The Stationary Office (April 2014). Accessible at http://www.publications.parliament.uk/pa/cm201314/cmselect/cmpubadm/760/760.pdf. para 32.

43 The force digests are available online here http://www.justiceinspectorates.gov.uk/hmic/publication/rape-monitoring-group-digests-data-and-methodology-2014.

44 *Caught Red-handed* pp. 15–16.

45 UK Statistics Authority *Overcoming Barriers to Trust in Crime Statistics: England and Wales* Monitoring Report 5 (May, 2010). Accessible at file:///C:/Users/orpheusinvelvet/Downloads/-images-overcoming-barriers-to-trust-in-crime-statistics-england-and-wales_tcm97–32230.pdf.

46 See links to the various reports here http://www.ons.gov.uk/ons/taxonomy/index.html?nscl=Crime.

47 https://www.gov.uk/government/collections/criminal-justice-statistics-quarterly.

48 See http://sentencingcouncil.judiciary.gov.uk/index.htm.

49 For example see the discussion in K. Soothill and S. Walby *Sex Crime in the News* London: Routledge (1991); C. Greer *Sex Crime and the Media: Sex Offending and the Press in a Divided Society* London: Routledge (2012); H. Benedict *Virgin or Vamp: How the Press Covers Sex Crimes* New York: Oxford University Press (1992).

50 See Chapter 4.

51 N. Christie, 'The ideal victim', in E. Fattah (ed.) *From Crime Policy to Victim Policy* Basingstoke: Macmillan (1986), pp. 17–30. This has later been considered in relation to the race of the victim see E. McLaughlin and K. Murji 'Ways of seeing: the news media and racist violence' in M. May, E. Brunsden and R. Page (eds) *Understanding Social Problems: Issues in Social Policy* Oxford: Blackwells (2001).

52 A full appraisal of how political agendas have shaped responses to crime is outside the remit of this textbook but a number of texts do provide historical and contemporary reviews. C.M.V. Clarkson and R. Morgan *The Politics of Sentencing Reform* Oxford: Clarendon Press (1995); D. Garland *The Culture of Control: Crime and Social Order in Contemporary Society* Oxford: Oxford University Press (2001); T. Newburn *Crime and Criminal Justice Policy* Harlow: Longman (2003); A. Barton and N. Johns *The Policy Making Process in the Criminal Justice System* London: Routledge (2012); J. Rowbotham, K. Stevenson and S. Pegg *Crime News in Modern Britain* London: Palgrave Macmillan (2013).

53 S. Cohen *Folk Devils and Moral Panics* (3rd edn) Oxon: Routledge (2002).

54 E. Butler-Sloss *Report of the Inquiry into Child Abuse in Cleveland* London: HMSO (1987).

55 C. Critcher 'Media, government and moral panic: the politics of paedophilia in Britain 2000–1' *Journalism Studies* (2002) 3(4) pp. 521–535.

56 J. Silverman and D. Wilson *Innocence Betrayed: Paedophilia, the Media and Society* Cambridge: Polity (2002) p. 150.

57 Prompting the *News of the World* to headline 'The evidence is overwhelming . . . we must have Sarah's law and end the killing', August 25, 2002 and the later well-publicized revelations that Ian Huntley had been investigated for numerous sexual offences (including offences against children) buttressed the *News of the World* claims. See reports in the *News of the World* June 26, 2005; July 3, 2005; September 18, 2005; November 13, 2005; February 5, 2006; June 18, 2006; June 25, 2006; November 12, 2006.

58 D. Howitt *Paedophiles and Sexual Offences Against Children* Chichester: Wiley (1995); Silverman and Wilson *Innocence Betrayed*.

59 See Kleinhans for discussion of the contextualization of the murder of Sarah Payne in light of the contemporary paedophilia concerns: M.M. Kleinhans 'Criminal justice approaches to paedophilic sex offenders' *Social and Legal Studies* (2002) 11(2) pp. 233–255.

60 For further discussion see L. Bunting 'Females Who Sexually Offend Against Children: Responses of the Child Protection and Criminal Justice Systems' NSPCC Policy Practice Research Series London (2005); M. Denov 'The myth of innocence: Sexual scripts and the recognition of child sexual abuse by female perpetrators' *The Journal of Sex Research* (2003) 40(3) pp. 303–314.

61 House of Commons Home Affairs Committee *Child Sexual Exploitation and the Response to Localised Grooming Second Report of Session 2013–14* London: The Stationery Office (2013). Accessible at http://www.publications.parliament.uk/pa/cm201314/cmselect/cmhaff/68/68i.pdf; *Serious Case Review into Child Sexual Exploitation in Oxfordshire: From the experiences of Children A, B, C, D, E, and F* Oxford: Oxford Safeguarding Children Board (February 2015). Accessible at http://www.oscb.org.uk/wp-content/uploads/SCR-into-CSE-in-Oxfordshire-FINAL-FOR-WEBSITE.pdf.

Chapter 2

The Female, the Male and the Child

Introduction

In this chapter we reflect on offences and offending by setting out the groups protected and criminalized by the law, establishing the historical, social and legal backdrop to our legal regulation and how the law exercises power over bodily autonomy. By this we mean the right to choose to engage in sexual activity and the manner in which that autonomy is protected or restricted by legal intervention. Many would be surprised that there is legal regulation concerning our sexual autonomy, but there are many examples the man or woman in the street would be familiar with – for example the criminalization of intercourse between a sister and brother and the sexual penetration of an animal. Although regulating these activities appears straightforward, it is a difficult task. An adult's right to sexual autonomy is not absolute and the law limits autonomy in order to protect individuals and society from harmful behavior. However what amounts to harmful behaviour and who should be subject to protection is mutable.

Historically the regulation of sexuality has been challenging. Not only does the law here intervene in the private realm but it seeks to establish legal principles that regulate activities heavily influenced by social stimuli when, as we know, the law does not change swiftly. Consider for example the social impact of *50 Shades of Grey*[1] and the effect this has had on conceptions of sadomasochism. Already cases such as *Peacock*[2] and *Walsh*[3] (discussed at Chapter 7) have demonstrated a gulf between the agencies of the criminal justice system and society in their estimation of what activities are obscene and undoubtedly this gulf will widen. Equally, matters such as same-sex marriage, sexual relations with distant relatives and the age of sexual consent have no clear social consensus and the law seeks to tread a careful balance between intrusion into the private realm and protecting the vulnerable. There are then many difficulties in effectively regulating sexual autonomy and historically this has been further nuanced by how autonomy has been managed with regard to your status as female, male or child. Today we are familiar with protectionist constraints upon children, by virtue of the age of consent for example, but you may be less familiar with how important gender has been in restricting autonomy. The discussion below is weighted toward the female – and this in itself tells you something about the historical conception of the male and the child in society and in the law.

Male and Female

Before we discuss how these different groups have been legally regulated it is important to understand how we decide who is male and female for the purposes of the law. Although this may not seem an important distinction in the modern day it has been important, as Justice Omerod sought to explain in 1970:

> Over a very large area the law is indifferent to sex. It is irrelevant to most of the relationships which give rise to contractual or tortious rights and obligations, and to the greater part of the criminal law. In some contractual relationships, e.g., life assurance and pensions schemes, sex is a relevant factor in determining the rate of premium or contributions. It is relevant also to some aspects of the law regulating conditions of employment, and to various State-run schemes such as national insurance, or to such fiscal matters as selective employment tax. It is not an essential determinant of the relationship in these cases because there is nothing to prevent the parties to a contract of insurance or a pension scheme from agreeing that the person concerned should be treated as a man or as a woman, as the case may be. Similarly, the authorities, if they think fit, can agree with the individual that he shall be treated as a woman for national insurance purposes, as in this case. On the other hand, sex is clearly an essential determinant of the relationship called marriage, because it is and always has been recognised as the union of man and woman. It is the institution on which the family is built, and in which the capacity for natural heterosexual intercourse is an essential element. It has, of course, many other characteristics, of which companionship and mutual support is an important one, but the characteristics which distinguish it from all other relationships can only be met by two persons of opposite sex. There are some other relationships such as adultery, rape and gross indecency in which, by definition, the sex of the participants is an essential determinant . . .[4]

Justice Omerod was speaking of how the law has used sex as a definitional factor – here sex refers to the biological and physiological characteristics that define men and women. Gender is quite different and refers to the social consequences for the individual of that assessment, the behaviours and attributes society considers appropriate for men and women – although the terms sex and gender are now typically used interchangeably. Deciding who is female or male may seem a straightforward task, and a necessary one as there is a legal duty to register a child's birth (including its sex) within 42 days.[5] But this assumes gender is both static and set at birth, when in actuality gender reassignment is not uncommon, with estimates of prevalence at 1 in 11,500 of our population.[6]

Biological sex has, as Justice Omerod indicated, been of some importance in regulatory law, the criminal realm and particularly for the marriage contract. Historically, the courts have intervened when property has been in question. For example, in the Scottish inheritance case of *Forbes-Sempill* (1967)[7] a male heir to a family estate sought to prevent his cousin Ewan (who had been registered at birth as a girl) inheriting the estate under the rules of primogeniture. Ewan, had 'changed sex' in the mid-1940s and obtained an amended birth certificate.

Despite this, Lord Hunter declared that although Ewan's genitals were predominately female in appearance Ewan's wife had asserted he was able to penetrate her satisfactorily and this was of far greater importance – consequently he was legally male and able to inherit. Of course until 2014[8] the law only recognized marriage between a man and a woman and the importance of establishing whether parties to a marriage were male and female had been central to establishing its validity[9] and it was this which first led our courts to consider what was meant by 'woman' in the context of marriage.

April Ashley, born George Jamieson and registered as male, married Arthur Corbett in 1963 and, the same year, Corbett filed a petition for a declaration that the marriage was null and void as, at the time of the ceremony, April was male. The case involved a lengthy discussion of April's transsexualism[10] which, as Lord Nicholls outlined in a later case, results in persons feeling "an unshakeable belief or feeling that they are persons of the opposite sex. They experience themselves as being of the opposite sex . . ."[11] Giving judgment in *Corbett v Corbett* (1970) Justice Omerod – well placed to hear the case being both medically and legally trained – favoured a biological test of sex:

> Having regard to the essentially heterosexual character of the relationship which is called marriage, the criteria must, in my judgment, be biological, for even the most extreme degree of transsexualism in a male or the most severe hormonal imbalance which can exist in a person with male chromosomes, male gonads and male genitalia cannot reproduce a person who is naturally capable of performing the essential role of a woman in marriage. In other words, the law should adopt, in the first place, the first three of the doctors' criteria, i.e. the chromosomal, gonadal and genital tests, and, if all three are congruent, determine the sex for the purpose of marriage accordingly, and ignore any operative intervention.[12]

The test he speaks of here is truly biological, requiring consideration of xx (female) or xy (male) chromosomes, the presence or absence of testes or ovaries and the external and internal sex organs. If these features are congruent then the decision is (legally) straightforward. In April's case they were, April was declared male and a decree of nullity of marriage granted. The test has not been looked back upon favourably, but the law rarely tackles these subtle questions well (consider for example sexual activity between underage children at Chapter 4) and Justice Omerod was adopting a simplistic test to tackle a multifaceted problem.

Perhaps we recall the *Corbett* decision with some distaste because of Justice Omerod's reference to the "essential role of a woman" in his judgment and April's inability to fulfil that role. Was he speaking of the ability to engage in intercourse (which April could, albeit with an artificial vagina) or the ability to procreate (which many married persons cannot)? Read in context, it appears Justice Omerod may have meant a woman was a woman from birth. Regardless, the decision confirmed that those who underwent gender reassignment would remain in their birth sex and could not have their new gender recognized in official records. They were denied the legal benefits of the acquired gender, such as marriage to the opposite sex, or a particular retirement age and they remained criminally liable for those offences that required a specific gender.[13]

Although *Corbett* was good law for more than 30 years steps were being taken in the civil realm to prevent discrimination, with the Sex Discrimination (Gender Reassignment) Regulations introduced in 1999.[14] This was the first time transsexual people had been explicitly protected against discrimination in employment and vocational training. Doubts were also being expressed about the Corbett test by the judiciary[15] most notably in *Bellinger v Bellinger* (2003)[16] where Lord Justice Thorpe had stated there was "no logic or principle in excluding one vital component of personality, the psyche" when deciding upon gender. While the Lords were sympathetic in *Bellinger* the ruling confirmed a change could only be a matter for parliament, not the justices. That decision followed an unequivocal pronouncement by the Grand Chamber of the European Court of Human Rights that the United Kingdom was in violation of the European Convention of Human Rights for failing to respect the private life of a post-operative male to female transsexual who was unable to change her birth certificate.[17] To this breach of Article 8 we may also add a breach of Articles 12 (right to marry)[18] and 14 (no discrimination in the application of human rights). The justices also drew attention to the fact the United Kingdom was in a group of only four of the 23 States of the Council of Europe that had not given legal recognition to a change of gender. The domestic legislative response was (then) swift and the Gender Recognition Act 2004 enacted. This Act was far more liberal than may have been expected given our legal history. The requirements, in brief, are that the applicant is aged over 18-year-of-age, has gender dysphoria, has lived in the acquired gender for two years, intends to continue to live in the acquired gender until death and has appropriate medical evidence to support their claim.[19] If this is complied with, a Gender Recognition Panel will issue a Gender Recognition Certificate and the applicant will be legally recognized in their acquired gender.

We have come a remarkably long way in a short time. The label of transsexual is now rarely used in legal and medical parlance and gender identity disorder or gender dysphoria is the clinical diagnosis for individuals, and when an individual transitions into their desired gender we term this their acquired gender. Such a transition is often discussed as a consequence of gender reassignment surgery (previously termed a 'sex change' operation) and there has never been a legal impediment to receiving surgery. The law does not require surgery to take place for an individual to be recognized in their acquired gender, but it does make provision for surgery to be accepted as part of the supporting evidence where it has taken place. The more complex cases, where biological criteria are not congruent, still cause social difficulties. Although this condition, termed intersex, has rarely troubled the courts[20] it does bring with it its own social and medical problems.[21]

The Marriage (Same Sex Couples) Act 2013 has now swept away dicta in *Hyde v Hyde* (1866)[22] and *Corbett* with individuals of the same biological sex legally able to marry. Although the Civil Partnership Act 2004 has provided a measure of equality by recognizing same-sex civil unions they are still regulated by a separate legal regime from marriage – and they are not open to couples of the opposite sex. By seeking to provide parity, the legislature has opened up a range of different legal couplings and it is perhaps time to revisit this area and tidy up the law.

Regulation of the Female

Female autonomy has historically been limited by social conventions supported and enforced by law. Women have been seen as an important commodity; it has of course been wives who produced legitimate children who could continue the family line. This is particularly important when you consider property and titles have historically been vested in male offspring, and it is of no surprise that the law adopted a paternalistic approach to the regulation of women. Moreover the propriety of a wife has historically reflected on her husband, so it has been in the interest of the law – something that has itself been male dominated – to robustly regulate the behaviour of the female. Morality exerts a heavy influence here; women were considered to be moral guardians and sexual impropriety a threat to society itself. The regulation of sexuality is here heavily entwined with the position of the woman as wife and this is addressed in some detail below.

Patriarchy and property

Patriarchy is a social system where the male is the authority figure, in terms of social construct, moral authority and (in a large part) the law. In our jurisdiction it is something people most readily associate with the nineteenth century where the father was often accepted as the dominant figure, with his wife and children subservient to his ultimate authority. In line with this, rather than examining the long legal history of patriarchy, we will take the nineteenth century period as our starting point with an eye to how the social and legal precedents set in this period continued to find expression in the modern day. Although our discussion concentrates upon the regulation of the female in marriage it is worth noting for the purposes of the law that the legal existence of the female has usually been subsumed by the dominant male, be that father or husband. As Blackstone expressed: "By marriage the very being or legal existence of woman is suspended, or at least it is incorporated and consolidated into that of a husband."[23] And the results of this were far reaching. In the civil realm property owned, inherited or earned belonged to the husband through a doctrine known as coverture and a women's position was as *feme covert* (a 'protected' woman). Coverture also excluded married women from entering into contracts, suing, or making a will on their own behalf. This denial of property rights also extended to a woman's claim to her children: legitimate children belonged in law to their father[24] – women had sole custody of illegitimate children. This principle was maintained in a moderated form by the Custody of Infants Act of 1839, which permitted a mother to petition the courts for custody of her children up to the age of 7, and for access to older children. It was not until 1873 that a new ethos was adopted and the Infant Custody Act 1873 put the needs of the child above those of either parent.

Property rights became progressively more positive for women with the enactment of the Matrimonial Causes Act 1857. This Act opened up the possibility of divorce to those other than the very wealthy, who previously had been able to take a case to the ecclesiastical courts to obtain an annulment or separation order. This order could later be formalized as a 'divorce' through a private Act of Parliament; strictly speaking divorce did not exist until 1857. The Act put divorce on a legal footing, moving jurisdiction to the civil courts, recognizing marriage as a contract and creating the Court for Divorce and Matrimonial Causes. Although the Act was a valuable step forward, recognizing women as *feme sole* (having separate legal relations), it promulgated a double standard by requiring a husband to prove only his wife's adultery for divorce; while a wife had to prove her husband's adultery, and also that he had either treated her cruelly, had deserted her, or had committed incest or bigamy. Divorce was then still not easy, nor cheap. Some relief for women came with the enactment of the Matrimonial Causes Act of 1878, providing the right to separation with maintenance when a wife was in danger and the husband had been convicted of aggravated assault. In effect this was a judicial separation giving women the custody of their children. Property rights were finally granted by the Married Women's Property Acts of 1870, 1874 and 1882, which gradually gave every married woman the right to hold property in her own name.

These civil principles were reflected in the social presumption that husbands could criminally injure their wives, and in legal manuals the right of a husband to beat his wife was noted as early as the 1600s. Punishment had to be reasonable, but what constituted excessive force was unclear. The situation improved, notably through the Aggravated Assaults Act 1853, which increased the fine for beating women and children – identifying this form of assault as something legally unacceptable. But the situation was not much improved, as John Stuart Mill, arguing in favour of women's suffrage, so forcefully asserted in 1867:

> I should like to have a Return laid before this House of the number of women who are annually beaten to death, kicked to death, or trampled to death by their male protectors; and, in an opposite column, the amount of the sentences passed in those cases in which the dastardly criminals did not get off altogether. I should also like to have, in a third column, the amount of property, the unlawful taking of which was, at the same sessions or assizes, by the same judge, thought worthy of the same amount of punishment. We should then have an arithmetical estimate of the value set by a male legislature and male tribunals on the murder of a woman, often by torture continued through years, which, if there is any shame in us, would make us hang our heads.[25]

Although the Matrimonial Causes Act 1878 went some way toward ameliorating the situation domestic violence continued, although it had become progressively less socially acceptable.[26] The difficulties in regulating this behaviour cannot be discussed in detail here but are well documented.[27] A husband's domain over his wife also extended to sexual violence and it is to how the law legitimized this we must now turn.

Conjugal rights

Conjugal rights are the rights conferred by the relationship of marriage, those of comfort and companionship by cohabitation. Conjugal rights have, of course, most readily been understood to be the right to have sexual relations with your partner. The contract of marriage does not and did not compel intercourse,[28] although, as we shall see below, rape was not considered possible between husband and wife.

Sexual rights have been heavily intertwined with marriage rights for females. When the age of consent was raised to 13 by the Offences Against the Person Act 1875 with it came the concomitant complication that a girl could marry at 12-years-of-age, but could not consent to sex outside marriage until 13. This difficulty was heightened by the 1885 Criminal Law Amendment Act that raised the age of consent to 16, while the age of legal marriage remained at 12 until 1929.[29] Thus marriage brought with it this special right of consent to sexual intercourse.

The language of conjugal rights most often arose in the writ for restitution for conjugal rights, where a deserted spouse could ask the court to order their husband or wife to return to the matrimonial home or suffer a penalty of imprisonment.[30] It was common for such writs to be brought in the nineteenth century, and earlier, by both men and women – but mainly men. These orders were not as drastic as they may appear – if a spouse suffered or feared ill-treatment a court would not compel them to return home. Not only was the marriage contract held to be enforceable through the writ but a wife was understood to hold inherent value, one economically quantifiable. For example civil claims for damages could be made against a wife's rapist, adulterer or lover. In *Macfazden v Olivant* (1805)[31] D "with force and arms" made an assault on P's wife and seduced her. P was considered to have been deprived of her comfort, society and fellowship and as Lord Chief Justice Ellenborough put it "as her body and mind had been corrupted she was therefore less qualified to perform the duties of the state of marriage". This value of a wife was twofold. Firstly, she held a pecuniary value consisting of her fortune, her assistance in her husband's business, her capacity as housekeeper and general role in the home. In *Lynch v Knight* (1861)[32] it was held a wife could be likened to a servant and thus monetary reparation could be made if she was corrupted. Secondly, there was the emotional and sexual role of the wife as consortium – this was closely linked to the purity, moral character, affection and role as wife and mother. A wife's moral behaviour was also held to reflect upon her husband, who could be compensated for, as was expressed in *Butterworth v Butterworth* (1920),[33] a "blow to his marital honour". Civil claims were based on this two-fold estimation of the value of the wife, until abolished by the Matrimonial Causes Act 1857, which replaced such actions with a statutory claim for damages.

This language of women as property was closely related to concerns that malicious women could take advantage of worthy men and, by the contract of marriage, take advantage of their fortune and good name. The writ for restitution of conjugal rights had moderated this concern by essentially enforcing the marriage contract but this was to be dealt a blow in the cause célèbre of late Victorian England, the Clitheroe abduction case.[34] In March 1891 Mr Jackson had seized his estranged wife Emily and confined her to the marital home after she had refused to accede to such a writ. Emily's family applied for a writ of habeas corpus (to produce the person alleged to be unlawfully detained before the court). Although initially rejected by the Queen's Bench Division, the Court of Appeal sat to consider its validity. Although the justices acceded there may have been a lingering principle of law allowing confinement of a wife if she was extravagant, or a right to restrain her if she were making to elope, they held there was no legal right to kidnap or confine a wife. It was an unpopular decision with the public, who gathered to boo and hiss at Emily and sing "He's a jolly good fellow to her husband".[35] Although the judgment may have been emancipatory in nature it meant, in the words of *The Times*, that the law:

> . . . seems to authorize deliberate desertion on the part of the wife who, if pos-
> sessed of private means, can substantially get rid at her pleasure of the obliga-
> tions of the marriage tie . . .[36]

So the writ had lost its teeth, spouses could refuse to return home and could not be forcibly compelled to do so by the courts. The writ was not abolished until 1970[37] but had already fallen out of favour as a method of forcing a spouse home for either financial or sexual reasons.[38]

By the end of the 1800s a wife could refuse to cohabit, but you will have noted one of the values of a wife was the right to sexual congress and many students of criminal law will have come across the case of *Clarence* (1888)[39] as this case is readily used as authority that men had an absolute right by marriage to sexual intercourse with their wives. The decision was not this simplistic, although the facts were. Charles Clarence, suffering from gonorrhea, passed the disease to his wife through sexual intercourse. Although his wife had consented to sex she did not know of her husband's condition and Charles was convicted by a jury of assault and grievous bodily harm. This conviction was later quashed by the Queen's Bench Division (in part) on the basis of the marital rape exception. As Justice Hawkins stated, by the marriage contract a wife confers upon her husband an "irrevocable privilege" to have sexual intercourse with her for the duration of the marriage. But this exemption, that a man had a right to sexual intercourse with his wife (and by logical extension sexual touching), was far from clear and certainly not undisputed.[40] This was a presumption with its roots in Sir Matthew Hale's statement that a man may not be guilty of the rape of his wife, because "by their mutual matrimonial consent and contract the wife hath given up herself in this kind unto her husband, which she cannot retract."[41] But this was not accepted as an unqualified presumption by all justices in *Clarence*, nor is it a statement grounded in any unequivocal case law. Later cases such as *Clarke* (1949)[42] began to erode the presumption, allowing consent to be revoked when a process of law (in this case a separation order) had shown a clear willingness to alter the marriage contract. This was taken further in *Steele* (1976)[43] where it was accepted that where a husband and wife live apart and where an undertaking has been given to the court by the husband not to molest the wife this had the same effect as an injunction, namely of eliminating the wife's matrimonial consent to intercourse. By no means were all martial rape cases decided in favour of the victim, but were the justices using these principles to avoid the presumption of marital consent? The law was finally settled in *R v R* (1991)[44] which 'abolished' the presumption,[45] as Lord Kinkel stated ". . . in modern times the supposed marital exemption in rape forms no part of the law of England"; this of course assumes it ever really did.

New threats to female autonomy through conjugal rights have now been recognized as the multicultural nature of England and Wales has required new provisions to tackle forced marriage, most notably the Forced Marriage Protection Orders introduced in 2008. This civil order can be sought by anyone threatened to marry against their will and a breach of the order is a criminal offence.[46] Third parties including relatives, friends and police officers can also apply for a protection order. These orders are essentially an injunction that prevents the threats and/or the marriage taking place and typically utilized by women.[47]

Virginity and female genital mutilation

In many cultures, physical proof of the virginity of brides has been demanded and virgins have traditionally held a high social and occasionally economic value. Although we are more used today to virginity being associated with high moral or religious values it has certainly played a part in our social construction of respectable femininity. A loss of virginity before marriage has been coupled to ideas of stigma and impurity and in some cases disqualification from marriage.[48] Consequently maintaining virginity has been an important tool in the regulation of women, if only through social approval and, as we have seen, women sullied through sexual intercourse outside marriage have been devalued. In our jurisdiction virginity has primarily found legal expression in debates regarding the regulation of female genital mutilation (FGM). Debates concerning FGM have only risen to prominence in the past few years – however it is not a procedure unfamiliar to England and Wales. FGM was advocated in limited nineteenth century circles as a treatment for women who were sexually abnormal, particularly those overly interested in sex and masturbation.[49] Today the term FGM has come to be associated with cultural practices out of step with our values and the law has taken a strong stance against its use. The practices of clitoridectomy and infibulation were initially criminalized by the Prohibition of Female Circumcision Act 1985, which criminalized those who carried out the act and those who were accessories to the same (s1(1)). The Female Genital Mutilation Act 2003, which replaced it, went further, criminalizing the same acts at ss1 and 2 and assisting a non-UK national to carry out FGM outside the United Kingdom on a UK national or permanent UK resident (s3) but included an extra-territorial offence extending sections 1–3 to any act done outside the United Kingdom to a UK national or permanent UK resident (s4).[50] The maximum sentence for these offences was also raised from 5 years to 14 years. An offence of failing to protect a girl under the age of 16 from the risk of genital mutilation was introduced in 2015. The offence essentially places a duty on those responsible for a girl at the time when an offence under section 1, 2 or 3 of the Act is committed where they saw a significant risk of a genital mutilation.[51] Anonymity for victims of FGM is also now enshrined in legislation.[52]

The rationale behind preventing women undergoing FGM is sound; it has no physical benefit and the process can cause very severe damage and even death. FGM has increasingly been recognized as violence against women[53] and modern responses have been subsumed under Governmental policy on Ending Violence against Women and Girls. At the point of writing there have been no successful prosecutions for FGM, a situation labelled by the Home Affairs Select Committee in 2014 as a "national scandal for which successive governments, politicians, the police, health, education and social care sectors all share responsibility".[54] There are numerous reasons for the failure to secure prosecutions, from the reticence of victims to report and the unwillingness of victims to give evidence to a failure to uncover cases and a low level of reporting by medical practitioners.[55] Consequently, along with providing a robust prosecution policy,[56] attention has increasingly turned to alternatives to the legal process including poster and leaflet campaigns, establishing the NSPCC FGM helpline and launching educational programmes. There is also a new focus on civil remedies and FGM Protection Orders modelled on Forced Marriage Protection Orders are now being used to prevent children being taken out of the country for the procedure.[57] Breach of the order is a criminal offence subject to a maximum penalty of 5 years' imprisonment.

But it is worth questioning whether we are protecting women through the criminalization of FGM, or restricting their autonomy. Opponents of FGM argue the procedure is not a rational choice and any desire to have it performed is based on a cultural anachronism that cannot be supported in the modern day. But we do not outlaw, for example, sizable breast augmentation, even when surgery poses dangers and the result may pose health risks. Perhaps then the regulation is better thought of as justifiably paternalistic.

Sexual offences

Although rape has long been a serious offence, when we speak of rape in historical terms (and indeed internationally) we are not discussing our current offence of rape. Until 1841 rape was a capital offence and, as with all capital offences, evidence had to be strong to maintain a conviction. Thus lesser charges were commonly used such as indecent assault and assault with intent to commit rape.[58] Equally, indecent assaults were often downgraded to common or aggravated assaults to ensure a conviction. As we know, rape was not considered to take place within marriage and a long line of authorities also held full penetration and force had to be present.[59] While this position was eroded in *Camplin* (1845)[60] there was still a lingering assumption that real rape involved an overpowering of the victim,[61] something only explicitly removed by the Sexual Offences Act 2003 (SOA 2003).[62] Of course, this requirement had aided prosecutors in proving a lack of consent but it also reflected the idea of a respectable woman as one who would vigorously defend her honour. Debates had also raged in the eighteenth and nineteenth century courts regarding the meaning of penetration and whether ejaculation had to take place for non-consensual sexual intercourse to be rape. Women were at a disadvantage, finding themselves in a situation where they could be sexually abused suggested a certain carelessness, and a willingness to speak out a lack of modesty. Juries were of course male, as were the police, prosecutors and judges. This was not an easy environment for female victims.[63]

This is not to say women have not been protected by the criminal law. The Sexual Offences Act 1956 (SOA 1956) updated the law and made explicit many offences that sought to protect women (and only women) from unlawful sexual intercourse. These included the offences of rape (s1),[64] procurement of sexual intercourse from a woman by threat or intimidation (s2), by false pretences or false representations (s3)[65] and applying drugs etc., to obtain sexual intercourse (s4). Indecent exposure was also phrased as an offence against women (s4 Vagrancy Act 1824, s28 Town & Police Clauses Act 1847) and it was an offence to abduct an unmarried girl from her parent or guardian (ss19, 20 SOA 1956). Likewise, offences relating to the exploitation of persons as prostitutes were ostensibly intended as protection for women and girls (ss22, 23 and 28 SOA 1956). It was not until 1976 that a definition of rape was set out in statute defining rape as vaginal intercourse with a woman who does not consent to it where the defendant knows that the person does not consent or is reckless as to whether that person consents to it.[66]

But protection in statute does not necessarily translate into protection in actuality and by the 1980s it was clear the criminal justice system was failing female victims. There was a low rate of conviction in rape cases,[67] various studies found police response to sexual offences lacking,[68] court processes traumatic and judicial responses unhelpful. How these have been reported on by the media is of equal importance. As Soothill has pointed out, the changing whims of media reporting impact upon public perceptions of the reality of rape, for example:

> The few cases which are given quite enormous attention heighten still further the contrast between some extraordinary cases of rape and the "normality" or reality of rape which is increasingly being captured in the court arena.[69]

The ideal victim and ideal model of a sexual offence may have been progressively eroded in substantive criminal law but it continues to hold sway socially and impact on the criminal justice system. Modern concerns have focused on rape myths and their impact on decision making throughout the criminal justice process. As Chapter 1 has touched upon, the law cannot be viewed in isolation from the social realm.

Prostitution

Linked to the significance of virginity and the consequent socio-legal 'protection' of womanhood has been the regulation of aberrant sexuality, particularly prostitution. The current law pertaining to prostitution is discussed at Chapter 6 and the law is now of course gender neutral, but here it is worth considering how and why female prostitution came to be regulated. Prostitution had traditionally been viewed as a deviant activity in modern history, but it was not until the nineteenth century that the law sought to control it in any systematic way. The Vagrancy Act 1824 created the legal category of 'common prostitute' outlining "any common prostitute behaving in a riotous or indecent manner in a public place or thoroughfare" was liable to a fine or imprisonment and section 54 of the Metropolitan Police Act of 1839 stipulated "any common prostitute loitering or soliciting for the purposes of prostitution to the annoyance of inhabitants or passers-by" would be subject to arrest and, if convicted, to a fine. In 1847 these powers were reiterated in the Town Police Clauses Act which allowed for the arrest of prostitutes soliciting in public places to the annoyance of passers-by or passengers. This early legislation makes it clear these women were to be governed as a nuisance but later regulation was more invasive, characterizing prostitutes as a danger. The Contagious Diseases Acts (1864, 1866, and 1869) condemned women living in certain garrison towns who were suspected of being common prostitutes to submit to a genital examination. If she (and it was only women) was found to be suffering from a venereal disease, she could be detained in a Lock hospital (i.e. a hospital which specialized in treating venereal diseases) until cured; if the examination was refused she could be sent to prison for three months. These Acts were of course driven by contemporary concerns regarding public health, a laudable cause, but they were a blunt instrument allowing the police autonomy over women's bodies and singling out women as the cause of disease with little effect on the spread of disease.[70]

The most notable legislative shift in regulating female sexual activity came in the Criminal Law Amendment Act 1885. Ostensibly passed to protect women and girls from themselves this Act raised the age of consent from 13 to 16 and strengthened existing legislation against prostitution by closing brothels and dance halls where prostitutes often worked, allowing children of prostitutes to be removed from their families and prohibiting landlords from renting rooms to prostitutes. In many ways the Act is reflective of the SOA 2003, criminalizing the procurement of women for sex by intimidation, drugs or deceit, preventing sex trafficking into, out of and within the United Kingdom and providing greater protection for children under 13 years of age. The 1885 Act clarified the law but ingrained the regulation of prostitution as a nuisance.

The next consideration for the law was driven by a clash between the Association for Moral and Social Hygiene, one of the aims of which was to secure the abolition of state regulation of prostitution, and the National Vigilance Association formed for the repression of criminal vice and public immorality. The resulting Street Offences Committee Report (1928), commissioned by the Home Office, had little effect on the law, but they did make this interesting and oft-quoted statement, which is perhaps reflective of the opposing aims of the interested parties:

> As a general proposition it will be universally accepted that the law is not concerned with private morals or ethical sanctions. On the other hand, the law is plainly concerned with the outward conduct of citizens in so far as that conduct injuriously affects the rights of other citizens. Certain forms of conduct it has always been thought right to bring within the scope of the criminal law on account of the injury which they occasion to the public in general. It is within this category of offences, if anywhere, that public solicitation for immoral purposes finds an appropriate place.

Thus prostitution was not to be decriminalized. The committee did make one significant recommendation – the term 'common prostitute' should be abolished. This terminology, used to denote a woman who was an habitual prostitute, was considered outdated in 1928 – as we will see this terminology was not abolished until 2009; again the law does not move swiftly.

The visibility of prostitutes was once again a concern in the post-war years and the Street Offences Act 1959 introduced stricter controls dispensing with the old language of annoyance and introducing the more simplistic terminology of it "shall be an offence for a common prostitute to loiter or solicit in a street or public place for the purpose of prostitution". This was a move that had been supported by the *Report of the Departmental Committee on Homosexual Offences and Prostitution 1957*, known as the Wolfenden Report, the next notable consideration of prostitution. Once again this Report had little practical impact on the law. The suggestions of the Committee, that higher penalties should be introduced for solicitation and the requirement of proving annoyance should be removed, had already being implemented. Wolfenden was not the last word on prostitution with the legal position debated throughout the 1970s and 1980s[71] but it was not until the twenty-first century that we saw notable changes to regulation discussed at Chapter 8, and even these are not substantial.

While public female sexual activity has been subject to regulation there has been little interest in female sexual offenders, with sexual offences considered a male predilection. In the nineteenth century sexual deviancy by women was contextualized in terms of the threat it posed to society – thus wives who strayed and women who prostituted themselves posed a danger to social mores over and above their own person. Women were largely considered passive, certainly in sexual matters,[72] and this was reflected in the absence of offences regulating child sexual abuse by females. Not only did the law rarely see fit to intervene – there was no corresponding offence of unlawful sexual intercourse when women had sex with young boys – but also the erroneous assumption that child sexual abuse is a male crime has deterred prosecutions for lesser offences. Those female offenders who have attracted popular attention in recent years have been viewed as being coerced by a male co-perpetrator. It appears we continue to cast women as less dangerous because incidences of sexual offending by women continue to be low and continue to pose a challenge to societal expectations of the female as a nurturing caregiver.[73]

The Male

Unsurprisingly the regulation of male sexuality has been the focus of sexual offences and restrictions on male autonomy have typically focussed on criminalizing behaviours considered 'unmanly', specifically same-sex sexual activity – and within this we can include the historic failure to recognize gender dysphoria. Circumcision of a male also raises some interesting questions regarding regulation of the sexes. Although female circumcision is absolutely prohibited, male circumcision for therapeutic or cultural reasons is lawful,[74] even when performed on a child who cannot consent.

Men have rarely featured as victims of sexual offences in legal discourse. Prior to 2003 a number of sexual offences could be committed only by men, and only women could be the victims and in any discussion of sexual offences men will typically be spoken of as offenders – is this characterization a fair one? It is one borne out by the statistics, the joint Official Statistics Bulletin of Sexual Offending in England and Wales reveals males accounted for 99 per cent of offenders found guilty of sexual offences in 2013.[75] This said, a new discourse of men as victims has been making headway in the past 15 years. Section 142 of the Criminal Justice and Public Order Act 1994 extended rape to anal intercourse, the eradication of homosexual offences has recognized same-sex sexual assaults and Government initiatives have been launched to support male victims.[76]

These statistics have not prevented men from being the subject of legal regulation and male sexual behaviour has been subject to legal constraint.

Homosexuality

While women found their sexuality constrained by the concept of ownership, male sexuality has been more closely governed though the criminalization of same-sex sexual activity. For example, Matthew Bacon described the offence of sodomy (unnatural sex) as one committed by men without the normal interest in women, defending the sentence of death as a remedy that prevented this vice from being passed to any children sired. Buggery, denoting anal sex or sex with an animal, had long been an offence and appeared in its most recent form in section 12 of the Sexual Offences Act 1956. Bestiality is one of the few offences that has consistently attracted social, legal and religious vilification but as a capital offence (until 1861) prosecutions and convictions were rare. The Buggery Act of 1533 made bestiality and anal sex with men, women or children[77] a secular crime when previously it had laid in the ambit of the church courts[78] and proscribed a capital sentence, reflecting the concern that men and women could be brought down to the level of lesser beasts and offspring could be sired.

Private male homosexual activity was not explicitly criminalized until 1885 as gross indecency, an offence conceived in the Criminal Law Amendment Act 1885, extended the regulation of male homosexual acts to those other than penetration, making it an offence for any male person to be party to, to procure or attempt to procure the commission of any act of gross indecency with another male person in public or private (s13). This essentially made male homosexual sexual acts (and female homosexuality was never subject to the same sanctions)[79] an offence until 1967 and was remarkably broad, encompassing activities where no physical contact was made.[80] Attempts to engage in homosexual activity were also regulated with importuning for an immoral purpose criminalized through the Vagrancy Act 1898, the Criminal Law Amendment Act 1912 and repeated in section 32 of the SOA 1956. By criminalizing sexual activity in both private and public these offences reflected contemporary concerns that homosexual men posed a threat – a stance, as we have seen, challenged by the Wolfenden Committee report. But as Sir David Maxwell Fyfe, who had led the opposition in the House of Lords to the implementation of Wolfenden argued, those convicted of homosexual offences should be subject to imprisonment "... because homosexuals in general were exhibitionists and proselytizers, and a danger to others, especially the young".[81] This criminalization of homosexual sexual activity had a number of repercussions. As Moran has outlined, social disapproval of homosexuals buttressed by criminalization provided ample opportunity for blackmail.[82]

In 1965 Lord Arran proposed the decriminalization of male homosexual acts but it was not until the Sexual Offences Act 1967 that we saw partial decriminalization as section 1 amended the law and decriminalized consensual private acts where both parties were 21-years-of-age.[83] Although the 1967 Act liberalized the law it did limit male homosexual activity to only two participants (at s1(2)(a)) and criminalized any consensual homosexual activity in public toilets (s1(2)(b) – a provision later echoed in the SOA 2003). The age of consent was eventually equalized by virtue of the Sexual Offences (Amendment) Act 2000.[84] Civil law also kept pace with social change and a number of Acts have sought to bring about equality – from the right to adopt in the Adoption and Children Act 2002 to the Equality Act 2010, which consolidated and extended anti-discrimination law in the provision of access to employment and private and public services. With the enactment of the SOA 2003 homosexual sexuality is now subject to the same criminal regulation as heterosexual relations – although the offence of sexual activity in public toilets may be, as Peter Tatchell has pointed out, an expression of continuing legal homophobia.[85]

One significant step toward remedying this historical homophobia was made with the Protection of Freedoms Act 2012, which allowed persons convicted under sections 12 and 13 of the SOA 1956 to apply to the Secretary of State for the conviction or caution to be disregarded (so removed from the official record) if certain conditions are met (ss92–94).[86]

The legacy of our criminalization of sexual activity between men is to be found in around 80 per cent of Commonwealth countries including India, Nigeria and Uganda.[87] The colonial export of English and Welsh law to these nations means many continue to regulate homosexual sex as unnatural. For example, section 377 of the Indian Penal Code attracted significant attention when its criminalization of anal and oral sex between men was challenged successfully as being in violation of the Indian Constitution,[88] a decision overturned four years later.[89] Nigeria continues to criminalize both carnal knowledge and gross indecency between men and Uganda's general offence against homosexuality prohibits all forms of sexual contact between men.

Protection of the male

With the regulation of 'unnatural' sexual relations between men there also came a degree of latitude to relieve men of liability for engaging in sexual acts considered normal but poorly judged. Explicit recognition of this in substantive law came in the form of "the young man's defence" (s6(3) SOA 1956), which provided a special defence for men who had unlawful sexual intercourse with a girl under the age of 16 (but not less than 13), if he was under the age of 24 and had not previously been charged with a like offence, and believed her to be 16 or over and had reasonable cause for the belief. This was a defence that only ever extended to young men – for example women charged with indecent assault under section 14 of the same Act could not make the same claim, sexual touching of a girl less than 16-years would be an irrefutable offence.[90] The defence is now reflected in the reasonable cause defence discussed at Chapter 3 but does demonstrate a certain historical leeway toward 'normal' male sexual relations – one bound up with the debates regarding the age of sexual consent. Indeed until the Sexual Offences Act 1993 there was also a legal presumption that a boy under the age of 14 was incapable of sexual intercourse and thus exempt from prosecution for rape, buggery and incest. This was of course a legal fiction assuming an imbecility of body, similar to the imbecility of mind provided for by *doli incapax* and was abolished by that Act for "natural or unnatural" sexual acts.

While substantive law provided limited protection for men, the agencies of the criminal justice system have implicitly and, at times, explicitly protected men. Consider for example the historically poor prosecution and conviction rates for rape – these have been linked to gendered presumptions, from an unwillingness to believe or support female victims to a willingness to buy into rape myths that devictimize women.[91] Historical ideas of manliness and sexual urges have buttressed these ideas of men as readily excused from violence (including sexual violence) against women[92] but, as commentators such as Weiner have demonstrated, appropriate behaviour towards women was considered a mark of a civilized man and reported violence against women declined in the latter half of the nineteenth century.[93]

Of course the historically gendered nature of the criminal justice system, with men in positions of power, has shifted and significant strides have been made to recognize and protect women and children from sexual victimization. However, as a report into the police handling of reports of offences committed by disc jockey and television presenter Jimmy Savile[94] and the sexual exploitation of children in Rotherham and Oxford suggest, the criminal justice system continues to be heavily weighted toward preferring the word of adult males over that of women and children.

The Child

The nineteenth century evidenced a confused approach to the very idea of childhood. Despite recognizing that childhood was an essentially innocent state, it was understood this was not something that could be maintained for all children. Although there was an ideal of innocence it was understood children could be deviant – by either virtue or position. Childhood was then a contested state in the nineteenth century although, chronologically speaking, the Victorian social commentator Mayhew suggested children were those aged less than 15-years-of-age, as children above this age had developed an "adult character" and were "beyond any influence of parent or state".[95] Similarly a Royal Commission set the age at below 14, suggesting that at 14 "the body becomes capable of enduring protracted labour".[96] Thus when we speak of the nineteenth century child we are often speaking of someone younger than our modern conception. However if the child was of the respectable middle or upper classes then the age of childhood could be significantly longer. Later in the period female children were also afforded a lengthier period of legally protected sexual innocence, something discussed further below.

Sexual victims

Regulation of girls was confirmed through the Offences Against the Person Act 1861.[97] The Act consolidated much of the historical provision regarding sexual offences and children and under this Act intercourse with a girl under the age of 10 years of age was charged as a felony. However, intercourse with a girl aged 10 to 12 years was a lesser misdemeanour offence. Regardless of the social conception of the innocence of childhood, these provisions offered little protection for those within the upper boundary of childhood.[98] After the 1861 Act the age of consent consistently rose, going from 12 to 13 years in 1875.[99] Social disquiet regarding one as young as 13 engaging in prostitution was harnessed by W.T. Stead, editor of the *Pall Mall Gazette*, through his own research regarding child prostitution. Public interest and social panic stirred up by Stead resulted in the age of consent being raised to 16 by virtue of the Criminal Law Amendment Act 1885.[100]

These were well-recorded shifts in the regulation of offences against children – but there are difficulties in addressing the historical child. Not only is the category of child a shifting one, but children were largely invisible as individuals until the early twentieth century. Childhood, as we understand the term in the twenty-first century, was not something experienced by all children. Children of the lower classes typically entered work as soon as they were capable and their childhood was barely distinguishable from adult life. The private realm was exactly that, private, and children had little bodily autonomy or integrity of their own.[101] There was awareness of the legislative deficiency that allowed parents to torture their children – and this included sexual abuse – without criminal sanction but the child as an autonomous individual with positive rights (outside of the working environment) was not recognized until the end of the century with the enactment of the Prevention of Cruelty to Children Act 1889, which allowed the state to intervene between parent and child in cases of wilful cruelty.[102] Incest was not a criminal offence until 1908 and therefore what we know to be the common paradigm of sexual abuse – abuse by close family members – would not have been an offence if the child had reached the age of consent.

This is not to say children were not recognized as victims of sexual offences in the nineteenth century although, as Jackson details, while cases were taken to court "probably less than a third" of the offenders were convicted.[103] As well as difficulties in establishing solid medical evidence children were not considered to be reliable witnesses[104] nor were respectable men (particularly fathers) readily accepted as offenders. Moreover, as Jackson makes clear, a child witness who could respond to questions about sexual activity had marked herself (and victims were usually female)[105] as immoral.[106] Good girls did not know the language of sexual activity. When these cases reached the press the loss of sexual innocence suffered by these victims was commonly presented in terms of its effects on the public realm rather than its impact upon the child. It was recognized that children could then be victims of sexual abuse, but concerns were articulated with regard to the moral effects on society, particularly in the field of prostitution.

As the welfare of the child became a significant policy issue post the Prevention of Cruelty to Children Act 1889 a welfarist position became more evident – although the law continued to very much reflect the Victorian position. The removal of the child from employment, the development of a national and regulated system of education and the Welfare State has shaped a modern conception of childhood as a protected space. Concerns regarding offending against children were periodically raised. However, as Smart points out, there was no exact term for child sexual abuse, with offences termed 'outrages', 'unlawful criminal or indecent assaults' or 'unlawful carnal knowledge'. Without the language of abuse it was difficult to conceive a particular problem to direct resources toward.[107] This said, some attempts were made to track offending behaviour. The Departmental Committee on Sexual Offences Against Young Persons (1925) recorded a significant rise in indecent assaults against the young, although incest had not increased and rape had decreased.[108] The report made many recommendations for the more effective prosecution of offenders, particularly in terms of adducing usable evidence from the child and abolishing the defence of 'reasonable belief' that a girl was over 16 – but these were not incorporated into the law. The later Cambridge Report (1957) showed a startling increase of 82.6 per cent of reported incidence of the defilement of girls under 13 years of age, and a 98.5 per cent rise for girls between 13 and 16 years of age between 1947 and 1954.[109]

Despite an attempt to raise the age of consent to 17 in the early 1900s[110] the age boundaries of 13 and 16 have been maintained. The SOA 1956 had consolidated the law preserving the offences of intercourse with a girl under 13 (s5), intercourse with a girl under 16 (s6), indecent assault on a woman (where a girl under 16 could not give any consent that would prevent an act being an assault) (s14) and the corresponding offence of indecent assault on a man (s15). The Indecency with Children Act 1960 extended the law to criminalize indecent conduct towards a young child (s1) making it an offence to commit an act of gross indecency with or towards a child under the age of 14, or to incite a child under 14 to commit such an act. This said, child sexual abuse was not taken terribly seriously until the late twentieth century, with victims often dismissed as fantasists[111] and men in thrall to their sexual instincts. In the light of these constraints and historic crimes unearthed by Operation Yewtree, Operation Hydrant (the Association of Chief Police Officers national coordination group for historic child abuse cases) and Operation Pallial (the NCA investigation into child abuse in Welsh care homes) it is clear that child sexual abuse has been historically under-reported and recorded. Statistical records of prevalence are hopelessly inadequate in this area.

While 16-years-of-age has endured as the upper end of consent, legislative provision regarding the child as a victim of sexual abuse has been informed in the modern period through social panics regarding the sexual safety of children. These concerns have been driven principally by media attention discussed at Chapter 1. The potential exploitation of the innocent child has been central to these changes and sexual innocence has been a quality extended to those of a higher age range. As we will see, the age of 18 has now been delineated as the uppermost end of childhood in certain circumstances, while those aged less than 13 have continued to be subject to more stringent protection.

Sexual perpetrators

This idea of childhood innocence has, to an extent, stymied research into children who sexually abuse. As children feature so readily in scandals and panics that reach the social realm children have rarely been considered as perpetrators.[112] Children and youths do of course commit sexual offences, but the prosecution was historically faced with additional hurdles to establishing criminal liability. We have already outlined above that young boys were deemed incapable of sexual intercourse but *doli incapax* provided an additional way of rebutting liability until the late twentieth century. In the nineteenth century children who had reached the age of criminal capacity (7-years-of-age), but were not yet of an age to be categorically judged an adult, required a more flexible notion, that of *doli incapax*. This principle provided that a child between 7 and 14 was to be initially presumed to be morally incapable of crime, on the basis he or she may not be capable of judging good from evil. It recognized that the child's ability to reason matured and that children may reach an adult standard of moral reasoning at different ages within this bracket. The minimum age was raised to 10 by section 16 of the Children and Young Persons Act 1963. Prior to the abolition of *doli incapax* in 1998, the child was afforded the unfettered capacity to reason to an adult standard at age 14.[113] This provision did not recognize a legislative end of childhood, but it did recognize a legislative end to childish reasoning.

Child sexual offenders have always been a statistically small group. By excluding rape by the under 14s and incest, taking into consideration the fluctuating age of consent, *doli incapax* and the physical inability of children to (usually) offend against adults this is unsurprising. Radford et al. (2012) found that 65.9 per cent of contact sexual abuse offences committed against children aged 0–17 were perpetrated by 'offenders' aged under 18.[114] Data obtained by the NSPCC likewise shows that between 2009 and 2012 5,028 child sexual abuse offences were reported where the perpetrator was under 18.[115] These reports do not necessarily translate into convictions, a welfare route may be taken or the child 'offender' may be below the age of criminal responsibility. That modern statistics point to a growth in child offenders undoubtedly says more about changes in legal regulation, social perceptions and a willingness to report and move forward with prosecutions than an increase in offending by children.

Conclusion

Many of the historic offences regulating sexual crime were, in the words of *Protecting the Public* (2002) "archaic, incoherent and discriminatory", and failed to reflect "changes in society and social attitudes".[116] This is not to say we have jettisoned all past offences, some addressed here are directly reflective of our modern position. For example our approach to street prostitution has changed very little since 1959 and, prostitution aside, female sexual offenders continue to be considered a lesser threat. The historical invisibility of the male victim and the historical unwillingness to accept the testimony of child victims of sexual abuse also echoes in our modern-day responses.

The SOA 2003 is the first substantive sexual offences Act to declare itself gender neutral and it is important to remember and reflect upon the antecedents to the Act. Not only have the issues discussed here shaped our current legal approach, but they continue to be live issues in society and throughout the criminal justice system. For example, the assumption that men may make a mistake about whether a sexual partner is of the age of consent is still given (albeit limited) credence in our substantive law and although there is now no legal impediment to prosecuting rape within marriage there may still be lingering social presumptions about the reality of consent.

While morality and proprietry were often paramount in shaping nineteenth and early twentieth century regulation, the welfare of the victim is now, if not supreme, at least central to regulation. In many ways the importance of whether a victim is male, female, a child or an adult has fallen away and in substantive law there is now strong legal protection for all classes of victims – particularly those deemed historically vulnerable. In the light of the inadequacies of these offences that had governed sexual offending the Home Office report, *Setting the Boundaries* (2000), sought to ensure that going forward the law would:

> Provide coherent and clear sex offences which protect individuals, especially children and the more vulnerable, from abuse and exploitation; enable abusers to be appropriately punished; and be fair and non-discriminatory in accordance with the ECHR and Human Rights Act.[117]

In meeting these terms of reference the review also appreciated it had to pay careful attention to society's views of what is right and wrong in sexual relationships and ensure it did not intrude into the private lives of consenting adults. The following chapters examine the offences that were enacted to achieve these goals.

Notes

1 E.L. James *50 Shades of Grey* London: Arrow (2012).
2 *R. v Peacock* unreported January 6, 2011 (Crown Ct (Southwark)).
3 *R. v Walsh (Simon)* unreported August 8, 2012 (Crown Ct (Kingston)).
4 *Corbett v Corbett* [1970] 2 All ER 33.
5 Births and Deaths Registration Act 1953. A sex classification can be altered later if there has been an error of fact or substance (s29).
6 Anon. *Trans: A Practical Guide for the NHS* London: Department of Health (2008).
7 *Re Forbes-Sempil* unreported, December 29, 1967 (OH).
8 The Marriage (Same Sex Couples) Act 2013.
9 By s11(c) of the Matrimonial Causes Act 1973 a marriage is void if the parties are not respectively male and female. This gave statutory effect to *Hyde v Hyde and Woodmansee* (1866) LR 1 P & D 130, although this case concerned the validity of plural marriages.
10 Transsexual is being used as the term here to denote people who believe their assigned sex at birth was wrong. The term transgender is sometimes used in the same way but can also be used to denote transvestites and others that move between gender boundaries. Cisgender has now begun to be used as an adjective to describe those whose gender corresponds to their assigned sex.
11 *Bellinger v Bellinger* [2003] UKHL 21.
12 *Corbett v Corbett* [1970] 2 All ER 33.
13 *R. v Tan (Moira)* [1983] 2 All ER 12.
14 Now superseded by the Equality Act 2010.
15 *J v ST (formerly J) (Transsexual: Ancillary Relief)* [1998] 1 All ER 431; *Bellinger v Bellinger* [2003] UKHL 21.
16 [2003] UKHL 21.
17 *Goodwin v United Kingdom* (2002) 35 EHRR 447.
18 *Rees v United Kingdom* (1986) 9 EHRR 56, ECHR; *Cossey v United Kingdom* (1990) 13 EHRR 622.
19 A requirement to provide a medical report giving details of treatment the applicant had undergone, or planned to undergo, is not incompatible with the ECHR. *Helen Carpenter v Secretary of State for Justice* [2015] EWHC 464 (Admin).
20 *W v W* (Nullity: Gender) [2001] 1 FLR 324.
21 For further discussion see J.J.W. Herring and P-L. Chau 'Defining, Assigning and Designing Sex' *International Journal of Law Policy and the Family* (2002) 16(3) pp. 327–367.

22 (1866) LR 1 P & D 130, 133. This case established that a marriage is void if the parties are not respectively male and female.

23 W. Blackstone *Commentaries on the Laws of England* Clarendon Press: Oxford (1765-69), Chapter 15, p. 430.

24 *R v De Manneville* 5 East 221, 102 Eng Rep 1054 KB (1804).

25 House of Commons debate May 20, 1867.

26 A. Clark 'Domesticity and the problem of wifebeating in nineteenth-century Britain: Working class culture, law and politics.' In S. D'Cruze (ed.) *Everyday Violence in Britain 1850–1950: Gender and Class* Harlow: Longman (2000) pp. 27–40.

27 S. Edwards '"Kicked, beaten, jumped on until they are crushed," all under man's wing and protection: the Victorian dilemma with domestic violence' in J. Rowbotham and K. Stevenson (eds) *Criminal Conversations* Columbus: Ohio State University Press (2005) pp. 247–266; M.J. Wiener, *Men of Blood: Violence, Manliness and Criminal Justice in Victorian England* Cambridge: Cambridge University Press (2006).

28 Although non-consummation of a marriage is grounds for annulment of a marriage.

29 Age of Marriage Act 1929.

30 Imprisonment became a sanction in 1857 when the action fell under the remit of the Divorce Courts. When the Matrimonial Causes Act 1884 reformed the law a refusal to accede to conjugal rights no longer led to imprisonment but was deemed to be desertion, which was then grounds for divorce.

31 [1805] East 6 387.

32 (1861) 9 HLC 577.

33 [1920] P 126.

34 *R. v Jackson* [1891] 1 QB 671.

35 *The Times* March 28, 1891. An effigy of Emily was also made to be burnt, a riot ensued and the police intervened, *The Times* March 30, 1891. Emily went on to become something of an activist for women's rights, publishing her concerns about coverture in *The Times* April 18, 20, 21, 22 and 23, 1891.

36 April 17, 1891.

37 Matrimonial Proceedings and Property Act 1970 s20.

38 An average of 35 petitions were made in the year 1965–1967. Law Commission, *Proposal for the Abolition of the Matrimonial Remedy of Restitution of Conjugal Rights* London: HMSO (1969).

39 [1888] 22 QBD 23.

40 See for example the statements of Justice Wills in the case.

41 Hale's Pleas of the Crown, Vol. I, 629.

42 [1949] 2 All ER 448.

43 (1976) 65 Cr App R 22.

44 [1991] UKHL 12.

45 Decision formalized in CJPO Act 1994 s142.

46 Family Law Act 1996 s63CA amended by Anti-social Behaviour, Crime and Policing Act 2014.

47 These are gender neutral and have been accessed by a small number of men. See Department for Children, Skills and Families, Research Brief No DCSF-RB128, *Forced Marriage: Prevalence and Service Response* London: National Centre for Social Research (July 2009).

48 M. Waller *English Marriage: Tales of Love, Money and Adultery* London: John Murray (2009).

49 This seems to have migrated as a process from treatments for men suffering from the same 'conditions' for which male circumcision was recommended. See O. Moscucci 'Clitoridectomy, circumcision and the politics of sexual pleasure in mid-Victorian Britain' in

A.H. Miller and J.E. Adams (eds) *Sexualities in Victorian Britain* Bloomington: Indiana University Press (1996).

50 The Act initially applied only to UK nationals or permanent UK residents, an issue identified as a loophole by campaigners against the practice. The law has now been amended and this is addressed at Chapter 10.

51 Female Genital Mutilation Act s3A inserted by the Serious Crime Act 2015 s72.

52 Female Genital Mutilation Act s4A inserted by the Serious Crime Act 2015 s71.

53 A. Sleator *The Female Genital Mutilation Bill* House of Commons Library Research Paper (March 24, 2003).

54 Home Affairs Committee *Female Genital Mutilation: The Case for a National Action Plan* Second Report London: The Stationary Office (2014). Accessible at http://www. publications.parliament.uk/pa/cm201415/cmselect/cmhaff/201/201.pdf.

55 Ibid.

56 Crown Prosecution Service, *Female Genital Mutilation Legal Guidance* http://www.cps. gov.uk/legal/d_to_g/female_genital_mutilation.

57 Female Genital Mutilation Act 2003 s5A inserted by the Serious Crime Act 2015. The first order was made by Bedfordshire police July 2015 just days after s5A came into force. The Serious Crime Act also places a duty on those who work in "regulated professions", which are healthcare workers and teachers, to notify the police if they discover FGM has been carried out on a girl (s5B).

58 For a discussion of how the print press can be used to illustrate the realities of rape in the nineteenth century see K. Stevenson 'Unearthing the Realities of Rape: Utilising Victorian Newspaper Reportage to Fill in the Contextual Gaps' *Liverpool Law Review* (2007) 28 pp. 405–423. K. Stevenson 'Crimes of Moral Outrage: Victorian Encryptions of Sexual Violence' in J. Rowbotham and K. Stevenson *Criminal Conversations Victorian Crimes, Social Panics and Moral Outrage* Columbus: Ohio State University Press (2005) pp. 232–246.

59 Sir Matthew Hale, *History of the Pleas of the Crown* London (1736) Vol. I, at p. 628.

60 *R. v Camplin* (1845) 1 Cox CC 220.

61 A. Clark 'Rape or Seduction? A Controversy over Sexual Violence in the Nineteenth Century', in *The Sexual Dynamics of History: Men's Power, Women's Resistance* London: Pluto Press (1983) and A. Clark *Women's Silence, Men's Violence: Sexual Assault in England 1770–1845* London: Pandora (1987).

62 But something that still finds expression in media reports of rape. For further discussion see K. Stevenson '"She Never Screamed Out and Complained": Recognising Gender in Legal and Media Representations of Rape' in J. Jones, A. Grear, R.A. Fenton and K. Stevenson *Gender, Sexualities and Law* London: Taylor & Francis (2010) pp. 121–134.

63 For further discussion see Clark *Women's Silence, Men's Violence*; J. Walkowitz *City of Dreadful Delight: Narratives of Sexual Danger in Late Victorian London.* London: Virago (1992); S. D'Cruze 'Sex, violence and local courts: working-class respectability in a mid-nineteenth-century Lancashire town' *British Journal of Criminology*, 39(1) (1999) pp. 39–55.

64 Although this was only by way of the rather oblique "It is felony for a man to rape a woman".

65 An offence that, if retained, may have surmounted some of the difficulties discussed at Chapter 3 regarding consent obtained by deception and SOA 2003 s76.

66 The Sexual Offences (Amendment) Act 1976 s1, amending the SOA 1956 s1.

67 S. Grace, C. Lloyd and L. Smith *Rape: From Recording to Conviction*, Research and Planning Unit. Paper 71. London: Home Office (1992); S. Lees and J. Gregory 'Attrition

in rape and sexual assault cases in England and Wales' *The British Journal of Criminology* (1996) 36 pp. 1–17.

68 J. Jordon 'Worlds apart? Women, rape and the police reporting process' *The British Journal of Criminology* (2001) 41 pp. 679–706; J. Temkin *Rape and the Legal Process* London: Sweet and Maxwell (1987); J. Temkin 'Plus Ca change: reporting rape in the 1990s' *The British Journal of Criminology* (1997) 37(4) pp. 507–528.

69 K. Soothill and S. Walby *Sex Crime in the News* London: Routledge (1991).

70 In 1886 the Acts were repealed. For further discussion see K. Baker 'The Contagious Diseases Acts and the prostitute: how disease and the law controlled the female body' *UCL Journal of Law and Jurisprudence* (2012) 1(1) pp. 88–119; J.R. Walkowitz, *Prostitution and Victorian Society: Women, Class, and the State* Cambridge: Cambridge University Press (1980); E. Bristow *Vice and Vigilance: Purity Movements in Britain since 1700* Colorado: Rowman and Littlefield (1977).

71 The law was considered by the Vagrancy and Street Offences Committee (1974–76) and the Criminal Law Revision Committee (1982–86); Criminal Law Revision Committee (1980), Fifteenth Report *'Sexual Offences'*, Cmnd 9213; Criminal Law Revision Committee (1982), *Working Paper on Offences Relating to Prostitution and Allied Offences*; Criminal Law Revision Committee (1984), Sixteenth Report *'Prostitution in the Street'*, Cmnd 9329.

72 See the work of L. Nead 'Seduction, prostitution, suicide: on the Brink by Alfred Elmore' *Art History* (1982) 5(3) pp. 308–322; C. Smart 'Disruptive bodies and unruly sex: the regulation of reproduction and sexuality in the nineteenth century' in Carol Smart (ed.) *Regulating Motherhood: Historical Essays on Marriage, Motherhood and Sexuality* London: Routledge (1992) pp. 7–32; Clark 'Rape or Seduction? A Controversy over Sexual Violence in the Nineteenth Century'.

73 T. Gannon and M. Rose 'Female child sexual offenders: towards integrating theory and practice' *Aggression and Violent Behaviour* (2008) 13(6) pp. 442–461.

74 *R. v Brown* [1994] 1 AC 212, *per* Lord Templeman.

75 Home Office *An Overview of Sexual Offending in England and Wales* London: Ministry of Justice, Home Office, and Office for National Statistics (2013).

76 The Male Rape Support Fund was created by the Ministry of Justice in 2014 to provide funding to charities and support organizations working for male victims.

77 *R. v Wiseman* (1718) Fortes Rep 91.

78 25 Hen. VIII c. 6.

79 In 1921 the House of Lords rejected the creation of an offence of gross indecency between women under the Criminal Law Amendment Bill.

80 *R. v Hunt* [1950] 2 All ER 291.

81 Cited in D. Kynaston *Family Britain, 1951–1957* London: Bloomsbury Publishing (2009) p. 332.

82 See the discussion in L. Moran *The Homosexual(ity) of Law* London: Routledge (1996) pp. 51–56.

83 These conditions did not decriminalize acts that took place in public toilets or involved more than two persons.

84 A response to the ruling in *Sutherland v United Kingdom* (1997) 24 EHRR CD 22-CD 35.

85 *New Statesman* October 13, 2003.

86 As sexual activity in a public toilet is still an offence convictions and cautions for s12 and s13 offences that took place in public toilets cannot be disregarded. There are calls for an automatic pardon to be given to all men convicted of these offences, without the need to apply to the Secretary of State.

87 For further discussion see Human Rights Watch 'This Alien Legacy: The Origins of "Sodomy" Laws in British Colonialism' December 2008. Accessible at http://www. hrw.org/reports/2008/12/17/alien-legacy.

88 *Naz Foundation v Govt. of NCT of Delhi*, 160 Delhi Law Times 277 (Delhi High Court 2009).

89 *Suresh Kumar Koushal and others v Naz Foundation and others* (Supreme Court of India 2013).

90 For further discussion see Cambridge Department of Criminal Science *Sexual Offences* London: MacMillan (1957).

91 S. Lees and J. Gregory *In Search of Gender Justice, Ruling Passions: Sexual Violence, Reputation and the Law* Buckingham: Open University (1997).

92 S. Rose *Limited Livelihoods: Gender and Class in Nineteenth-Century England* Berkeley and Los Angeles: University of California Press (1992); M. Roper and J. Tosh (eds) *Manful Assertions: Masculinities in Britain Since 1800* London: Routledge (1990); N. Tomes 'A Torrent of abuse: crimes of violence between working class men and women in London 1840–1875' *Journal of Social History* (1978) 11 pp. 328–345.

93 M.J. Wiener *Men of Blood: Violence, Manliness and Criminal Justice in Victorian England* Cambridge: Cambridge University Press (2006).

94 HMIC, *"Mistakes Were Made." HMIC's Review into Allegations and Intelligence Material Concerning Jimmy Savile Between 1964 and 2012* London: HMIC (2013). Accessible at http://www.justiceinspectorates.gov.uk/hmic/media/review-into-allega tions-and-intelligence-material-concerning-jimmy-savile.pdf.

95 Mayhew continued: "It is just beyond that age (or the age of puberty) that, as our prison statistics and other returns show, criminal dispositions are developed, 'self will' becomes more imperious and headstrong, that destructive propensity, or taste, which we term the ruling passion or character of the individual is educed, and the destiny of the human being, especially when apart from the moulding and well-directed care of parents or friends, is influenced perhaps for life." H. Mayhew *London Labour and the London Poor* Vol. I London: Penguin Classics (1985) (first published in this format 1861–1862 London: Charles Griffin and Co. p. 162).

96 *Employment of Children in Factories First Report of the Commissioners with Minutes of Evidence and Reports of District Commissioners* London: HMSO (1833).

97 Replacing corresponding provisions in the Offences against the Person Act 1828.

98 As Stevenson has highlighted, ss50 and 51 reiterated the 1828 provisions that carnal knowledge with a girl under 10 remained a felony, and between 10 and 12 a misdemeanour. The Act maintained the position that it was no offence to have sexual intercourse with a girl under 12 who "freely consented . . . however ignorant of the carnal connection she may be." K. Stevenson 'Observations on the law relating to sexual offences: the historic scandal of women's silence' *Web Journal of Current Legal Issues* [online] 4 (1993).

99 The Offences against the Person Act 1875 38 & 39 Vict c. 94 s4.

100 For further discussion of Stead's campaign see A. Brown and D. Barrett *Knowledge of Evil: Child Prostitution and Child Sexual Abuse in Twentieth-century England* Cullompton: Willan (2003).

101 G.K. Behlmer *Child Abuse and Moral Reform in England, 1870–1908* Stanford, CA: Stanford University Press (1982). This is not to say abuses against children were not recognized and Pollock provides ample evidence of abuses being legally condemned: L. Pollock *Forgotten Children: Parent-Child Relations from 1500 to 1900* Cambridge: Cambridge University Press (1983).

102 Prevention of Cruelty to and Protection of Children Act 1889.

103 In the period 1830–1914. L. Jackson *Child Sexual Abuse in Victorian England* London: Routledge (2000).

104 *The Times* August 25, 1890. An accusation of indecent assault against two little girls in August of that year resulted in a complaint of interference by the National Society for the Prevention of Cruelty to Children Officer. It was alleged he had rewritten the child's statement and coached the child on what to say on the stand. *The Times* noted Mr Bedford, solicitor for the defence, stated: "He thought the Court should know the facts and view the information on the Society in the future with suspicion." The Society disputed these facts but the element of distrust toward child witnesses clearly hindered the number of cases reported and/or brought to court.

105 Offences against boys and girls could be prosecuted as indecent assault for which the Assault of Young Persons Act 1880 fixed an age of consent at 13.

106 Jackson *Child Sexual Abuse in Victorian England* pp. 99–100.

107 C. Smart 'A History of Ambivalence and Conflict in the Discursive Construction of the "Child Victim" of Sexual Abuse' *Social & Legal Studies* (1999) 8 pp. 391–409.

108 *Departmental Committee on Sexual Offences against Young Persons*, Report, CrMD. No. 256 (1925) para 9, at 9.

109 The Cambridge Department of Criminal Science, *Sexual Offences* (1957) p. 12.

110 In an amendment proposed by the Criminal Law Amendment Bill 1917.

111 See discussions in J. La Fontaine *Child Sexual Abuse* Cambridge: Polity Press (1990).

112 Some notable research has taken place. M. Erooga and H. Masson *Children and Young People Who Sexually Abuse Others: Current Developments and Practice Responses* (2nd edn) London: Routledge (2006); S. Hackett, H. Masson, M. Balfe and J. Phillips 'Individual, family and abuse characteristics of 700 British child and adolescent sexual abusers' *Child Abuse Review* (2013) 22 pp. 232–245.

113 The presumption was abolished by virtue of the Crime and Disorder Act 1998 s34.

114 L. Radford, S. Corral, C. Bradley, H. Fisher, C. Bassett, N. Howat et al *Child Abuse and Neglect in the UK Today* London: NSPCC (2012).

115 Data obtained from 34 of 43 police forces across England and Wales. NSPCC, People Who Abuse Children an NSPCC Research Briefing June 2014. Accessible at: http://www.nspcc.org.uk/globalassets/documents/information-service/research-briefing-people-who-abuse-children.pdf.

116 Home Office Protecting the Public London: HMSO (2002), para 4.

117 Home Office Setting the Boundaries: Reforming the Law on Sexual Offences London: Home Office (2000), para 0.3.

Chapter 3

Consent and Sexual Offences

Introduction

An absence of consent is central to the commission of a number of sexual offences. For some it forms part of the definition of the offence itself and, for others, the capacity to legally consent is prohibited by the offence. The law then seeks to prescribe what amounts to real consent for sexual activities; if consent is found not to be genuine due to for example, threats of violence, deception concerning a crucial feature on which consent was based or the inability of the complainant to consent due to age, then there is no legal consent.

We are, in this chapter, primarily concerned with the four offences that require the prosecution to prove absence of consent: sections 1–4 of the Sexual Offences Act 2003 (SOA 2003). But there are other areas of the law where consent has been a disputed issue. Sadomasochism, the giving or receiving of pain for the purposes of sexual pleasure, has not been accepted as a sexual practice and is neither criminalized nor regulated under the SOA 2003. However the distinction between 'normal' sexual practices (including where these transmit human immunodeficiency virus (HIV)) and sexual violence is far from clear, and sexual activity that may give rise to liability for violent offences must be considered.

This chapter will detail the statutory provisions and leading cases but with an eye to highlighting conflicts in this area. It will also give some consideration as to how evidence is brought before the court to address the issue of consent and whether the criminal justice system has appropriately responded to the calls for greater victim support to improve the rates of reporting, attrition and conviction, which have been discussed in Chapter 1.

The Offences

All the offences that follow require that the accused has the intention for the relevant act. Thus if, for example, the touching is accidental then the offence is not made out.

Section 1 – Rape

Section 1 of the SOA 2003 follows the convention established in previous legislation by leading with the offence of rape. If the Act is at any point hierarchical it is
here, with rape considered the most serious sexual offence, carrying a potential life
sentence.

The offence itself is straightforward and requires the intentional penetration by
A (the defendant) of the vagina, anus or mouth of another person (B) with a penis,
where B does not consent to the penetration, and A does not reasonably believe that
B consents. That the offence encompasses anal and oral rape is important – these
orifices have not always been within the ambit of rape; non-consensual anal penetration only became rape in 1994[1] and oral penetration was introduced by the SOA
2003 itself.[2] These orifices also include any of the proscribed orifices that have been
surgically created (s79(3)).

Penetration is "a continuing act from entry to withdrawal" (s79(2)) and
includes penetration of the slightest degree.[3] Rape has always been distinguished
from the lesser sexual offences as it requires penile penetration. This has led many
commentators to claim rape can only be committed by a man and it is true there
is a long history of case law that claims rape cannot be committed by a female as
principal offender. However these cases were decided before the Gender Recognition Act 2004. It is submitted here that there is no reason the law would fail to
acknowledge a rape committed by someone who has legally transitioned to female
but retained their penis. To suggest otherwise would be to undermine the contention that rape is a particularly serious offence as it is an offence "of a particularly
personal kind" carrying "risks of pregnancy and disease transmission and should
properly be treated separately from other penetrative assaults".[4]

Oral penetration was included in the *actus reus* of the offence for this very
reason, to recognize the personal nature and inherent risks in penile penetration.
Forced oral sex used to be prosecuted only under indecent assault (now sexual
assault). It was recognized a lesser offence did not capture the severity of the act –
particularly when the victim is a child[5] – and its inclusion is to be welcomed.

We discuss any extraneous features that have to be present for rape to be
proven and the *mens rea* below – and we have already addressed marital rape at
Chapter 2. At this point it is worth noting penetration has to be intentional and
non-consensual, with no reasonable belief in consent by A. The shift to reasonable
belief rather than honest belief is discussed below and is a departure from the common criminal law subjectivist position we see in the *mens rea* for offences such
as the non-fatal offences. There is however some leeway as section 1(2) states:
"Whether a belief is reasonable is to be determined having regard to all the circumstances, including any steps A has taken to ascertain whether B consents." So
now we must look at what is reasonable in the circumstances, a contextual objective test that allows for the personal quirks or disabilities of A to be taken into
consideration. Academics such as Tempkin and Ashworth have questioned how
"all the circumstances" will be taken into account asserting "The broad reference
to 'all the circumstances' is an invitation to the jury to scrutinise the complainant's behaviour to determine whether there was anything about it which could have
induced a reasonable belief in consent."[6] This could open the door to rape myths
and stereotypes being used to discredit a complainant – and, as the Stern Review

(2010) demonstrates, rape myths are still prevalent.[7] Choice examples cited by the review include:

- 26–29 per cent (of people questioned) feel that a woman is at least partially responsible for her own rape if she had been drunk or was behaving in a flirtatious manner (2005).
- 17 per cent think a woman is partially responsible for her own rape if she was walking alone in a dangerous or deserted area (2005).
- 21 per cent of people feel that a person should take responsibility for being raped if they act flirtatiously (2010).
- 64 per cent of people feel that a person should take responsibility for being raped if they drink to excess/blackout (2010).
- 39 per cent of 18–24-year-olds think a person should accept responsibility for being raped if they go back to the assailant's house for a drink (2010).[8]

As the matter of consent is of course left to the jury they may be influenced by these myths in deciding upon the existence of a reasonable belief.[9] The presumptions discussed below go some way toward ameliorating this positon, but the Crown Prosecution Service (CPS) have been sufficiently worried by the existence of rape myths and stereotypes that they now offer some guidance to their own prosecutors about why and how they should be discounted.[10] Trial judges can also give warnings to the jury about rape myths when summing up, "particularly in areas where there is a danger of a jury coming to an unjustified conclusion without an appropriate warning".[11] Agencies of the criminal justice system have also taken significant steps toward improving processes for victims and these are explored further below.

Section 2 – Assault by penetration

Assault by penetration at section 2 was an offence introduced by the SOA 2003. This makes it an offence to penetrate the vagina or anus of another person with a part of A's body or anything else, where the penetration is sexual, B does not consent to the penetration and A does not reasonably believe that B consents. The offence covers serious sexual assaults (those that pre-2003 would have been charged as indecent assault) where penetration is not by a penis, making it overtly gender neutral. Successful prosecutions have involved penetration with a dildo,[12] digital penetration,[13] and penetration with a bottle and handle of a knife.[14]

That we required an offence commensurate in seriousness to rape in the law for non-penile penetrations was largely uncontested. It also provides a useful alternative to section 1 when the complainant is unsure (and it cannot be proven) what has penetrated them and carries the same maximum sentence. By including the requirement that the penetration must be sexual the offence ensures medical examinations and body searches are excluded. An assessment of whether the penetration is sexual is made by the jury on the basis of the guidance given at section 78 of the Act, which sets out that any penetration, touching or other activity is sexual:

If a reasonable person would consider that:

(a) whatever its circumstances or any person's purpose in relation to it, it is because of its nature sexual, or

(b)   because of its nature it may be sexual and because of its circumstances or the purpose of any person in relation to it (or both) it is sexual.

This slightly convoluted test boils down to 'an act is sexual if a jury believe it to be sexual'. The first limb allows jurors to conclude an act is sexual because it is by its very nature sexual, such as intercourse or oral sex. By reference to circumstances and purpose the second limb allows a consideration of broader issues. For example, the physical location of the act may be relevant, using a finger to administer a suppository in a care home for example, which would not be sexual if the purpose was medical, but could be if the purpose were sexual gratification by the carer. This is the meaning of sexual throughout the Act.[15]

Section 3 – Sexual assault

The SOA 2003 swept away the old indecent assault offences,[16] which were widely acknowledged to have become overly complex; requiring an assault coupled with the conditions of indecency, indecent intention and lack of consent.[17] Historically the indecent assault offence had proven surprisingly problematic, with conflicting case law regarding whether a hostile intent was required.[18] Adding a further layer of complexity in *Sutton* (1978),[19] where A had photographed boys and touched the boys to pose them, the court had stated the legislative sections were limited to assaults that were inherently indecent. *Court* (1989)[20] exemplifies the approach now reflected in the current law. A shop assistant had struck a 12-year-old-girl on her buttocks a number of times and, in response to police questioning as to motive, had replied "I don't know – buttock fetish." The House of Lords clarified that whether this amounted to an indecent assault depended upon where a jury found "right-minded persons would consider the conduct indecent or not".[21]

The sexual assault offence at section 3 of the SOA 2003 requires that there is an intentional touching of B, that the touching is sexual, B does not consent to the touching and A does not reasonably believe that B consents. "Sexual" carries the meaning at section 78 above. "Touching" is defined in section 79(8) SOA 2003 to include touching with any part of the body, with anything else, through anything. Any touching will then suffice, from overt groping to touching of clothing.[22] It may be assumed that indirect assaults, such as that which David Selfe has highlighted of throwing "a quantity of water over B, in order to soak her breasts through her T-shirt", are included,[23] but that touching such as that in *Sergeant* (1997)[24] where B was forced to masturbate into a condom is excluded, although this would be captured by section 4. Such a distinction between direct and indirect sexual assaults is perhaps unsatisfactory: the victim in *Sergeant* would undoubtedly consider himself a victim of what we would (at least) colloquially consider to be a sexual assault.

By replacing the indecency requirement with the requirement that the touching must be sexual, the offence has undoubtedly been simplified, although as Selfe has commented section 78 may exclude fetishist touching not deemed to be of a nature your average juror would find sexual unless that sexual motive is revealed.[25]

Section 4 – Causing a person to engage in sexual activity without consent

Section 4 makes it an offence for a person (A) to intentionally cause another person (B) to engage in sexual activity without that person's consent, if he does not reasonably believe that B consents. The offence is wide, taking in any form of sexual activity, from causing the complainant to penetrate themselves with objects,[26] masturbate the offender,[27] masturbate themselves,[28] perform oral sex on a third party[29] and engage in sex with animals.[30] This offence is also available for what is colloquially known as 'female rape', i.e. a female who forces a man to have sex with her. The offence is set to capture contact and non-contact offences, but has had the effect of cleaving off certain acts into this new category of sexual offending that may more straightforwardly be considered an assault.

The breadth of this offence has been taken into account in the legislation and section 4(4) delineates those acts sufficiently serious to warrant a maximum sentence of imprisonment for life as: where the activity caused was penetration of B's anus or vagina, penetration of B's mouth with a person's penis, penetration of a person's anus or vagina with a part of B's body or by B with anything else and penetration of a person's mouth with B's penis. For all other acts on conviction on indictment imprisonment is for a maximum of 10 years.

This approach of essentially prioritizing the penetration of some orifices over others has some drawbacks. Restricting oral penetration to a human mouth by B's penis excludes the oral penetration of animals. These would have to be dealt with as other less serious acts for sentencing purposes. Likewise forced anal and vaginal penetration of an animal – and as the pornography chapter shows us this is not an unusual sexual deviation[31] – is also considered a lesser offence for sentencing purposes. By prioritizing instances where the complainant him/ herself has been penetrated the offence fails to recognize the severity of being forced to penetrate.

Consent pre-SOA 2003

The *actus reus* requirements of these offences have caused few problems. It has been consent that has occupied the appeal courts for many years and we will now turn briefly to how the common law had dealt with consent prior to the SOA 2003.

Broadly speaking under the law prior to 2003 consent was negatived if the complainant was mistaken about the nature of the act to which he was consenting or to the identity of the person he had given consent to. By virtue of *Morgan* (1976)[32] consent was also judged subjectively – if A honestly thought B was consenting then he could not be intending to have sexual intercourse without consent. These principles developed through the common law and some are broadly reflected in the SOA 2003. As the SOA 2003 drew upon these common law principles we do need to briefly reflect upon them.

In *Clarence* (1889),[33] discussed at Chapter 2, the justices considered whether A's failure to disclose his sexual disease had negatived his wife's consent to sex.

The earlier case of *Flattery* (1877)[34] where A had sexual intercourse with B telling her it was medical treatment for the fits she was suffering, had concerned a different point of law than that at question in *Clarence*. In *Flattery* consent had been obtained by fraudulent conduct concerning the nature of the act: A had induced B to believe that she was undergoing medical treatment or examination and this clearly negated consent to sexual activity.[35] Cases where an injurious condition was withheld from the complainant (such as gonorrhoea or syphilis) had been held to negate consent to sexual activity in limited circumstances but these were not binding in Clarence where sections 20 and 47 of the Offences Against the Person Act 1861 had been charged.[36] Heard by 13 justices there is no clear ratio to *Clarence*, but the majority did accept that the only types of deception or mistake that would vitiate consent were those relating to the nature or condition of the act that was being consented to, or the identity of the perpetrator of the act.[37] *Tabassum* (2000)[38] addressed the same point in the modern context where the defendant had conducted breast examinations on the pretence he was collecting data for a cancer-screening programme.[39] Dismissing his appeal against conviction the Court of Appeal sought to draw a distinction between consent to the nature of the act (the touching) and its quality (medical purposes not indecent behaviour) and held there was no consent to the quality of the act. This distinction was not particularly helpful, with quality previously understood to be part of the nature of an act.[40]

Consent was also held not to be present if the complainant did not have the knowledge or understanding, by age, illness or disability, to consent,[41] was unconscious[42] or intoxicated to the point they could not consent.[43]

A fraud as to identity was also held to vitiate consent, but this was generally recognized and affirmed in the CJPOA 1994 that it was impersonation of a husband that vitiated the wife's consent. It was left to the courts in *Elbekkay* (1995)[44] to clarify that the rule relating to impersonation of a husband applied equally to impersonation of a boyfriend.

DPP v Morgan[45] dealt with the difficult issue of a mistake of *mens rea* when A claimed a belief in consent to the act of sexual intercourse after the complainant's husband told him his wife liked to pretend to be raped, then bound and gagged her and invited A to have intercourse with her. Morgan later told the court that if he had known the true situation he would not have had sex with his friend's wife. A majority of their Lordships held if a person honestly believed that the woman was consenting to intercourse he should not be convicted, even where that belief was not based on reasonable grounds. This statement of the law could, and often was, considered an expression of the old patriarchal agenda to excuse men of rape.[46]

The lingering principle that consent was submission induced by fear, force or fraud discussed at Chapter 2 was defeated in *Olugboja* (1982).[47]

Using these principles jurors were to conclude whether consent was given "applying their combined good sense, experience and knowledge of human nature and modern behaviour" to the facts of each case.[48] This left a significant amount of discretion to the jury and the Government's White Paper *Protecting the Public* (2002) then sought "to make statutory provision that is clear and unambiguous".[49]

Consent and the Sexual Offences Act 2003

Clarity in the meaning of the definitional term of consent was central to the development of the SOA 2003. In the White Paper the Home Office stated one aim in reforming the law was clarification of consent:

> It is vital that the law is as clear as possible about what consent means in order to prevent miscarriages of justice that result in an innocent party being convicted or the guilty walking free. Juries must decide that they are sure, beyond reasonable doubt, whether the complainant was consenting or not.[50]

The SOA 2003 then, for the first time, provided a statutory definition of consent. This legislation has not yet been fully tested; however as Lady Justice Hallett commentated in 2007: "As enacted, the legislation on this topic has not commanded totally uncritical enthusiasm. For some it goes too far, and for others not far enough."[51]

Consent is directly addressed at sections 74–76 and the offences necessarily include consent as a definitional element. The offences at sections 1–4 require that B does not consent to the penetration, and A does not reasonably believe that B consents. Consent is then effectively addressed through three questions: whether A in fact consented, and (if A did not) did B believe A consented and was this belief reasonable. Section 1(2)[52] provides some guidance on how to assess whether a belief is reasonable, stating regard must be given to "all the circumstances, including any steps A has taken to ascertain whether B consents".[53] These circumstances are not limited to factual circumstances concerning the sexual act, but extend to the personal characteristics of A, including youth, learning disabilities and mental disorders – but only in appropriate circumstances. To avoid section 1(2) opening the door to belief in consent for sexual predators the Court of Appeal have clarified:

> . . . beliefs in consent arising from conditions such as delusional psychotic illness or personality disorders must be judged by objective standards of reasonableness and not by taking into account a mental disorder which induced a belief which could not reasonably arise without it.[54]

The characteristics taken into account in objective tests have consistently been a cause of concern for the criminal law and it appears it may be the case again here.

Consent can be withdrawn at any time during sexual activity and the reality of consent can be addressed in historical context if that is relevant, for example where B had been groomed by A when B was a child and the question for the jury is the reality of consent when B is an adult.[55]

Section 74 – The 'definition' of consent

Section 74 provides that a person consents if he agrees by choice and has the freedom and capacity to make that choice. The terms within this definition are so oblique that this cannot be a definition of consent *per se* but guidance for decision making. Moreover as Tempkin and Ashworth comment:

> it might be thought that 'freedom' and 'choice' are ideas which raise philosophical issues of such complexity as to be ill-suited to the needs of criminal justice – clearly those words do not refer to total freedom or choice, so all the questions about how much liberty of action satisfies the 'definition' remains at large.[56]

Capacity is also a problematic term that the Explanatory Notes to the Act do little to elucidate, stating that a person might not have sufficient capacity because of his age or because of a mental disorder. However, if you are a person with a mental disorder impeding choice or under 16-years-of-age the Act already makes provision for assuming a lack of consent (see Chapters 4 and 5). In actuality capacity has come to be primarily addressed under case law concerning intoxication. In the leading case of Bree (2007)[57] the complainant had drank substantial amounts of alcohol and Bree had returned home with her. Both parties agreed the complainant was drunk, but while Bree asserted the complainant had encouraged and consented to sexual intercourse she maintained she had not. Bree was convicted and appealed. The Court of Appeal sat to address the effect of voluntary alcohol consumption and consent. Quashing the conviction they stated:

> If, through drink (or for any other reason) the complainant has temporarily lost her capacity to choose whether to have intercourse on the relevant occasion, she is not consenting . . . However, where the complainant has voluntarily consumed even substantial quantities of alcohol, but nevertheless remains capable of choosing whether or not to have intercourse, and in drink agrees to do so, this would not be rape.[58]

Although the trial had been complicated by the prosecution changing their arguments part of the way through the case, the ratio was quite clear; a drunken consent can still be real consent. Commentators such as Wallerstein have questioned why the law would allow consent in these circumstances when drunken suspects cannot be interviewed by the police, drink driving is prohibited and valid contracts cannot usually be executed.[59] But this approach is clearly a practical approach to a difficult problem, preserving the autonomy of people to have sex when drunk.

The inclusion of freedom in the consent test is a clear nod to *Olugboja* and reflects the dictum of Lord Justice Dunn in that case who had stated "every consent involves a submission, but it by no means follows that a mere submission involves consent".[60] Ensuing submission does not equate to consent is important and the inclusion of the term 'freedom' captures this. However the emergent case law has gone further than may have been anticipated.

Conditional consent

This is an issue that has recently arisen in relation to section 74, principally due to the narrow interpretation of section 76 discussed below. In short the evolving case law has taken the approach that where consent is given on the basis of some condition that is a crucial feature, and the complainant had been deceived about this crucial feature, then consent may be negated. A series of cases have accepted this proposition, most recently in R *(on the application of F) v The DPP* (2013),[61] an application for judicial review of a decision not to prosecute where the court considered an episode when the complainant consented to sexual intercourse on the clear understanding that her partner would not ejaculate inside her vagina. He deliberately ejaculated inside her. The question for the court was whether ejaculation without consent could transform consensual intercourse into rape. The court stated:

> She was deprived of choice relating to the crucial feature on which her original consent to sexual intercourse was based. Accordingly her consent was negated. Contrary to her wishes, and knowing that she would not have consented, and did not consent to penetration or the continuation of penetration if she had any inkling of his intention, he deliberately ejaculated within her vagina. In law, this combination of circumstances falls within the statutory definition of rape.

The similar case of *Assange v Swedish Prosecution Authority* (2011)[62] – a judicial review of an extradition order – reached the same conclusion when a deliberate decision not to use a condom was made by A when B had made it clear this was a condition of intercourse.

These are surprising decisions, opening the door to rape where a man deceives a woman about having a vasectomy or causing a person to engage in sexual activity without consent where a women lies about taking contraceptive pills. *McNally* (2013)[63] takes this further.[64] The case involved an internet relationship between Justine McNally, a young female who had misrepresented herself as a male called "Scott" and built up an online relationship with another young woman for a number of years. When the parties met McNally had continued the ruse and, in the course of an ongoing sexual relationship, had penetrated the complainant orally and digitally. Convicted at trial on six counts of assault by penetration, McNally appealed. The Court of Appeal dismissed McNally's appeal as she had consistently held herself out as a male and the court determined "deception as to gender can vitiate consent" as the sexual nature of the acts is different where the complainant is deliberately deceived by a defendant into believing the latter is a male. The court stated the complainant had chosen to have sexual encounters with a male and her freedom to choose whether or not to have a sexual encounter with a female was removed. The justices emphasized that there had been an active deception, and it may be assumed that mere mistakes as to gender are outside of the ambit of section 74. The earlier Gemma Barker case (2012)[65] had similarly accepted a guilty plea to sexual assault when Gemma presented herself as a male in order to sexually touch a number of her friends by stating and disguising herself as male.

McNally establishes a difficult precedent in light of the Gender Recognition Act 2004 where transitioning persons are living in their acquired gender role.[66] The Law Commission were alive to such difficulties in their 2000 review of consent pointing out: ". . . it seems likely that a court permitting a jury to convict on such grounds would be held to have infringed the transsexual's rights under Article 8, and the possibility should therefore be eliminated".[67]

They conclude:

> . . . an apparent agreement to a sexual act by another should not be disregarded merely because it is given under the impression that the other is male whereas the other is in fact female, or vice versa, where the other has undergone sex-reassignment surgery.[68]

One would expect transgender persons to be given careful consideration and CPS policy advises where there is such a deception, in additional to the general Public Interest Test, additional considerations should be taken into account, including whether the offending occurred as a result of gender uncertainty and the duration of the relationship between the suspect and complainant.[69]

These cases reopen the old question of whether a failure to disclose HIV status can vitiate consent. In *B* (2006)[70] this had been answered in the negative, as Lord Justice Latham stated:

> All we need to say is that, as a matter of law, the fact that the appellant may not have disclosed his HIV status is not a matter which could in any way be relevant to the issue of consent under Section 74 in relation to the sexual activity in this case.[71]

A deception about a positive HIV status (or any other sexually transmitted disease) will then not negate consent for the purposes of sexual intercourse, but it will open the defendant up to liability for offences against the person, an issue discussed below.

Usefully the justices in *McNally* did state that circumstances in which consent may be vitiated are not limitless and some deceptions (such as in relation to wealth, age or marital status) will not be sufficient to vitiate consent. But questions remain. What of undercover police officers such as Mark Kennedy et al, who had sexual relationships with animal rights activists by virtue of pretending to be activists themselves,[72] or the person who lies about their religion?[73] These may very well be crucial features on which consent is based and, as the law stands, it is unclear whether they will be operative deceptions.

Section 75 – Evidential presumptions

The presumptions at sections 75 and 76 do not define consent but raise presumptions. Section 75(1) provides that where A did the relevant act and knew that any of the circumstances detailed at section 75(2) existed, B is presumed not to have consented, unless sufficient evidence is adduced to raise an issue as to whether they consented. A is to be taken not to have reasonably believed the complainant consented unless sufficient evidence is adduced to raise an issue as to whether he reasonably believed it. In *Ciccarelli (Yuri)* (2011)[74] the court stated that before the question of reasonable belief in consent could be left to the jury, some evidence had to be adduced to support the reasonableness of A's belief that B had consented to the sexual act. In the *Ciccarelli* case this meant there had to be reasonable evidence to support A's belief that B had consented to being touched while asleep – when A and B had only met on a number of occasions and did not have a relationship.

The exhaustive list of circumstances at section 75(2) are that:

(a)   any person was, at the time of the relevant act or immediately before it began, using violence against the complainant or causing the complainant to fear that immediate violence would be used against him;

(b)   any person was, at the time of the relevant act or immediately before it began, causing the complainant to fear that violence was being used, or that immediate violence would be used, against another person;

(c)   the complainant was, and the defendant was not, unlawfully detained at the time of the relevant act;

(d)   the complainant was asleep or otherwise unconscious at the time of the relevant act;

(e)   because of the complainant's physical disability, the complainant would not have been able at the time of the relevant act to communicate to the defendant whether the complainant consented;

(f)   any person had administered to or caused to be taken by the complainant, without the complainant's consent, a substance which, having regard to when it was administered or taken, was capable of causing or enabling the complainant to be stupefied or overpowered at the time of the relevant act.

A prosecutor may then seek to rely on one of these presumptions and, if the defence fails to rebut them, then no consent will be found. It is for the judge to decide whether sufficient evidence has been raised for the question of consent to be left to the jury. The evidence adduced has to support a reasonable belief in consent, if it is merely 'fanciful' or 'speculative' the judge can direct the jury to convict (if the offence is otherwise made out).[75]

This section has generated little case law. There is perhaps a straightforward reason for this; when Carline and Gunby sought the opinions of barristers they found "It was felt that the use of a presumption only served to further complicate the trial and they were therefore avoided by both barristers and Judges."[76] Certainly many of the circumstances outlined in section 75 also fall squarely within the ambit of (the less complicated) section 74 and, for example, should the defendant rebut section 75(2)(a) it will still be for the prosecution to prove, beyond reasonable doubt, that the offence has been made out.

The requirement that A must have knowledge of the circumstances at section 75(2) provides something of a brake on raising the presumption. If A claims no knowledge of B's disability (s75(2)(e)) should this fail to trigger the presumption? There are also some definitional problems. The requirement of immediacy at section 75(2)(a) and (b) seems to exclude a threat of future violence, something the criminal law has struggled with in other areas.[77] These sections are broad enough to encompass threats of violence that do not come from A and we can assume violence embraces the common law offence of battery given a threat of violence amounts to an assault; but again clarification would be welcomed. That the threat must be one of violence does exclude other common threats – as Women Against Rape London suggested:

> Rape by police officers, immigration officials, doctors, landlords, employers, heads of children's homes and others in positions of power, is particularly hard

to report. If the rapist can then successfully defend himself on the grounds that the victim "consented," the door is wide open for further abuse . . . Threats to the welfare or security of a child are frequently used against women by partners or ex-partners . . . Women – and children – must not be left vulnerable to such threats. Financial duress is also commonly used where there are children involved.[78]

Setting the Boundaries had initially recommended a wider presumption encompassing "threats or fear of serious harm or serious detriment of any type to themselves or another person"[79] but these threats can of course be considered through section 74 and, as the consultation paper sets out, there may be considerable difficulties in deciding the limits of what amounts to a 'threat' if it is not restricted to violence.

Section 75(2)(d) puts the case of *Larter & Castleton* (1995)[80] on a statutory footing raising an evidential presumption where B is asleep or unconscious. These are expressed as very particular conditions, potentially causing difficulty in situations such as those in *Bree* where it may be difficult to establish whether B was unconscious or merely intoxicated. Moreover these are expressed as static states, but many complainants may move in and out of consciousness. Section 75(2)(f) raises the issue of intoxication. A late addition to the Bill, this section is meant to deal with drink spiking after concerns were raised about Rohypnol being used to sedate potential victims of sexual offences.[81] The presumption does of course also include where a drink is adulterated with alcohol and raises the interesting issue that involuntary intoxication – or blameless intoxication – can raise a presumption when voluntary intoxication does not.

Section 76 – The conclusive presumptions

The presumptions at section 76 are irrebuttable; therefore if any of the circumstances listed below exist then it is to be conclusively presumed that B did not consent to the relevant act and that A did not believe that the complainant consented to the relevant act. The circumstances at section 76(2) are that:

(a)   the defendant intentionally deceived the complainant as to the nature or purpose of the relevant act;
(b)   the defendant intentionally induced the complainant to consent to the relevant act by impersonating a person known personally to the complainant.

In the light of section 74 and the evidential presumptions there has been significant criticism of this new regime. Tempkin and Ashworth question the hierarchical nature of situating section 76 as conclusive, asking:

Are the three categories intended to reflect some kind of moral hierarchy, so that the most serious cases of non-consent give rise to irrebuttable presumptions and the next most serious to rebuttable presumptions, with the remainder falling within the general definition? Or is the organising principle one of clarity and certainty, so that it is the clearest cases (not necessarily the worst) that give

rise to irrebuttable presumptions and the next clearest to rebuttable presumptions, with the remainder falling within the general definition? Or is it a mixture
of the two, with an added element of common law history?[82]

It seems strange that being beaten into submission raises a rebuttable presumption –
when engaging in sexual activity due to fraud raises a conclusive presumption. But
this is how the law has been set. As you can see these presumptions have a long
legal history, reflecting the cases of *Flattery* etc. discussed above. Using the term
'purpose' does also perhaps clarify what may have been intended by the term 'quality' in *Tabassum* but also perpetuates a legal fallacy that the nature of an act can
be divided from its purpose. Perhaps the best we can say is that these frauds have
a long history of proving problematic and section 76 seeks to tackle this as clearly
as possible. However it is the limits of section 76(2)(a) that have caused significant
difficulty for the courts.

In *Devonald* (2008)[83] A was convicted of an offence under section 4 SOA 2003
after impersonating a young woman online to induce the complainant (B) to masturbate in front of a webcam in order to embarrass him. The complainant, a young
man, had been in a relationship with the daughter of A and the online seduction
of him was an elaborate hoax, with A posing as a young woman named Cassey.
The issue was whether B had consented to the masturbation and the trial judge
ruled it was open to the jury to conclude that the complainant was deceived as to
the purpose of the act of masturbation. On appeal A submitted that the SOA 2003
section 76(2)(a) dealt with deception as to the act rather any surrounding circumstances and B had understood the act in which he had engaged was sexual. The
Court of Appeal held it was open to the jury to conclude that B had been deceived
as to the purpose of the masturbation as he had been deceived into believing that
he was indulging in sexual acts with and for the sexual gratification of the young
woman. This gave a surprisingly broad interpretation to the nature of the act.

Jheeta (2007)[84] adopted a far narrower approach. B had begun a sexual relationship with A and, after a few months, had received threatening text messages
and telephone calls; these were from A, but B did not know that. B also received
text messages pretending to be various police constables and, whenever she tried to
end her relationship with A, she received text messages from these 'police officers'
telling her that she should sleep with him, otherwise she would receive a fine. When
arrested, A admitted sexual intercourse had taken place whilst the complainant was
not truly consenting and was advised to plead guilty to rape on the basis that his
behaviour fell within the ambit of section 76. Sitting to consider the safety of the
conviction Sir Igor Judge upheld the conviction, but stated:

> On the written basis of plea the appellant undoubtedly deceived the complain-
> ant. He created a bizarre and fictitious fantasy which, because it was real enough
> to her, pressurised her to have intercourse with him more frequently than she
> otherwise would have done. She was not deceived as to the nature or purpose
> of intercourse, but deceived as to the situation in which she found herself. In our
> judgment the conclusive presumption in section 76(2)(a) had no application, and
> counsel for the appellant below were wrong to advise on the basis that it did.

B had not been deceived as to the nature or purpose of the sexual intercourse, but deceived as to the situation in which she had found herself – and this was outside section 76. However, in the light of A's clear admissions in interview and his guilty plea, it was clear B had not exercised a free choice for the purpose of section 74 of the Act and so had not truly consented.

We are then faced with two very different readings of nature, one that considers the wider context and one that looks only to the nature of the specific sexual act. In *Jheeta* Sir Igor Judge attempted to clarify how narrow the presumption was, making it clear that pre-2003 cases such as *Linekar* (1995)[85] would not now fall within section 76. In *Linekar* A had promised to pay a prostitute £25 for intercourse, but had no intention of paying. The trial judge left it to the jury to consider whether this fraud vitiated a consent given on the basis that A would pay and A was convicted. The conviction was quashed as the consent given by the prostitute was held to be real consent: a promise to pay was not a fraud that could vitiate consent. While *Jheeta* and *B* (below) declare this situation would not now fall within section 76 there is now an argument it could fall under section 74.

These divergent interpretations of section 76 were addressed by the Court of Appeal in *B*.[86] A had used false identities to cause his girlfriend to engage in sexual acts over the internet and was charged with seven offences of causing a person to engage in sexual activity without consent contrary to section 4(1) SOA 2003 in that he had deceived her as to the purpose of the relevant act. The prosecution predictably relied upon the broad construction of section 76 in *Devonald*; the defence on its narrower construction in *Jheeta* and *Assange*. As with *Devonald* the crux of the matter was whether there had been a deception as to purpose. On appeal against conviction the court addressed whether there had been a deception within the ambit of section 76(2)(a):

> The complainant knew full well what she was being asked to do and what she did in fact do, namely perform a sexual act for the benefit of the camera. She could have been in no doubt that the motive was at least in part sexual gratification. If so, on one view, even if one were to extend the definition of purpose to include the appellant's intention, as has been suggested, there is here no evidence going to the issue of deceit as to his purpose.[87]

In explicit disapproval of *Devonald* the court stated:

> Those engaging in a sexual act may have a number of reasons or objectives and each party may have a different objective or reason. The Act does not specify whose purpose is under consideration. There is, therefore, a great danger in attempting any definition of the word purpose and in defining it too widely. A wide definition could bring within the remit of section 76 situations never contemplated by Parliament.[88]

This practical judgment acknowledges the difficulties inherent in an expansive definition of section 76, and we could add to this that section 76 effectively removes from the defendant the right to challenge the reality of consent and thus should not be broadly construed. But the limits of section 76 do cause practical difficulties for section 74. Is the list of deceptions at section 76 nature, purpose and impersonation, an exhaustive list of legally relevant deceptions? Should any other deceptions be dealt with under section 74 or have they been implicitly excluded by the prescriptive nature of section 76?

Sexual History Evidence, Special Measures and Anonymity

Where consent is disputed it will fall to the jury to make a decision on the basis of the evidence presented at trial (where the judge leaves the question to the jury). Historically evidence could readily be adduced to rebut denials of consent in sexual cases and defence counsel were given the opportunity to portray complaints as not only untruthful about whether consent had been given in the particular case, but whether the complainant was more generally disreputable. For example, evidence could be given that the complainant was a common prostitute[89] as this was considered relevant to the issue of consent.[90] Although women could be questioned on their sexual history there was not unfettered discretion to discredit their testimony, as Justice Byles, set out in 1871: "I think it quite clear that the prosecutrix in a charge of rape, or attempt at rape, cannot be contradicted by persons who swear that they have had connection with her, for a rape may be committed upon a prostitute."[91] This was rather a liberal statement for the time, and was by no means observed in all cases. By the early 1970s it was settled law that the complainant could be cross-examined about her reputation (including moral character), any previous sexual intercourse between herself and the defendant and evidence could be called to contradict any denials. The complainant could also be questioned about sexual intercourse between herself and other men, but no evidence could be called to contradict denials on that point. A woman's respectability was then a matter that could go to the very heart of the case, as Lord Justice Stephenson forcefully put it:

> In an age of changing standards of sexual morality it may be harder to say where promiscuity ends and prostitution begins, and it may be unnecessary to decide on which side of the dividing line the particular conduct falls which a man charged with rape may wish to prove. Evidence which proves that a woman is in the habit of submitting her body to different men without discrimination, whether for pay or not, would seem to be admissible.[92]

As unpleasant a statement as this was, it was not until the decision in *Morgan* (1976) that widespread concern prompted the appointment of the Heilbron Committee, sitting to consider the state of the law and make recommendations for change. As well as recommending complainant anonymity[93] the Committee suggested sexual history evidence should only be introduced in limited circumstances.[94] This was given legislative effect by the Sexual Offences (Amendment) Act 1976, section 2 which limited questioning on sexual history to where it would be "unfair to that defendant to refuse to allow the evidence to be adduced or the question to be asked" giving the trial judge ultimate discretion.[95] It was this discretion that caused the matter to be readdressed. As Tempkin has stated, the legislation was understood to be "deeply flawed, permitting a wide use of sexual history evidence whenever it was deemed by the trial judge to be relevant to the issue of consent".[96] Change came when a Home Office working group[97] sat to once again consider the operation of the law and found that the Sexual Offences (Amendment) Act, section 2 was widely interpreted and sexual history evidence admitted too readily – concluding that "the existing law is not achieving its purpose".[98]

Sections 41–43 of the Youth Justice and Criminal Evidence Act 1999 (YJCEA) then sought to tighten and clarify the law, continuing to restrict sexual history evidence but providing a number of gateways to admissibility set out at section 41(3) and (5). The Act also restated that any question regarding sexual behaviour must be justified on the ground that to refuse it would render any conviction unsafe. Once again these measures were not without criticism[99] and have since been eroded by a reintroduction of judicial discretion to allow sexual history evidence where it cannot be introduced through one of the gateways.[100] This said, there is no evidence sexual history evidence is being readily admitted and judges do appear to be taking a narrow approach.[101] Moreover the objective focus at section 1(1)(c) SOA 2003[102] limits how relevant sexual history may be to a defendant's belief in consent.

Special measures are available for all vulnerable witnesses and are a provision that help relieve the stress associated with giving evidence in court.[103] Vulnerable witnesses include children, discussed at Chapter 4, but also those whose quality of evidence is likely to be diminished because they fall within the criteria of the YJCEA 1999. These include those who suffer from a mental disorder (as defined by the Mental Health Act 1983) (s16(2)(a)(i)), have a significant impairment of intelligence and social functioning (s16(2)(a)(ii)), or have a physical disability or are suffering from a physical disorder (s16(2)(b)). Provision can include screening the witness in court (s23), giving evidence from a remote location by a live link (s24), clearing the court to give evidence 'in private' (s27), the removal of wigs and gowns (s26), and giving video-recorded evidence in chief (given in support of the case) (s27). These measures are also available for victims of sexual offences and section 101 of the Coroners and Justice Act 2009 inserted section 22A into the YJCEA to make provision for adult complainants in sexual offence trials for the automatic admissibility of a video-recorded evidence in chief, unless this would not be in the interests of justice. There have been some concerns that the use of these measures could distance the jury from the victim and lead them to doubt the credibility of the victim, but research thus far does not suggest this is the case.[104]

For certain sexual offences[105] the complainants are given lifelong anonymity under the Sexual Offences (Amendment) Act 1992 and names cannot be revealed on any media platform. Complainants can waive this right by applying to the court, or it can be lifted by the court where it is in the interests of justice to do so. The accused has no similar right to anonymity.

When first introduced anonymity (in rape cases) was for all parties, including the accused;[106] this was to protect those found innocent or those falsely accused.[107] Although there have periodically[108] been calls for this to be reintroduced, it seems unlikely this would find much support following the convictions of several well-known sexual offenders such as entertainer Rolf Harris, whose conviction took place after victims came forward after his initial arrest was publicized. The police maintain the name of the accused needs to be released in order to identify further victims and that those who make false allegations will be charged with offences including perverting the course of justice, wasting police time and perjury.

Consent and Sadomasochism

Sexual activity brings with it the right to consent to injury when it is an accidental by-product of the sexual activity and where that activity has been consented to.[109] *Dica* (2004)[110] takes this principle further with consent negating liability for both actual bodily harm and grievous bodily harm where consent (and this must be informed consent)[111] is given to running the risk, not the certainty, of injury in the course of normal sexual activity. *Dica* was a case of HIV infection but the ratio is broader than that, as Lord Justice Judge stated:

> In our judgement the impact of the authorities dealing with sexual gratification can too readily be misunderstood. It does not follow from them, and they do not suggest, that consensual acts of sexual intercourse are unlawful merely because there may be a known risk to the health of one or other participant. These participants are not intent on spreading or becoming infected with disease through sexual intercourse. They are not indulging in serious violence for the purposes of sexual gratification. They are simply prepared, knowingly, to run the risk – not the certainty – of infection, as well as all the other risks inherent in and possible consequences of sexual intercourse, such as, and despite the most careful precautions, an unintended pregnancy.[112]

This case then deals with consent to reckless injury in the course of normal sexual activity. The difficulty here often comes from delineating what activities are understood to be violent (and therefore prohibited by law) and which are sexual (falling under the *Dica* principle). In *Boyea* (1992)[113] B was convicted of indecent assault after inserting his hand into a woman's vagina causing injuries. However it was recognized:

> the court must take account of the fact that social attitudes have changed, particularly in the field of sexual relations between adults. As a generality, the level of vigour in sexual congress which was generally acceptable, and therefore the voluntarily accepted risk of incurring some injury was probably higher now than it was in 1934.

This raises the question of which sexual practices will be deemed an acceptable part of sexual intercourse. As Professor J.C. Smith prophetically commented in 1992, this will be a matter for the jury and what we deem to be acceptable intercourse may be nuanced as "What is good for ordinary heterosexual intercourse will not necessarily be good for the practice of 'perversions' or what the Sexual Offences Act 1956 treats as 'unnatural' intercourse."[114]

Although the SOA 2003 has done away with the explicit concept of unnatural intercourse it continues to find expression in sexual practices that are not considered 'normal' and it has been in the field of sadomasochism that consent has been most vigorously contested. The infliction of pain for sexual pleasure is something the judiciary have firmly rejected as a sexual practice, as was made clear in *Brown* (1993).[115] *Brown* has already been mentioned in Chapter 1 and concerned a group of homosexual men who had engaged in consensual sadomasochistic practices, such as whipping, piercing and branding. None of the men suffered injuries requiring medical attention, but it was held by the House of Lords that their injuries amounted to bodily harm for the purposes of the Offences Against the Persons Act 1861, irrespective of whether they consented or not. Lord Templeman stated "sadomasochism is not only concerned with sex. Sado-masochism is also concerned with violence" and:

> In principle there is a difference between violence which is incidental and violence which is inflicted for the indulgence of cruelty. The violence of sadomasochistic encounters involves the indulgence of cruelty by sadists and the degradation of victims. Such violence is injurious to the participants and unpredictably dangerous. I am not prepared to invent a defence of consent for sadomasochistic encounters which breed and glorify cruelty and result in offences under ss47 and 20 of the 1861 Act.

The ratio of this case was that one cannot validly consent to intentional or reckless infliction of injury that is more than transient or trifling.[116]

The opinion of Lord Templeman has been cited as "moral rhetoric"[117] and an opinion that reveals a "powerful emotional and visceral reaction of disgust"[118] and the majority opinion as evidence of "repugnance to the sexual morality of the sadomasochist".[119] We know the law can and does build or legitimize moral boundaries, but this is not the only justification for the decision in *Brown*. As Edwards states: "The law is about protecting from harm, the weak and the vulnerable, not for protecting the excesses of the cruel and violent, to satisfy their libidos"[120] and this is indeed the ethos we see reflected in offences governing sexual activity. *Brown* was not establishing a new legal principle. In *Donovan* (1934)[121] the appellant asked a 17-year-old girl to accompany him to his garage where he beat her with a cane. Justice Swift outlined, "If an act is unlawful in the sense of being in itself a criminal act, it is plain that it cannot be rendered lawful because the person to whose detriment it is done consents to it."[122] Thus violence cannot be privileged and subject to a different regime from activities such as prize fighting[123] just because it has a sexual undertone. Not all justices in *Brown* agreed with this approach. Lord Mustill stated that the case was about the criminal law of violence when it should have been about the criminal law of sexual relations and Lord Slynn argued that adopting a paternalistic approach was not helpful.

Brown was a clear case of intentional physical injury – the participants were gaining pleasure from the pain inflicted. In the later case of *Emmett* (1999)[124] the consensual activity involved restricted breathing (with D placing a bag on his partner's head) and an element of danger (pouring lighter fluid on her breasts and setting fire to it). This was not with the intention of causing injury; breathing was merely restricted and lighter fluid ordinarily burns without causing injury to the skin. However there was clearly an objective risk of injury and D was convicted on the basis of a foresight of bodily harm. *Emmett* was redemptive in one respect.

Comments such as Lord Lowry's "Sadomasochistic homosexual activity cannot be regarded as conducive to the enhancement or enjoyment of family life or conducive to the welfare of society" and Lord Jauncey of Tullichettle's "When considering the public interest potential for harm is just as relevant as actual harm . . . the possibility of proselytization and corruption of young men is a real danger" had left a lingering sense of homophobia. The decision in *Wilson* (1996),[125] where a husband had branded his wife – where *Brown* had been distinguished on a number of grounds, including the fact the activity took place in the marital home and a brand was akin to tattooing – had further ingrained the idea that the law was validating homophobia. *Emmett* made clear that sadomasochistic activities between heterosexuals are subject to the same legal restrictions.

Many would argue, and indeed the appellants in *Laskey, Jaggard and Brown v UK* (1997)[126] did, that the criminalization of sadomasochism that resulted in bodily harm was an interference with their Article 8 rights. Article 8 of the European Convention on Human rights provides that everyone has the right to respect for his private and family life but this is a right that is qualified by the necessity to prevent crime, protect health or morals or to protect the rights and freedoms of others. *Laskey* was the appeal from *Brown* to the European Court of Human Rights where the appellants argued their activities had been consensual, private and had resulted in no lasting injuries. But Article 8 is a qualified right and the right of the State to prosecute, convict and sentence the defendants involved no breach of Article 8 and was recognized by the court as a necessary and proportionate interference (within the meaning of Article 8(2)). The court emphasized the right of the state to protect health and (to a far lesser extent) public morality. It was evident that it would have been difficult for the United Kingdom to successfully argue for a margin of appreciation grounded in morality alone. In *Dudgeon* (1981) the European Court of Human Rights had pronounced:

> Although members of the public who regard homosexuality as immoral may be shocked, offended or disturbed by the commission by others of private homosexual acts, this cannot on its own warrant the application of penal sanctions when it is consenting adults alone who are involved.[127]

Despite the clear moral thread that runs through the majority opinions in *Brown* (and undoubtedly some of this is homophobia) it was the physical harm that flowed from these activities and the potential threat to public health this posed that was accepted as sound legal justification.

As *Boyea* indicates the law here has to be considered in its contemporary context. It is difficult to know what decisions are being reached in the lower courts but there are indications that social tolerance of what is an acceptable part of normal sexual activity may have increased. For example, in *Lock*[128] where a man caused actual bodily harm to his partner (bruises to the buttocks) during a sadomasochistic encounter he was acquitted.[129] *Peacock* (2012)[130] (discussed at Chapter 7) similarly suggests moral boundaries regarding acceptable sexual behaviour may have shifted, or are at least out of line with current police and CPS guidance.

In 1995 the Law Commission suggested the level of bodily interference in sadomasochistic encounters to which one can validly consent should be raised, so anything less than seriously disabling injury might be consented to.[131] This suggestion has not been acted upon, although clearly the jury can, and almost certainly are, exercising their own discretion to establish new moral boundaries. The outstanding question now is what amounts to sexual activity? Could the changing level of acceptable vigour in sexual activity recognized in *Boyea* embrace sadomasochism? If sadomasochism were embraced as a normal sexual practice it would then be regulated by *Dica*.

The Criminal Justice Process

Some would argue too much attention is paid to the substantive law when considering why there are continuing problems with attaining convictions for rape and associated offences and that more attention should be paid to criminal justice processes. The Stern Review accepted this in their comprehensive review of public authority responses to rape complaints[132] and made a number of recommendations that have since been implemented.[133] These include a fuller exploration of conviction rates in rape cases, the establishment and extension of Sexual Assault Referral Centres that provide specialist help and support for victims of sexual offences and Association of Chief Police Officers Rape Support Programme specialist training for staff involved in rape investigations aimed at tackling rape myths. Independent Sexual Violence Advisors, trained support workers who provide targeted assistance to victims of sexual violence through all stages from report to post-conviction, have also grown in number since Baroness Stern called for a greater focus on victim care.[134] There has also been a general shift away from a consideration of the credibility of the victim in sexual offence cases to the credibility of the allegation, and this has been reflected in numerous policy and service documents for the police and CPS.[135] The establishment of CPS Rape and Serious Sexual Offence units and the introduction of the CPS Victims' Right to Review scheme,[136] introduced to make it easier for victims to seek a review of a CPS decision not to bring charges or to terminate proceedings, shows a serious commitment by the CPS to improve the landscape for complainants. The Sexual Violence against Children and Vulnerable People National Group[137] is also proposing policy and implementing proposals from reports such as the Savile Inquiry. A 2012 Government consultation on the protection and support available for victims and witnesses also made a number of recommendations for improving the processes in place.[138] More generally the Code of Practice for Victims of Crime[139] now sets out the key entitlements for victims of all criminal offences and outlines the support available during investigation, prosecution and post-trial, the duties placed on criminal justice system personnel and how to make a complaint.

In recognition of the serious impact of sex offences on victims, the Sentencing Council has also comprehensively overhauled its sentencing guidance and its latest incarnation[140] came into effect April 2014 and adopts a structured approach to sentencing. The document provides general offence ranges that set out the variety of sentences appropriate for each type of offence. For each offence, there are categories reflecting degrees of seriousness for both harm (category 1, 2 and 3) and culpability (category A or B). For example, for section 1 the offence range is 4–19 years' custody and category 1 harm includes factors such as extreme psychological or physical harm, serious degradation/humiliation and prolonged detention or a sustained incident. Category A culpability includes a significant degree of planning, the use of alcohol or drugs on the victim to facilitate the offence, an abuse of trust and the offence being racially or religiously aggravated. These categories are then mapped against one another to give a starting point for the offence (15 years in this case) and a more specific range of appropriate offences (13–19 years' custody). Aggravating and mitigating factors can then be taken into consideration to decide whether there should be an upward or downward adjustment from the starting point. Aggravating factors include the targeting of a particularly vulnerable victim, the location and timing of the offence, the use of a weapon to frighten or injure and the presence of others, particularly children, at the time of the offence. Mitigating factors include: no previous convictions, remorse shown, previous good character and whether the offender has a mental disorder or learning disability. Any assistance given to the prosecution[141] and a guilty plea can be taken into consideration to reduce the length of the sentence.[142] The court will also decide whether any ancillary orders should be made or automatically apply. In the case of sexual offences this will usually be a sexual harm prevention order (discussed at Chapter 10).[143]

For bodily harm caused through sadomasochism any offences charged are of course understood to be offences of violence and are subject to sentencing under the regime for these offences.[144] If the injury has been caused through a sexual encounter this may be a mitigating factor where ostensible consent to the risk of injury has been given.

Conclusion

For the offences addressed above the SOA 2003 clearly makes provision for most, if not all, forms of non-consensual sexual offending. Whether it has drawn these boundaries correctly is another matter. Many would argue that penetration without consent should amount to rape regardless of the part of the body that is used. There are also a number of overlaps between the offences, so in some circumstances sexual assault and causing a person to engage in sexual activity without consent may overlap.

Consent is still an unsettled area of the law and it is hard to predict how the courts will deal with emerging issues such as conditional consent. It is obvious that section 74 is going to be subject to significant judicial attention that will hopefully reflect our contemporary understanding of consent.

Consent and the offences cannot be considered outside the landscape in which they operate and the criminal justice process has, in recent years, done much to improve the situation for complainants. Victims have increasingly become central to the administration of justice, with support mechanisms put in place to improve victim support and engagement. It will be interesting to see whether these processes will improve rates of reporting, attrition and conviction in the coming years.

Notes

1 S42 of the Criminal Justice and Public Order Act 1994.
2 See Chapter 2.
3 This is the meaning of penetration throughout the Act.
4 Home Office *Setting the Boundaries: Reforming the Law on Sex Offences* London: Home Office (2000), para 2.8.4.
5 Discussed at Chapter 4 in reference to s5 SOA 2003.
6 J. Temkin and A. Ashworth 'The Sexual Offences Act 2003: (1) Rape, sexual assaults and the problems of consent' *Criminal Law Review* May (2004) pp. 328–346.
7 Baroness Stern *A Report by Baroness Vivien Stern CBE of an Independent Review into How Rape Complaints Are Handled by Public Authorities in England and Wales* London: Home Office (2010).
8 Ibid. p. 51.
9 There are some indications from mock jury trials that these stereotypes may not wield as great an influence as has been generally accepted. For further discussion see the work of L. Ellison and V. Munro including L. Ellison and V. Munro 'Of "Normal Sex" and "Real Rape": exploring the use of socio-sexual scripts in (Mock) jury deliberation' *Social and Legal Studies* (2009) 18(3) pp. 1–22 and L. Ellison and V. Munro 'Reacting to rape: exploring Mock Jurors' assessments of complainant credibility' *British Journal of Criminology* (2009) 49(2) pp. 202–219.
10 See http://www.cps.gov.uk/legal/p_to_r/rape_and_sexual_offences/societal_myths.
11 *Per* Latham LJ in *R.* v *D* [2008] EWCA Crim 2557.
12 *R.* v *McNally* [2013] EWCA Crim 1051.
13 *R.* v *Cooper (Declan Alexander)* [2014] EWCA Crim 946; *R.* v *Barclay (David)* [2012] EWCA Crim 2375.
14 *R.* v *Oliver Jean Plunkett* [2007] EWCA Crim 1957.
15 Apart from s71 and s15A discussed at Chapter 4.
16 SOA 1956 ss14 and 15.
17 Indecent assault (on a woman) (s14 SOA 1956), indecent assault (on a man) (s15 SOA 1956) discussed at Chapters 2 and 4.
18 Where children were concerned. *R.* v *Mason* (1968) 52 Cr App R 12; *Faulkner v Talbot* (1982) 74 Cr App R 1.
19 (1978) 66 Cr App R 21.
20 *R.* v *Court* [1989] AC 28 (HL).
21 By finding that no specific intent of indecent assault had to be established, the offence was held to be one of basic intent and thus intoxication could not be a defence; see also *DPP v H* [1992] C.O.D. 266.
22 *R.* v *H (Karl Anthony)* [2005] EWCA Crim 732.
23 D.W. Selfe 'Sexual assault and the Sexual Offences Act 200 touch too far' *Criminal Lawyer* (2006) 165 pp. 3–5.
24 [1997] Crim LR 50, CA.
25 Ibid.
26 *R.* v *B* [2013] EWCA Crim 823.
27 *R.* v *Ayeva (Sharif)* [2009] EWCA Crim 2640.
28 *R.* v *Devonald* [2008] EWCA 527.
29 *R.* v *Azam (Kamber)* [2007] EWCA Crim 3376.
30 *R.* v *H and R* [2008] EWCA Crim 1202.
31 Discussed at Chapter 7.
32 [1976] AC 182.

33 (1889) 22 QB 23.

34 [1877] 2 QBD 410.

35 Similarly in *Williams* [1923] 2 KBD 340 A was a singing coach who told one of his pupils he was performing an act to open her air passages to improve her singing (and she consented to this act). Again, he was having performing a sexual act and it was held her consent was vitiated by fraud as to the nature of the act.

36 See footnote 67.

37 After a number of conflicting decisions the Criminal Law Amendment Act 1885 s4 defined as rape the act of fraudulently impersonating the husband of a woman to successfully obtain her consent to intercourse.

38 [2000] 2 Cr App R 328.

39 Similarly in *R. v Green* [2002] EWCA Crim 1501 there was a deception as to the nature of the physical act when young men were wired up to monitors while they masturbated ostensibly to assess their potential for impotence, when it was in fact for the defendant's own sexual gratification.

40 For further discussion see J.C. Smith case comment, Crim LR (2000) Aug pp. 686–689.

41 *R. v Howard* [1956] 3 All ER 684; *R. v Lang* (1975) 62 Cr App R 50.

42 *Larter & Castleton* [1995] Crim LR 75.

43 *R. v Camplin* (1845) 1 C & K 746.

44 [1995] Crim LR 163.

45 [1976] AC 182.

46 For further discussion see J. Temkin *Rape and the Legal Process* London: Routledge and Kegan Paul (1987).

47 [1982] QB 320.

48 *R. v Olugboja per* Dunn LJ.

49 Home Office *Protecting the Public* London: HMSO (2002), para.30.

50 *Protecting the Public*, para 28.

51 *R. v Bree* [2007] EWCA Crim 804 para 22.

52 Also at ss2(2), 3(2) and 4(2).

53 If A is intoxicated this cannot be taken into to consideration in an estimation of reasonableness: *R. v Grewal* [2010] EWCA Crim 2448.

54 *R. v B* [2013] EWCA Crim 3 para 40.

55 *R. v C* [2012] EWCA Crim 2034.

56 J. Temkin and A. Ashworth 'The Sexual Offences Act 2003: (1) Rape, sexual assaults and the problems of consent' *Criminal Law Review* May (2004) pp. 328–346.

57 [2007] EWCA Crim 804.

58 At para 34.

59 Shlomit Wallerstein ' "A drunken consent is still consent" – or is it? A critical analysis of the law on a drunken consent to sex following Bree' *Journal of Criminal Law* (2009) 73(4) pp. 318–344.

60 At 322.

61 [2013] EWHC 945 (Admin).

62 [2011] EWHC 2849 (Admin).

63 [2013] EWCA Crim 1051.

64 Gayle Newland, 25, was also convicted in 2015 of 3 counts of assault by penetration against a woman who had believed she was in a sexual relationship with a man. Newland had established contact with the victim, also a 25-year-old woman, through a Facebook profile set up in the name of a fictitious young man, "Kye Fortune" and during their 2-year relationship "Kye" always required the victim wear a blindfold. *R. v Newland* Unreported November 12, 2015 (Crown Ct (Chester)).

65 [2012] EWCA Crim 1593.
66 See Sharpe for criticism of the decision in *McNally*: A. Sharpe 'Criminalising sexual intimacy: transgender defendants and the legal construction of non-consent' *Criminal Law Review* (2014) 3 pp. 207–223.
67 Law Commission *Consent in Sex Offences: A Policy Paper: Appendix C of Setting the Boundaries.* London: Home Office (2000).
68 Ibid.
69 See http://www.cps.gov.uk/legal/p_to_r/rape_and_sexual_offences/consent/#b01.
70 [2006] EWCA Crim 2945; [2007] 1 WLR 1567.
71 There are old decisions where deception regarding a disease vitiated consent. *R. v Bennett* (1866) 4 F & F 1105; *R. v Sinclair* (1867) 13 Cox CC 28.
72 See the civil case of *AKJ et al v Metropolitan Police Commissioner* [2013] EWHC 32 (QB).
73 In Israel Sabbar Kashur, a Muslim who told his sexual partner he was Jewish, was convicted of sex by deception in 2010.
74 [2011] EWCA Crim 2665.
75 Ibid.
76 A. Carline and C. Gunby 'Barristers' Perspectives on Rape and the Sexual Offences Act 2003' *Criminal Law and Justice Weekly* (2010) 174(3) pp. 472–474; A. Carline and C. Gunby '"How an ordinary jury makes sense of it is a mystery." Barristers' Perspectives on Rape, Consent and the Sexual Offences Act 2003' *Liverpool Law Review* (2011) 32(3) pp. 237–250.
77 *R. v Burstow* [1997] UKHL 34; *R. v Hasan* [2005] UKHL 22.
78 Cited in http://lawcommission.justice.gov.uk/docs/Consent_in_Sex_Offences.pdf pp. 58–59.
79 *Setting the Boundaries* para 2.10.9.
80 *R. v Larter and Castleton* [1995] Crim LR 75.
81 For further discussion see E. Finch and V. Munro 'The Sexual Offences Act 2003: intoxicated consent and drug assisted rape revisited' *Criminal Law Review* October (2004) pp. 789–802.
82 J. Temkin and A. Ashworth 'The Sexual Offences Act 2003: (1) Rape, sexual assaults and the problems of consent' *Criminal Law Review* May (2004) pp. 328–346.
83 [2008] EWCA 527.
84 [2007] EWCA Crim 1699.
85 [1995] 2 CAR 49.
86 [2013] EWCA Crim 823.
87 Para.22.
88 Para.19.
89 *R. v Clay* (1851) 5 Cox 146.
90 *R. v Greatbanks* [1959] Crim LR 450, CCC.
91 *R. v Holmes (Henry)* (1871) LR 1 CCR 334.
92 *R. v Krausz* (1973) 57 Cr App R 466.
93 Sexual Offences (Amendment) Act 1976 s4. Complainant anonymity has since been extended to other sexual offences: Sexual Offences (Amendment) Act 1992 s2.
94 Heilbron Committee *Report of the Advisory Group on the Law of Rape* London: HMSO (1975).
95 Something that has garnered significant criticism: S. Easton 'The use of sexual history evidence in rape trials' in M. Childs and L. Ellison *Feminist Perspectives on Evidence* London: Cavendish Publishing (2000); J. Temkin 'Sexual history evidence – the ravishment of Section 2' *Criminal Law Review* (1993) (3) pp. 3–20.
96 J. Temkin 'Sexual history evidence – beware the backlash' *Canadian Criminal Law Review* (2003) 4 pp. 217–242.

97 Home Office *Speaking up for Justice – Report of the Interdepartmental Working Group on the Treatment of Vulnerable or Intimidated Witness in the Criminal Justice System* London: Home Office (1998).

98 *Speaking up for Justice* para 9.63.

99 D. Birch 'Rethinking sexual history: proposals for fairer trials' *Criminal Law Review* July (2002) pp. 531–553; J. Temkin 'Sexual history evidence – beware the backlash; L. Kelly, J. Temkin and S. Griffiths *Section 41: An Evaluation of New Legislation Limiting Sexual History Evidence in Rape Trials* London: Home (2006).

100 *R. v A (No 2)* [2001] UKHL 25.

101 *R. v Bahador (Hussein)* [2005] EWCA Crim 396; *R. v Gjoni (Kujtim)* [2014] EWCA Crim 691.

102 And the corresponding reasonable belief subsections at sections 2–4 SOA 2003.

103 Measures introduced to give effect to the recommendations of Home Office *Speaking Up for Justice – Report of the Interdepartmental Working Group on the treatment of Vulnerable or Intimidated Witness in the Criminal Justice System* London: Home Office (1998).

104 L. Ellison and V. Munro 'A special delivery? Exploring the impact of screens, live links and video-recorded evidence on Mock Juror deliberation in rape trials' *Social Legal Studies* March (2014) 23(1) pp. 3–29.

105 This includes the offences in Part 1 of the Sexual Offences Act 2003 except those in ss64, 65, 69 and 71.

106 Sexual Offences (Amendment) Act 1976.

107 The prevalence of false allegations is unclear and best estimates are at around 8–11 per cent see HMCPSI and HMIC *Without Consent: A Report on the Joint Review of the Investigation and Prosecution of Rape Offences* London: HMCPSI and HMIC (2007). A. Feist, J. Ashe, J. Lawrence, D. McPhee and R. Wilson *Investigating and Detecting Recorded Offences of Rape* Home Office online report 18/07, London: Home Office (2007).

108 For the last comprehensive review see Ministry of Justice *Providing Anonymity to Those Accused of Rape: An Assessment of Evidence* London: Ministry of Justice Research Series 20/10 (2010).

109 *R. v Simon Slingsby* [1995] Crim LR 570; *R. v Meachen (David Nigel)* [2006] EWCA Crim 2414.

110 [2004] EWCA Crim 1103.

111 *R. v Konzani* [2005] EWCA Crim 706.

112 Para 47.

113 [1992] Crim LR 574.

114 J.C. Smith 'Indecent assault – defence of consent – whether injury more than "transient or trifling" – take account of current day social attitudes to sexual activity among consenting adults. Case Comment' *Criminal Law Review* August (1992) pp. 574–576.

115 *R. v Brown* [1994] 1 AC 212.

116 Some violence to the person is lawful: surgery, male circumcision for cultural or medical reasons, tattooing, ear-piercing and regulated violent sports including boxing.

117 D. Gurnham 'Legal authority and savagery in judicial rhetoric: sexual violence and the criminal courts' *International Journal of Law in Context* (2011) 7(2) pp. 117–137.

118 E. Chan and H. Gommer 'Sexually biased case law' *The Original Law Review* (2011) 7(4) pp. 155–171.

119 J. Tsang 'State interference and sadomasochism' *UCL Jurisprudence Review* (2005) 12 pp. 161–179.

120 S. Edwards 'No defence for a Sado-Masochistic Libido' *New Law Journal* (1993) 143(6592) pp. 406–407.

121 [1934] 2 KB 498.

122 Consent *can* be given to an injury that is less than transient or trifling.

123 *R. v Coney* (1882) 8 QBD 5; *A-G's Reference(No 6 of 1980)* [1981] 2 All ER 1057.

124 [1999] EWCA Crim 1710.

125 [1996] 3 WLR 125.

126 *Laskey, Jaggard and Brown v UK* (1997) 24 EHRR 39.

127 *Dudgeon v The United Kingdom* (1981) 4 EHRR 149 para 60.

128 Unreported January, 2012 (Crown Ct (Ipswich)).

129 They had entered into a contract to allow Mr Lock "dominion" over his partner; however a contract to enter into a sadomasochistic relationship is unenforceable: see *Sutton v Mishcon de Reya* [2003] EWHC 3166.

130 Unreported January 6, 2011 (Crown Ct (Southwark)).

131 Law Commission *Consent in the Criminal Law* London: HMSO (1995) para 2.1.9.

132 Home Office, Baroness Stern, *The Stern Review – An Independent Review into How Rape Complaints Are Handled by Public Authorities in England and Wales* London: Home Office (2010).

133 In response to the report the Government accepted 21 out of the 23 recommendations. The Cabinet Office *The Government Response to the Stern Review: An independent Review into How Rape Complaints Are Handled by Public Authorities in England and Wales* London: The Cabinet Office (2011).

134 Victim care and proper engagement by agencies of the criminal justice system with victims was also the focus of the report by Sara Payne, the then Victims Champion. S. Payne *Redefining Justice: Addressing the Individual Needs of Victims and Witnesses* London: Home Office (2009).

135 CPS *Policy for Prosecuting Cases of Rape* Accessible at https://www.cps.gov.uk/publications/prosecution/rape.html. ACPO and CPS Protocol between the Police Service and Crown Prosecution Service in the Investigation and Prosecution of Rape (2015). Accessible at http://www.cps.gov.uk/publications/agencies/cps_acpo_rape_protocol_v2.pdf. The Rape Monitoring Group chaired by chaired by Her Majesty's Inspectorate of Constabulary monitors criminal justice agencies responses to rape. http://www.justiceinspectorates.gov.uk/hmic/about-us/working-with-others/rape-monitoring-group.

136 Detail accessible at http://www.cps.gov.uk/publications/docs/vrr_guidance_2014.pdf. The policy was introduced after a Court of Appeal decision made clear victims should have a right to review: *R. v Christopher Killick* [2011] EWCA Crim 1608.

137 For details of the progress report and action plan see https://www.gov.uk/government/publications/sexual-violence-against-children-and-vulnerable-people-national-group.

138 Including the better provision of information and updating of victims and witnesses, better use of Victim Impact Statements and improving mechanisms for complaint. Ministry of Justice *Getting It Right for Victims and Witnesses* London: The Stationary Office (2012). Accessible at https://consult.justice.gov.uk/digital-communications/victims-witnesses/supporting_documents/gettingitrightforvictimsandwitnesses.pdf.

139 A revised Code came into effect on 10 December 2013. Accessible at https://www.gov.uk/government/publications/the-code-of-practice-for-victims-of-crime.

140 https://www.sentencingcouncil.org.uk/wp-content/uploads/Final_Sexual_Offences_Definitive_Guideline_content_web1.pdf.

141 Sections 73 and 74 Serious Organised Crime and Police Act 2005.

142 Subject to taking into account when the plea was given and the circumstances that resulted in the plea: s144 of the Criminal Justice Act 2003.

143 More information on how sentences are reached is available here: https://www.sentencingcouncil.org.uk/about-sentencing/how-sentences-are-worked-out.

144 Sentencing Council *Assault Definitive Guideline* (2011). Accessible at: https://www.sentencingcouncil.org.uk/wp-content/uploads/Assault_definitive_guideline_-_Crown_Court.pdf.

Chapter 4

Sexual Offending Against Children

Introduction

If the role of law is to protect the vulnerable in society, then there can be no more important section of society to protect than our children. As has been seen in Chapter 2, the definition of a child has changed throughout history, the general trend being that the age at which someone is considered to be a child for the purposes of sexual activity has gone steadily upwards. There has also been a significant change in society's attitude towards what we now call 'child sexual abuse', with the issue being reported more widely, thus raising public awareness.

Much of the recent reported allegations of child abuse relate to historic abuse, i.e. abuse which took place many years ago but may not have been reported at the time, or not prosecuted. Some accusations relate to well-known public figures, including politicians.[1] Allegations made against Jimmy Savile, the former DJ and television presenter, were reported in detail and, as Chapter 1 has discussed, reports of sexual offending against children have increased sharply since the Savile Inquiry and there is further discussion about this in Chapter 5. Systemic failures in protecting children from sexual abuse have increasingly been the focus of inquiries. For example, Peter Wanless and Richard Whittam QC reviewed information that had been provided to the Home Office information regarding child abuse from 1979 to 1999[2] and the Independent Inquiry into Child Sexual Abuse (which opened in 2015) will be looking at whether public bodies and other non-state institutions have properly protected the children in their care.[3] As well as allegations made against public figures, there were a number of high-profile investigations into street grooming in Peterborough, Oxford and Rochdale, which involved groups of men befriending vulnerable girls, giving them gifts of money, drugs or alcohol and then sexually abusing them, including passing them around to other men for sex.[4] As a result of these reports, the issue of child abuse, particularly child sexual exploitation, is now quite high in the public consciousness.[5]

While we know, as Chapter 1 discussed, that the perpetrators of sexual abuse are more likely to be a family friend or to be acquainted with the child rather than being a stranger, estimating the prevalence of child sexual abuse is difficult because it is known that some children do not report such abuse. However, reports suggest the numbers are high. A 2011 National Society for the Prevention of Cruelty to Children (NSPCC) study found that nearly a quarter of young adults (24.1 per cent) had experienced sexual abuse during childhood.[6] The Office of the Children's Commissioner's Inquiry into child sexual exploitation reported 2,409 children were known to be victims of sexual exploitation by groups or gangs between August 2010 and October 2011.[7]

There is no legal definition of the term 'child sexual abuse' but the World Health Organization defines is as "the involvement of a child in sexual activity that he or she does not fully comprehend, is unable to give informed consent to, or for which the child is not developmentally prepared, or else that violate the laws or social taboos of society".[8] There is no one offence of 'child sexual abuse'; instead there are many different offences that can be committed against children that will be considered in this chapter. Historically, contact offences had been the focus of the law here (child abuse images aside) but as the dangers posed to children have become better understood non-contact offences have been crafted to better reflect offending behaviour. The terminology of child sexual exploitation[9] has also increasingly been used to capture the variety of offending behaviour and recognize that children have been sexually victimized by perpetrators by not only violence and oppression, but also subtle coercion.[10] Child sexual exploitation is inherent in many of the offences discussed at this chapter and at Chapter 5 which considers abuse of a position of trust, i.e. abuse that takes place in an institutional setting, such as schools or hospitals and within the family. Exploitation is also central to the offences of pornography and prostitution discussed in later chapters.

The age of consent

It is well known that the age of consent is this country is 16 years. By 'age of consent' we mean the age when the law says that children can legally consent to sexual activity. In fact, there is no legal provision that uses the phrase 'age of consent'. Instead, there are a number of different sexual offences that can be used to charge those who engage in sexually activity with children. In most cases, the age of 16 is used as the age beneath which a child is deemed to be unable to consent. However, as we will see in the following chapter, this is too simplistic and there are some offences where a child is regarded as someone under the age of 18. We will also see that although offences against children are targeted principally at adults, it is also possible for a child to commit a sexual offence against another child.

Age limits are arbitrary and, as discussed above and at Chapter 2, the age of consent has been, and continues to be, disputed.[11] However there are a number of reasons why it may be thought necessary to set an age of consent. The most important is that it protects young people from abuse and exploitation by others, who may seek to persuade them to engage in behaviour that is inappropriate for a child, or even would result in significant harm. There is also the risk of unwanted pregnancy for young girls but also the belief that children should not grow up too soon. There have been many concerns recently regarding the sexualization of children in society. For example, in 2011 the Department of Education published a report in which it was stated that nearly nine out of ten parents surveyed agreed with the statement that "these days children are under pressure to grow up too quickly".[12] However, it has already been noted that historically the concept of childhood is a fairly recent one in this country and the age of consent has been much lower in the past.[13]

There is no consensus around the world about what age it is appropriate for children to engage in sexual activity. In Europe the majority of countries have an age of 16 but some, e.g. France (15 years) and Italy (14 years), have a lower age. Spain has fairly recently raised the age from 13 to 16. In the United States the age depends on state law and ranges from 16–18 (in California the age is 18 years). Japan has an age of consent of 13 years.

One of the problems with legislating for sexual behaviour in relation to children is to find a way to protect the vulnerable from abuse, while at the same time not unnecessarily criminalizing normal teenage behaviour. The law attempts to do this by making it illegal for a person to have sex with a child, irrespective of whether that child consented or not, but this also has the side effect that children, in effect, do not have a right to a sex life. Article 8 of the European Convention on Human rights (ECHR) provides the qualified right to respect for a private and family life and the protection of children can be seen to be a proportionate response to the claim that the right to a private life has been breached. Fixing a specific age of consent could be seen as a blunt tool to achieve the required protection and it has been suggested that a fairer way to resolve the issue is to consider whether an individual child has the capacity to consent on a case-by-case basis. However, there are significant problems with this approach, not least the basis on which such children could be assessed as capable. One suggestion would be to adopt the same tests as were established in the case of *Gillick v West Norfolk and Wisbech Area Health Authority* (1986).[14] This House of Lords case established the principle that doctors should be able to give contraceptive advice or treatment to those under the age of 16 without parental consent, provided that the child has the maturity and understanding to truly consent to the treatment. It gives rise to the contradictory situation where an under-aged child could be assessed as capable of consenting to being prescribed contraceptives, while still under the age of consent for sexual intercourse. However, another consideration is that if such a test was applied to consent for the purpose of sexual intercourse, then there would always be an incentive for offenders to plead not guilty and to seek to bring expert evidence as to the maturity of the individual child. This could result in significant distress to the child who would have to give evidence about its own level of maturity. In addition, there is the question of whether it is ever acceptable that a child of 12 should have to give evidence about whether or not they consented to sexual activity.

Some of these issues are considered further below, in the section on section 13 (child sex offences committed by children and young persons).

The Sexual Offences Act 1956

The Sexual Offences Act 2003 (SOA 2003) completely overhauled the law on sexual offences against children. However, any offences committed before 1 May 2004 (when the SOA 2003 came into force) are charged under the previous legislation.

As many prosecutions for child sex abuse are historic and the SOA 2003 sought to remedy problems with the old law we must briefly consider the law preceding 2003 – the background to these offences was explored in more detail at Chapter 2.

Prior to the SOA 2003, offences were gender specific, had inconsistent sentences and varying defences. Most were contained in the Sexual Offences Act 1956 (SOA 1956).

Section 5 SOA 1956 made it an offence for a man to have unlawful sexual intercourse with a girl under the age of 13. This offence could only be committed by a man, and only a girl could be a victim. It was a serious offence punishable with up to life imprisonment.

Under section 6 SOA 1956, it was an offence for a man to have unlawful intercourse with a girl under the age of 16. This offence had a maximum penalty of 2 years' imprisonment. For this offence, there was a specific defence (which did not apply to the section 5 offence) which became known as 'the young man's defence' discussed at Chapter 2. This defence apparently viewed a younger man with more sympathy than an older man, who presumably should know better. There was a further defence where there was an invalid marriage but the man had reasonable grounds to believe that the girl was his wife. This was intended to cover situations where someone had married under the legal age (16 years) either because they married abroad or because a mistake as to age was made.

One of the main criticisms of the section 6 offence was that there was a 1-year time limit for prosecutions. This means that this offence cannot be charged when accusations of historic child sexual abuse are made, since the 1-year time limit would be long past. For this reason, many historic child sex abusers are charged with indecent assault instead.

Indecent assault was an offence under section 14 SOA 1956. This offence could be committed by either men or women but the victim had to be female. The section specifically stated that a girl under the age of 16 years could not in law give any consent that would prevent an act being an assault for the purposes of the section.[15] There was no time limit for prosecutions and so sexual intercourse with a girl under 16 could be charged as indecent assault even if it had taken place many years previously.[16]

All the offences above relate to sexual activity with a girl. There was no equivalent to the sections 5 and 6 offences in relation to boys. However, under section 15 SOA 1956 it was an offence for a person to make an indecent assault on a man. Section 46 SOA 1956 made clear that 'man' included a boy and a boy under the age of 16 years could not give consent in law. It was decided in *Hare* (1934)[17] that 'person' could include a woman. So, a woman who had sexual intercourse with a boy under the age of 16 could be convicted of indecent assault. The maximum penalty for this offence was 10 years (substantially less than the maximum sentence of life imprisonment under section 5 but substantially more than the 2-year maximum under section 6).[18]

In addition to the above offences, the Indecency with Children Act 1960 made it an offence for any person to commit an act of gross indecency with a child under the age of 14. There was a maximum penalty of 10 years' imprisonment.

As can be seen, the legislation showed an inconsistent approach to sexual activity with a child, with widely varying penalties. In 2000 the review of the law relating to sexual offences *Setting the Boundaries: Reforming the Law on Sexual Offences* noted:

> The present structure of offences has been built up over time, and added to piecemeal primarily in order to protect girls and boys from older men. It does not form a coherent code, nor one that reflects what we now know of the patterns of child sexual abuse. It deals differently with different kinds of sexual abuse depending on the nature of the act, so providing varying levels of protection for boys and girls.[19]

With coherence and the protection of the vulnerable central to the new regime, the review recommended offences against children be comprehensively overhauled.

The Current Law – Sexual Offences Act 2003

Offences against children can be broadly split into two types: those relating to children under 13 and those relating to children under 16. There is sometimes an overlap between these offences. Many of the elements of the offences are similar but they are not identical and the available defences are different. However, the question of consent of the child is irrelevant for all of the offences.

Children under the age of 13

Retaining a set of offences that protected children younger than 13 was considered essential, reflecting a socially acceptable limit to childhood that, while arbitrarily established, continued to have relevance in the twenty-first century. Debating the Sexual Offences Bill it was noted that the age boundary:

> . . . reflects the provisions of existing sexual offences legislation, whereby cases involving victims below that age trigger higher maximum sentences than those in which the victims are aged 13 or over, but under 16. We have already debated the age at which people mature and whether that age is rising, falling or staying the same. We have drawn the conclusion that as 13 is the age at which children enter their teenage years and which is recognised by society as marking a significant step towards maturity, it seems appropriate for 13 to be the age threshold below which any ostensible consent to sexual activity should not be deemed to be legally significant. Regardless of whether a child under the age of 13 may have the necessary understanding of sexual matters to give ostensible consent to sexual activity, we firmly believe that the law has a duty to protect all children from engaging in sexual activity at such an early age.[20]

While the age of consent continues to generate debate, this lower threshold has rarely been challenged. This said, the strict liability of these offences – so if a defendant honestly or even reasonably believes a child is 13-years-of-age or older this does not negate liability for the offence – has been a matter of debate. This has particularly been the case when the offender is also a young person, something discussed further below.

Section 5 – Rape of a child under 13

Under section 5 of the SOA 2003, a person commits an offence if he intentionally penetrates the vagina, anus or mouth of another person with his penis and the other person is under the age of 13. Although the section refers to a person rather than a man, the offence involves penetration by a penis and so can only be committed by a man (or a male to female transsexual who still has a penis). The victim could be either a boy or a girl. Although the section is headed 'rape of a child' it is important to realize that there is no requirement for the prosecution to prove that any force or even persuasion was used. The point of the offence is that consent is irrelevant and a defendant should not be able to argue that the child was a willing participant. The offence is then driven by the *actus reus*, and the *mens rea* only relates to whether the penetration was intentional (this is also the case for section 6).

The use of the word rape to describe the offence is highly judgemental and reflects the fact that a child under 13 should not be considered to be capable of legal consent. However, in practice, it is the case that sometimes a child under this age has in fact consented to the sexual activity. For example, in *Corran* (2005),[21] an appeal against sentence, it was clear that the 12-year-old girl did consent to sexual intercourse. Ben Corran met her while she was in the company of older girls, all of who were aged 15 or 16 and she told him she was 16 and was in year 11 at school. Over a few weeks the relationship developed and culminated in consensual sex. The girl did not complain but told her mother, who reported the matter to the police. Corran was found guilty of rape of a child, as consent was irrelevant. However, on appeal his sentence of 2 years' detention was quashed and substituted with a conditional discharge for 6 months. This clearly illustrates the point that consent does not excuse the defendant but it can be taken into account for sentencing. There is no excuse of reasonable belief that the child is over the age of 13, so the fact that she was in the company of older girls and lied to him about her age was irrelevant to the conviction.

The section 5 offence can also be committed by children over the age of criminal responsibility. This is illustrated by the case of *G v United Kingdom* (2011),[22] which concerned a 15-year-old boy who had sexual intercourse with a 12-year-old girl, who had told him that she was 15. The complainant alleged the intercourse was not consensual but was terrified of attending court. G was charged with rape of a child under section 5 and pleaded guilty, but on the basis that he believed she had consented and that she was 15 years old. He was sentenced to a 12-month detention and training order, as well as being made subject to the notification requirements of the sex offenders register. He appealed against conviction and sentence. He argued that his conviction under section 5 was in contravention of Article 6 ECHR, in that it violated his right to a fair trial and the presumption of innocence, as the offence was one of strict liability. In addition, he argued that it violated his right to a private life under Article 8 because it was disproportionate to charge him with rape under section 5 when he could have been charged with the lesser offence of section 13 (see below). Although the Court of Appeal allowed his appeal against sentence, substituting a conditional discharge, his appeal against conviction was dismissed. A further appeal to the House of Lords was also dismissed and the defendant therefore applied to the European Court of Human Rights. His application was ruled inadmissible. The decision of the court made clear that the interference with his rights was for a legitimate aim as the state is under an obligation to protect vulnerable people from sexual abuse. The state had not therefore exceeded the available margin of appreciation by creating a strict liability offence called 'rape of a child', which has no defence of consent or mistaken belief as to the child's age.[23]

The maximum penalty for this offence is life imprisonment.

Section 6 – Assault of a child under 13 by penetration

Section 6 SOA 2003 makes it an offence for a person to intentionally penetrate the vagina or anus of another person with a part of his body or anything else, where the penetration is sexual and the other person is under 13 years. This offence is gender neutral and so can be committed by a man or a woman on a boy or a girl. Although the offence still involves penetration it is much wider than section 5 in that the penetration can be by other parts of the body, such as a finger or a tongue, or can involve other objects. Although the section heading uses the word "assault" it only covers sexual penetration and not the wider concept of assault generally found in the criminal law. Again, consent is irrelevant and the maximum penalty is life imprisonment.

Section 7 – Sexual assault of a child under 13

Section 7 SOA 2003 provides that a person commits an offence if he intentionally touches someone under the age of 13 and that touching is sexual. As above, the offence is gender neutral and consent is irrelevant. The only *mens rea* is for the touching. The maximum penalty is 14 years' imprisonment. The word "assault" does not mean that any assault is an offence; as Chapter 3 explored there must be some actual touching.

The meaning of sexual and touching

As has already been considered at Chapter 3, the definition of sexual at section 78 allows a jury to decide what is sexual in the circumstances. Clearly, some actions would always be regarded as sexual because of their nature, e.g. sexual intercourse or oral sex with a child. However, there may be other actions that are not necessarily sexual, such as medical procedures or normal parental care of a child (such as bathing), which would not normally be regarded as sexual unless there were other circumstances or purposes that showed a sexual motive. Undressing a child to put them to bed would not be sexual but undressing a child for sexual gratification certainly would be.

'Touching' is defined in section 79(8) SOA 2003. It includes touching with any part of the body, with anything else, through anything and specifically includes touching amounting to penetration. This is an extremely wide definition and it is intended to be so. It would cover touching a child through their clothing and with an item such as a toy. However, it must be remembered that the touching does have to be sexual for the defendant to be guilty of an offence. Accidental touching of a child's body through clothing would almost certainly not be regarded as sexual by a jury.

Section 8 – Causing or inciting a child under 13 to engage in sexual activity

This offence and its co-offence at section 10 is perhaps closer to what we would typically think of as grooming than the section 15 offence discussed below. It is an offence under section 8 SOA 2003 to intentionally cause or incite a child under the age of 13 to engage in a sexual activity. This is wider than section 7 in that there is no need to show touching, so this could cover other sexual activity that did not involve touching, e.g. inciting a child to act out certain sexually suggestive actions without touching the child at all. Again the causing or inciting must be intentional and this is the only *mens rea* required. The penalty for this offence depends on the nature of the sexual activity. The maximum sentence of life imprisonment only applies if the activity involved penetrative acts, whereas the maximum penalty for non-penetrative acts is 14 years – still a serious penalty.

'Causing' is different from 'inciting' a child to engage in sexual activity. A person (A) causes another (B) to engage in sexual activity without consent if B, for example, engages in the activity as a consequence of A exerting a capacity that he possesses to control or influence B's acts. Here the sexual activity actually has to take place. Whereas, the essence of the offence of incitement is the *encouragement* of a person under 13 to engage in such activity. It has to be intentional or deliberate, and the defendant has to know what they are doing. However, given that the essence of the offence is incitement, it is not a necessary ingredient, and the prosecution does not have to prove that the defendant intends that the incited activity should actually take place.[24] Although the incitement must have been communicated to at least one child, it does not matter that it is not possible to identify any specific or identifiable person to whom the statement was addressed.[25]

Some of these points are well illustrated in *Grout (Phillip)*.[26] The 18-year-old defendant was a helper at a local church group and became friendly with the 12-year-old complainant, H, with whom he exchanged mobile numbers and e-mail addresses. They were also in contract via their computer webcams. On one occasion the defendant asked H to show him her bra over the webcam. She said that she was scared and so showed him her bra strap by pulling the corner of the neck of her jumper so that it was visible to the defendant on his computer screen. He was convicted of an offence under section 8. On appeal, his conviction was quashed on the basis of errors made by the trial judge's directions to the jury. The court held that section 8(1) of the SOA 2003 created at least two separate offences: intentionally *causing* a child to engage in sexual activity and intentionally *inciting* a child to engage in sexual activity, the elements of each were different and the indictment needs to clearly identify which offence the defendant is being charged with. If a defendant was charged with inciting, the prosecution did not have to prove that the defendant intended that the actual sexual activity should take place. Grout's conviction was unsafe as the jury had been asked to consider other possible offences, for which there was no evidence to support conviction.

There is no definition of 'activity' in the SOA 2003 but in *Grout* the court was prepared to accept that 'activity' on the part of the child could embrace the activity of conversation, sending a text or using instant messaging. Whether the action of showing the defendant her bra was sexual needed to be decided by the jury in accordance with the definition of sexual in section 78 SOA 2003. It is the activity of the *child* that must be sexual, not the defendant.

Children under the age of 16

The next set of offences all relate to children under the age of 16. They can also be committed against children under 13 and so there is necessarily some overlap with the offences discussed above. It seems that it was the intention of Parliament that where a complainant is under 13 then the more serious offences examined above should be charged, and this is generally what happens. Therefore, the offences below are really aimed at complainants who are between the ages of 13 and 16 years. It could be argued that we do not need the overlap at all. However, if someone was charged under section 9 with sexual activity with a child who was between 13 and 16, then proof that the child was under 13 would relieve the defendant of liability. The defendant would therefore be found not guilty and would have to be acquitted and recharged under section 13. The risk of this happening seems to be the reason for the overlap. However, the overlap does also mean that it is possible for a defendant to be charged with the lesser offence under section 9 rather than rape of a child under section 5, for example. However, as we have already seen above in relation to *G v United Kingdom*,[27] the European Court of Human Rights rejected a claim that a charge of rape of a child under section 5 (rather than the less serious charge under section 13) was a breach of Article 6 and it is generally the case that the more serious offence would be charged where the child was under 13.

The elements of some of the following offences are very similar to those offences discussed above. However, generally, where the child is between 13 and 16 there is an excuse of reasonable belief that the child is over 16, which would mean the offence was not made out; this does not apply where the child is under 13. No belief, however reasonable, that the child is over 13 would be a defence.

Consent of the child is irrelevant to all these offences.

Section 9 – Sexual activity with a child

Under section 9 SOA 2003, a person aged 18 or over (A) commits an offence if he intentionally touches another person (B), the touching is sexual and either B is under 16 and A does not reasonably believe that B is 16 or over, or B is under 13.

This offence is much wider than the offences under section 5 or 6. The *actus reus* embraces sexual intercourse, or other penetrative acts, but also covers *any* sexual touching. As at section 7 the touching must be intentional. The meanings of the words 'sexual' and 'touching' are set out in sections 78 and 79 SOA 2003 and have been discussed above. The definitions therefore result in a wide range of sexual activity being covered by this offence, including touching through clothing. This will be considered in more detail below, in relation to section 13 (child sex offences committed by children and young persons).

The maximum penalty for this offence is 14 years' imprisonment.

Section 10 – Causing or inciting a child to engage in sexual activity

A person (A) aged 18 or over commits an offence if he intentionally causes or incites a child under the age of 16 (B) to engage in a sexual activity. For the offence to be proved, the prosecution has to show that A did not reasonably believe that B was 16 or over, or that B was under 13. This offence closely mirrors the one contained in section 8, and so the meaning of 'cause' and 'incite' would be the same as the meanings used for the purpose of section 8. The penalties for this offence depend on the type of activity, with the maximum being 14 years' imprisonment for activity that involves penetration.

Section 11 – Engaging in sexual activity in the presence of a child

It is an offence for a person over 18 to intentionally engage in a sexual activity, for his own sexual gratification, when a child is present or is in a place from which the activity can be observed. The defendant must know or believe that the child is aware, or must be intending that the child should be aware of the sexual activity. A child is someone under the age of 16.

This could cover a broad range of behaviour. For example, if two adults engaged in sexual intercourse in the presence of a child for their own gratification, this would be an offence. However, it would also cover the situation where an adult was alone, such an adult who masturbated in the presence of a child for his own gratification.[28] It is important to realize that the sexual activity must be for the sexual gratification of the adult, not the child. The reference to "a place from which the activity can be observed" is intended to apply to a situation where the child is not actually physically in the same room, but nevertheless can see the activity, for example through a window or via a webcam.[29]

As usual, consent of the child is irrelevant. There is an excuse of reasonable belief that the child is over 16, but there is no such defence where the child is under 13. The maximum penalty is 10 years' imprisonment.

Section 12 – Causing a child to watch a sexual act

A person aged 18 or over commits an offence if they intentionally cause a child to watch a third person engaging in sexual activity or to look at the image of any person engaging in sexual activity for the purpose of sexual gratification. A child is someone under the age of 16 and consent is irrelevant. As above, it is the sexual gratification of the defendant which is the issue, not that of the child. Again, there is a defence of reasonable belief that the child is over 16, but there is no such defence if the child is under 13.

Section 79(4) SOA 2003 provides that an image means a moving or still image and includes an image produced by any means, so obviously includes photographs, pseudo-photographs, digital images and films.[30]

Clearly, this offence applies where an adult shows a child pornographic images[31] but also would apply where the defendant causes the child to watch another person engaging in sexual activity in the presence of the child. The maximum penalty is 10 years' imprisonment.

The issue of sexual gratification of the defendant was considered in *Abdullahi* (2007).[32] The defendant was in his early 30s and the child was a boy of 13 years who was visiting the defendant's younger brother. The defendant played various pornographic films to the child, which depicted men and women having sex as well as homosexual activity. Later, there was a conversation about sexual matters and this was followed by the defendant touching the boy's penis. The reported case was an appeal against conviction for an offence under section 12. The trial judge had directed the jury that they would have to be satisfied that Abdullahi had caused the boy to look at the pornography for the purpose of obtaining sexual gratification at the time, or to provide sexual gratification to himself later. Abdullahi submitted that this direction was too wide. The court held (dismissing the appeal) that sexual gratification does not have to be taken immediately, i.e. it is not required that sexual gratification and the viewed sexual act, or display of images, are contemporaneous. The offence can be committed where the defendant's purpose involves immediate or *deferred* gratification. In the context of the case, this would include showing the boy the images with a view to putting him in a mood to provide sexual gratification to the defendant later.

Section 13 – Child sex offences committed by children and young persons

The offences in sections 9–12 are all expressly aimed at offenders over the age of 18 but it is clear that young people can also be abusers. The NSPCC report referred to above stated that 65.9 per cent of the contact sexual abuse reported by children and young people up to the age of 17 was perpetrated by other children and young people under the age of 18.[33]

The SOA 2003 deals with this issue in section 13, which provides that a person under 18 commits an offence is he does anything that would be an offence under sections 9–12 if he were aged 18. However, if the defendant is under 18 then the maximum penalty is only 5 years' imprisonment. So, a young person who is over the age of criminal responsibility can be guilty of sexual activity with a child, causing or inciting a child to engage in sexual activity, engaging in sexual activity in the presence of a child, or causing a child to watch a sexual act because of section 13, albeit at a reduced sentence.

The problem with this is that the provision effectively criminalizes what many would consider to be normal teenage sexual experimentation. A national study of sexual attitudes and lifestyles in 2013 found that approximately 29 per cent of young women and 31 per cent of young men said that they had heterosexual intercourse before the age of 16.[34] The definitions of 'sexual' and 'touching' in sections 78 and 79 are so wide that this figure would probably be very much higher if it included all sexual activity and not just sexual intercourse. So, the kind of sexual touching that many young people engage in could theoretically result in a conviction under section 13 for sexual activity with a child. This problem of how to protect vulnerable children from abuse from others, while not unnecessarily criminalizing consensual teenage behaviour, was discussed during the passage of the SOA 2003 through Parliament. One MP even offered a bottle of champagne to anyone who could adequately resolve the problem.

Criminalizing activity between consenting teenagers also presents an opportunity for parental moralizing whereby:

> . . . parents, disapproving of their children's sexual choices, can attempt to enforce their choices on the child by reporting the child's partner to the police. This may be of particular concern to gay children, whose parents, if possessed of a disapproving 'morality', may wish to punish their children's partners.[35]

The best the legislature could come up with in answer to these concerns was s13 – and the Crown Prosecution Service (CPS) guidelines aim to avoid prosecutions where both parties are genuinely consenting. It must be remembered that the CPS have a discretion to prosecute and it is generally not regarded as being in the public interest to prosecute for consensual sexual activity between young people.

The CPS guidelines point out that where both parties to sexual activity are under 16, then they may both have committed a criminal offence. However, the overriding purpose of the legislation is to protect children and it was not Parliament's intention to punish children unnecessarily or for the criminal law to intervene where it was wholly inappropriate. Consensual sexual activity between, for example, a 14- or 15-year-old and a teenage partner would not normally require criminal proceedings in the absence of aggravating features. The relevant considerations taken into account by the CPS when making a decision whether to prosecute include:

(a) the respective ages of the parties;
(b) the existence and nature of any relationship;
(c) their level of maturity;
(d) whether any duty of care existed;
(e) whether there was a serious element of exploitation.[36]

So we are left with a situation where technically two young people who engaged in sexual touching are committing an offence, but in reality it is unlikely that they will be prosecuted unless it is doubtful that there was genuine consent or there is some element of abuse or exploitation. This places significant responsibility on the agencies of the criminal justice system both in terms of choosing whether to charge and in choosing an appropriate charge where both parties are of a similar young age.

Section 14 - Arranging or facilitating commission of a child sex offence

A person commits an offence under section 14 if he intentionally arranges or facilitates something that he intends to do, intends another person to do, or believes that another person will do, in any part of the world, which involves the commission of an offence under sections 9–13. This offence can be committed by anyone over the age of criminal responsibility. It covers taking preparatory steps with the intention of committing an offence. It could include arranging travel, access to children,[37] allowing facilities to be used, supplying equipment such as sex toys (or even ordinary toys meant to put a child at ease in order to facilitate the commission of an offence). Again this is an intention offence and the defendant must intentionally arrange or facilitate something he intends or believes will be done. The maximum penalty is 14 years' imprisonment.

The case of *Robson (John Paul)* (2009)[38] made clear that an arrangement may be made without the agreement of anyone else and a defendant may take steps by way of a plan without involving anyone else. The appellant in the case was appealing against a conviction, following a retrial, for attempting to arrange the commission of a child sex offence contrary to section 14. He had been a client of a sex worker (M) and he asked her if she knew of any girls of around 12-years-of-age. M said that she did not know any such girls. Over the course of some weeks, he phoned and texted M asking her to find him a 12-year-old girl. M never agreed to his request. Robson argued that what he had done was incapable of being an attempt to arrange, since there had to be agreement to the arrangement by someone else for there to be an attempt, and no arrangement would have been made until the girl herself had agreed to it. However, the Court of Appeal did not accept this argument and held that the fact that M did not agree did not mean that he had not attempted to make an arrangement. It was not necessary for the child to have agreed before there was an arrangement either; Robson was still making an arrangement for something that, if done, would have been a child sex offence.

During the passage of the SOA through Parliament there was some concern that this offence would criminalize the activities of those who gave advice to children on sexual matters. There was particular concern about healthcare workers, who may give children advice on contraception, and even agony aunts writing in magazines for young people. As a result of these concerns a specific defence was included in section 14, which is meant to protect such advisers from prosecution. Therefore, it is not an offence for someone who is acting for the protection of a child to arrange or facilitate something for the purposes of:

(a)   protecting the child from sexually transmitted infection;
(b)   protecting the physical safety of the child;
(c)   preventing the child from becoming pregnant; or
(d)   promoting the child's emotional wellbeing by the giving of advice.

This defence only applies where the person is not acting for the purpose of obtaining sexual gratification or for the purpose of causing or encouraging the activity constituting the offence (s14(3)).

Section 15 – Meeting a child following sexual grooming

Before the SOA 2003, there was no equivalent offence relating to the sexual groom-ing of children. The introduction of the section 15 offence was particularly in response to internet grooming of children and young people, through social media sites, e-mails, etc. However, the section does not make the act of grooming itself an offence. Section 15 (as amended by the Criminal Justice and Immigration Act 2008 and Criminal Justice and Courts Act 2015) provides that:

A person ('A') aged 18 or over commits an offence if:

(1) A has met or communicated with another person ('B') on at least one or more occasions[39] and subsequently:

    (a) A intentionally meets B,

    (b) A travels with the intention of meeting B in any part of the world or arranges to meet B in any part of the world, or

    (c) B travels with the intention of meeting A in any part of the world,

(2) A intends to do anything to or in respect of B, during or after the meeting mentioned in (1)(a) to (c) and in any part of the world, which if done will involve the commission by A of a relevant offence,

(3) B is under 16, and

(4) A does not reasonably believe that B is 16 or over.

The first point to note is that it is the travelling or meeting (or arranging to meet) which constitutes the *actus reus* of the offence, not the act of grooming. So, to be guilty under section 15, a defendant must have done something more than merely contacting or communicating with the child. The point of this offence is to allow a prosecution in circumstances where the child has not actually been abused. Thus, the offender is prevented from actually engaging in any sexual activity with the child. If the objective is to protect children from sexual abuse, then this is one way of trying to achieve that aim but some would argue that the offence does not go far enough, as someone who sexually grooms a child, even if they do not actually arrange to meet, is a threat to the safety of children and this is now dealt with under section 15A. Although the offence was originally created as a response to internet grooming, it is not confined to communications via electronic means. It would also cover face-to-face meetings with a child.[40] The recent street-grooming cases men-tioned in the introduction to this chapter are an example of this.

For a prosecution to succeed there must be the intention to commit a relevant offence, so travelling to meet a child for innocent purposes, e.g. to take part in a game or other event, would be outside the scope of the offence. A relevant offence is any offence in the SOA 2003 and so covers all the child sex offences discussed in this chapter, as well as those discussed in other chapters. It also extends to anything done outside the country that would be an offence if done in England and Wales. Whether the prosecution can prove the necessary intention beyond reasonable doubt will depend upon the extent to which the circumstances sur-rounding the grooming, and perhaps the meeting itself, reveal the purpose. It may be clear because the communications are of a sexually suggestive nature, but they may not be and so other evidence will have to be used to show that the defendant intended to commit a relevant offence against the child, especially where the individual has no previous convictions for child sexual offences. In G^{41} the court made clear that the only requirement prior to an intentional meeting was that there was a communication. There was no requirement that the communication itself be sexual in nature, and the title of the offence is then misleading in this respect. Of course the intention to commit a sexual offence had to be proved and in that case there was ample evidence to show the defendant's intention, including the fact that he had condoms in his pockets when he picked the 12-year-old girl up from school. *Mohammed (Raza)* (2006)[42] concerned a 55-year-old man who met and communicated with a 13-year-old girl on a number of occasions. She eventually contacted him and asked him to pick her up in his van, which he did. The police were informed and, after a while, they found and stopped the van. He claimed that he was taking her out for fish and chips and they were looking for a fish and chip shop. However, when their mobile phones were analysed there were a number of intimate and suggestive text messages found and this was sufficient for a conviction under section 15.

The consent of the child is not a defence but there is an excuse of reasonable belief that the child is over 16. This could apply, for example, where someone contacts a child via the internet and the child lies about their age but the belief does have to be reasonable and so might not apply where the child is contacted via a chatroom specifically designed for children.

The maximum penalty is 10 years' imprisonment.

Section 15A – Sexual communication with a child

In 2014 the NSPCC ran a campaign that suggested that a new offence was needed to tackle those offenders who communicate sexually with a child and have no intention of meeting or travelling to meet them.[43] In response to this the Serious Crime Act 2015 introduced the offence of sexual communication with a child which inserted section 15A into the SOA 2003. This makes it an offence for a person aged 18 or over (A) to intentionally communicate with a person under 16 (and A does not reasonably believe that B is 16 or over) for the purpose of obtaining sexual gratification. The communication must itself be sexual, or it must be intended to encourage the child to make a communication that is sexual, whether to the offender or a third party. The offence carries a maximum sentence of 2 years.

Sexual is given its own definition here and a communication is sexual if:

(a)   any part of it relates to sexual activity, or
(b)   a reasonable person would, in all the circumstances but regardless of any person's purpose, consider any part of the communication to be sexual (s15A(2)).

In line with section 78 this leaves the jury considerable discretion in deciding whether a communication is sexual. Sexual gratification is expected to carry the same meaning as expounded in *Abdullahi* (2007).

Offences at sections 8 and 10 SOA 2003 already cover inciting or causing a child to engage in sexual activity; these offences are made out whether or not the activity encouraged (say, undressing or taking a photo) actually takes place and clearly these offences should be charged when appropriate as they have higher maximum sentences.

Thankfully this offence does not criminalize the issues of sexting between similarly aged teenagers[44] – although, as Chapter 7 discusses, where the communication features an indecent photograph of a child this will be a criminal matter even when both parties are children.

Possession of a paedophile manual

The Serious Crime Act 2015 created a new offence of possession of any item that contains advice or guidance about abusing children sexually (s69(1)). "Abusing children sexually" embraces any act that is an offence under Part 1 of the Sexual Offences Act 2003 (s69(8)(a)). "Item" is a purposefully broad term that can cover materials that are printed, electronic or recorded and that are comprised of words, images or sound. This offence seeks to plug a perceived gap in regulation by criminalizing the possession of advice on how to abuse and/or groom a child. It has a number of specific defences that mirror those provided for the pornography offences discussed at Chapter 7. These defences protect those who have a legitimate reason for being in possession of the item (s69(2)(a)), or where the defendant had not read, viewed or listened to the item, and did not know, and had no reason to suspect, that it contained advice or guidance about abusing children sexually (s69(2)(b)) or the item was sent to the defendant without request and it was not kept for an unreasonable time (s69(2)(c)).

Although it is likely the production and dissemination of these materials would already be captured by existing offences this specific offence was enacted to ensure that the possession of these materials could be appropriately punished.[45]

The offence carries a maximum sentence of 3 years.

Exceptions to aiding, abetting and counselling

Section 73 of the SOA 2003 provides a general exception to a charge of aiding, abetting or counselling of a sexual offence against a child where a person is acting for the purpose of:

(a)   protecting the child from sexually transmitted infection;
(b)   protecting the physical safety of the child;
(c)   preventing the child from becoming pregnant; or
(d)   promoting the child's emotional wellbeing by the giving of advice.

This exception only applies where the person is not acting for the purpose of obtaining sexual gratification or for the purpose of causing or encouraging the activity constituting the offence. It closely mirrors the defence in section 14 discussed above. As was the case in section 14, the exception aims to protect those who provide young people with advice on sexual matters.

Sentencing

When the offender is over the age of 18 the same sentencing provision applies as set out at Chapter 3. Reflecting the seriousness of offending against children these offences also have higher starting points for custody, although there is provision for non-custodial offences in exceptional cases.[46]

Sexual offender treatment programmes are considered at Chapter 10 and there is provision for offenders to be rehabilitated or controlled in the community, but the sentencing focus here is still very firmly on the protection of the public through the use of custody. It is notable the 2014 sentencing regime has put a focus on whether children have been exploited and/or groomed (by an individual or a gang) and/or whether a position of trust has been abused in assessing the culpability of offenders. In response to new understandings of child abuse and exploitation the Sentencing Council have also removed the mitigating factor of "ostensible consent", from the new guidelines, as the Council explains:

> In the previous guideline there were child sex offences labelled as involving 'ostensible consent' – that is, where a child over 13 has apparently agreed to sexual activity. The Council believes that this is the wrong way of looking at these offences as children do not consent to their own abuse. The new guideline therefore looks more at the offender's actions and behaviour towards the victim.[47]

How far the demeanour of the child should be taken into account in sentencing has also caused some difficulty.[48] At Chapter 3 we related some of the prevalent rape myths that may cause significant difficulties in attaining a conviction. Perhaps surprisingly we also find statements that children are complicit in sexual abuse expressed at the sentencing stage. For example, in a case where a 24-year-old man had sex with a 10-year-old-girl and was charged with the section 5 offence the trial judge commented:

> One of the problems I face is the moral situation which this case gives rise to. Here is a young woman of 10 who is taken to the park within three-quarters of an hour of meeting a 24 year old and they have sex together . . . This was not sexual activity of affection it was of animal desire by both.[49]

These comments on the sexuality of some young children may not be incorrect, but they do illustrate a dichotomy in our approach to child protection that is oft reported in the media without the legal context.

Ostensible consent and mistake as to age has often been afforded considerable weight at the sentencing stage, particularly when the offenders are young men. For example, in C (2011)[50] two 12-year-old girls had arranged to meet six young men and, after being denied access to a party they all expected to attend, the girls got into two cars with the men and were driven to a park. The men (aged 18–21) believed the girls to be 16 years old. One of the girls, 'consented' to oral sex with five of the men and vaginal intercourse with one man; the other girl 'consented' to sexual intercourse with one of the men. All the men were convicted of the section 5 offence and appealed against their sentences of 2 years. On appeal the character, appearance and behaviour of the young girls was considered and, as Stevenson highlights, the judgment of Lord Justice Moses is littered with comments that suggest weight should be given to the appearance of the girls when sentencing as, while both girls were under 13, there was "nothing in their physical appearance to suggest they were under 16".[51] The sentences were quashed and replaced with sentences of detention in a young offender institution (for those aged less than 21) or imprisonment, suspended for 12 months.

As section 5 is a strict liability offence these matters cannot affect liability and, while we may appreciate that they should be given credence in determining an appropriate sentence, it is difficult to reconcile this with the ideal of child protection in the substantive offences. It is even more difficult to reconcile the sentences here with those in *Attorney General's References (Nos 11 and 12 of 2012)*[52] where, in similar circumstances, the offenders received sentences of 7 years' detention. Hopefully the new Council guidance will provide a more consistent approach to sentencing.

For youth offenders (those less than 18-years-of-age) special considerations must be taken into account.[53] For all young offenders the courts are trying to balance the rights of victims with the rights of child offenders, whose welfare must also be taken into consideration. For sexual offences normal teenage sexual experimentation is also a consideration, as the Sentencing Council outlines:

> When sentencing a young offender whose offence involves sexual activity but there is no evidence of a coercive or abusive relationship or of anything other than consensual activity, a court will need to be aware that a desire to explore gender identity or sexual orientation may result in offending behaviour. Depending on the seriousness of the offending behaviour, offender mitigation may arise where that behaviour stems from sexual immaturity or confusion.[54]

These are very similar considerations to those in the CPS guidance set out above.

Credibility and Special Measures

As Chapter 2 explored, child victims have had some difficulty making their voice heard in accusations of sexual assault. This situation is now considerably improved. One of the results of the Savile Inquiry and the various grooming inquiries has been to bring to light the filtering of cases that has taken place by the police and the CPS. As the House of Commons Affairs Committee noted:

> Clearly it is right and necessary for prosecutors to weigh the strengths and weaknesses of a case before taking it to court and it is not in anyone's interest to pursue cases that have no prospect of success. However, as the Director of Public Prosecution has acknowledged, until recently the CPS approach to credibility of victims of child sexual exploitation as witnesses was inappropriately cautious and risked leaving the whole category of child sexual exploitation victims unprotected by the criminal justice system. This was because the standard CPS

test for credibility would, if unadjusted, almost always find against a child sexual exploitation victim. This was based partly on victims' prior history of involvement with the police and social services and partly on internal inconsistencies in their accounts, some of which were a result of substance misuse initiated by the groomer. The confusion about whether or not these children were 'consenting' to sexual activity (though the law clearly says that they cannot) was also a factor which influenced police decisions.[55]

In response to this the CPS now produce detailed guidance for dealing with reports made by children.[56] Multi-agency guidance is also produced by the Government to clarify the positive duties placed on criminal justice, welfare, health and other agencies who have contact with children.[57] Detailed guidance for the police on responding to child exploitation is also provided by the College of Policing[58] and the police together with other welfare services are also part of the Local Safeguarding Children Boards who work to safeguard and promote child welfare.[59] Councils have also been advised that they need to take steps to actively safeguard children in their locality with a need for appropriate policies and procedures to tackle child sexual exploitation.[60] These provisions, together with a general social shift toward accepting the reality of child sexual offending has created an environment in which accusations by children should be taken more seriously.

This is only the first hurdle. Once a case reaches court this can be an intimidating atmosphere for children and special measures, as outlined at Chapter 3, are available for all child witnesses – this is inclusive of victims – (defined as those under 18), but not for child defendants. Section 29 Youth Justice & Criminal Evidence Act 1999 allows witnesses to be questioned and give evidence through a court-approved intermediary, but this currently excludes defendants. There have been suggestions in the past that this should be an option for defendants[61] on the grounds of equality of arms, and a common law power to appoint intermediaries has now been recognized.[62] The cross-examination of a child by an accused in person is also prohibited.[63]

As cases may involve both children as witnesses and defendants one may expect that child defendants would be afforded the same protection as witnesses but this is not the case. For defendants aged under 18 the Youth Courts may hear cases. This system is different to the adult system, as it is both structured to address the needs of young people and custody is considered as a last resort. For more serious cases, and this would include offences against children, child defendants can appear in Magistrates and Crown Courts where some provision can be made to accommodate young offenders. These accommodations include: proceedings should be explained to defendants, trials should be conducted in language the defendants can understand, courtrooms should be arranged so all participants are on the same level, robes and wigs should not be worn and frequent breaks should be taken.[64]

Conclusion

As has been seen, the offences relating to children in the SOA 2003 are wide ranging. In trying to achieve the aim of protecting children from abuse almost every possible kind of sexual activity has been criminalized. However, this has not necessarily been done in the simplest way, with some offences overlapping others. There are also different age thresholds and age limits that sometimes make it difficult to understand which of the offences apply to a particular situation. Some would argue that section 13, which effectively criminalizes normal teenage sexual behaviour, is a step too far, but the CPS charging guidelines mitigate against any harshness in the law. In the end it could be argued that the objective of protecting the vulnerable from abuse should outweigh any other considerations.

Improvements still need to be made in how the criminal justice system and welfare agencies respond to offending against children. There is now a wealth of guidance for these agencies and whether this will help child victims achieve justice in the future is something that will continue to be the subject of significant attention.

Notes

1 See 'Timeline: 1980s child abuse allegations' *BBC News*, February 4, 2015. Accessible at www.bbc.co.uk/news/uk-politics-28195580 for further information.

2 Where no evidence of a systematic cover up of child sexual abuse was found, although record-keeping by the relevant agencies was criticized: Home Office *An Independent Review of Two Home Office Commissioned Independent Reviews Looking at Information Held in Connection with Child Abuse from 1979–1999* London: Home Office (2014). Accessible at https://www.gov.uk/government/uploads/system/uploads/attachment_data/file/372915/Wanless-Whittam_Review_Report.pdf.

3 The Independent Inquiry into Child Sexual Abuse has yet to issue any reports but its website holds information on its progress and terms of reference accessible at https://childsexualabuseinquiry.independent.gov.uk.

4 House of Commons Home Affairs Committee *Child Sexual Exploitation and the Response to Localised Grooming Second Report of Session 2013–14* (June 2013) London: The Stationery Office; A. Jay OBE *Independent Inquiry into Sexual Exploitation in Rotherham (1997–2013)* Rotherham: Rotherham Metropolitan Borough Council (2014); Oxford Safeguarding Children Board *Serious Case Review into Child Sexual Exploitation in Oxfordshire: From the Experiences of Children A, B, C, D, E, and F* Oxford: Oxford Safeguarding Children Board (February 2015). Accessible at http://www.oscb.org.uk/wp-content/uploads/SCR-into-CSE-in-Oxfordshire-FINAL-FOR-WEBSITE.pdf.

5 For a discussion of the background to the grooming reports and the methods used by street groomers see S. Berelowitz, et al *"If only someone had listened" The Office of the Children's Commissioner's Inquiry into Child Sexual Exploitation in Gangs and Groups Final Report* London: Office of the Children's Commissioner (2013). Accessible at http://www.childrenscommissioner.gov.uk/sites/default/files/publications/If_only_someone_had_listened.pdf.

6 L. Radford et al *Child Abuse and Neglect in the UK Today* London: NSPCC (2011).

7 S. Berelowitz *"If only someone had listened" The Office of the Children's Commissioner's Inquiry into Child Sexual Exploitation in Gangs and Groups Final Report* London: Office of the Children's Commissioner (2013). Accessible at www.childrenscommissioner.gov.uk/content/publications/content_743.

8 World Health Organisation *Preventing Child Maltreatment: A Guide to Taking and Generating Evidence* Geneva: World Health Organisation (2006) p. 10.

9 For example see the reports and definitions of child exploitation advanced by Banardo's: Barnardo's *Puppet on a String: The Urgent Need to Cut Children Free from Sexual Exploitation* Ilford: Barnardo's (2011). Accessible at http://www.barnardos.org.uk/ctf_puppetonastring_report_final.pdf; Barnardo's *The Tangled Web: How Child Sexual Exploitation Is Becoming More Complex* Ilford: Barnardo's (2013). Accessible at http://www.barnardos.org.uk/the_tangled_web.pdf.

10 The UK National Working Group for Sexually Exploited Children and Young People has developed a definition of child sexual exploitation that is used to inform practice and statutory guidance. This sets out "Sexual exploitation of children and young people under 18 involves exploitative situations, contexts and relationships where young people (or a third person or persons) receive 'something' (e.g. food, accommodation, drugs, alcohol, cigarettes, affection, gifts, money) as a result of them performing, and/or another or others performing on them, sexual activities. Child sexual exploitation can occur through the use of technology without the child's immediate recognition; for example being persuaded to post sexual images on the Internet/mobile phones without immediate payment or gain. In all cases, those exploiting the child/young person have power over them by virtue of their age, gender, intellect, physical strength and/or economic or other resources. Violence, coercion and intimidation are common, involvement in exploitative relationships being characterised in the main by the child or young person's limited availability of choice resulting from their social/economic and/or emotional vulnerability." See http://www.nwgnetwork.org.

11 M. Waites *The Age of Consent: Young People, Sexuality, and Citizenship* Basingstoke: Palgrave Macmillan (2005); N. Piyan 'Satiating the saturnine child: sex, sin and shame' *UCL Juris. Rev.* (2008) 14 pp. 221–245; D. O'Gara 'Protecting young girls from themselves: Part 2 – The development of the mistake as to age defence in England and Wales and Canada' *Irish Law Times* (2007) 25(13) pp. 212–216.

12 Department for Education *Letting Children Be Children, Report of an Independent Review of the Commercialisation and Sexualisation of Childhood* London: Stationary Office (June 2011). Accessible at https://www.gov.uk/government/uploads/system/uploads/attachment_data/file/175418/Bailey_Review.pdf.

13 For a discussion of how these historical preconceptions are presenting in the current law see K. Stevenson 'It is what "Girls of Indifferent Character" do . . . complications concerning the legal age of sexual consent in the light of R v C (2011)' *Journal of Criminal Law* (2012) 76(2) pp. 130–139.

14 [1985] UKHL 7.

15 *R. v K* [2001] UKHL 41, it was held a defendant could be acquitted where the victim was under 16 if the defendant had held an honest belief that the complainant was aged 16-years-of-age or over.

16 Although this is not without its difficulties: see *R. v Cottrell (Steven)* [2007] EWCA Crim 2016.

17 [1934] 1 KB 354.

18 Section 2 of the Indecency with Children Act 1960 increased the maximum sentence from 2 years to 5 years where the offence was committed against "a girl under thirteen who is stated to have been so in the indictment".

19 Home Office, *Setting the Boundaries: Reforming the Law on Sexual Offences*, para 3.2.3.

20 *Per* Mr. John Randall. Hansard, HC Standing Committee B, 3rd Sitting, September 11, 2003, col.102.

21 [2005]2 Cr App R (S) 73.

22 (37334/08), EHRLR 2011, 6, 747–749.

23 For further discussion see *European Human Rights Law Review* (2011) 'Case Comment, G v United Kingdom (37334/08)' 6 pp. 747–749.

24 *R. v Walker* [2006] EWCA Crim 1907.
25 *R. v Jones (Ian)* [2007] EWCA Crim 1118.
26 [2011] EWCA Crim 299.
27 *G v United Kingdom* (Application number 37334/08).
28 *R. v Bowling (Stephen David)* [2008] EWCA Crim 1148; [2009] 1 Cr App R (S.) 23. *R. v WH* [2005] EWCA Crim 1917 (CA (Crim Div)).
29 See *R. v Michael Thomas Alderton* [2014] EWCA Crim 2204; *R. v Scott Allan Henderson* [2012] EWCA Crim 2024.
30 The offence has also been committed by way of FaceTime, an application that can be used for video calls on mobile phones: *R. v Adam Storer* [2013] EWCA Crim 2700.
31 *R. v Shaun Burford* [2015] EWCA Crim 615.
32 [2007]1 WLR 225.
33 Radford, et al *Child Abuse and Neglect in the UK Today.*
34 C.H. Mercer and C. Tanton et al 'Changes in sexual attitudes and lifestyles in Britain through the life course and over time: findings from the National Surveys of Sexual Attitudes and Lifestyles'. Accessible at www.thelancet.com, vol. 382, November 30, 2013.
35 S. Knight 'Libertarian critiques of consent in sexual offences' *UCL Journal of Law and Jurisprudence* (2012) 1(1) pp. 137–165.
36 See http://www.cps.gov.uk/legal/s_to_u/sexual_offences_act.
37 *R. v Jordan (Nicholas James)* [2006] EWCA Crim 3311; *R. v JR* [2008] EWCA Crim 2912.
38 [2009] EWCA Crim 1472.
39 Originally the section referred to two occasions but this was reduced to one by s36 Criminal Justice and Courts Act 2015.
40 Although, as McLaughlin argued in 2009, grooming has typically been understood by the public as an online process. S. McLaughlin Online sexual grooming of children and the law *Communications Law* (2009) 14(1) pp. 8–19.
41 [2010] EWCA Crim 1693.
42 [2006] EWCA Crim 1107.
43 NSPCC 'Flaw in the Law'. Accessible at http://www.nspcc.org.uk/fighting-for-childhood/campaigns/flaw-law.
44 Although commentators still have some reservations about how sensitive this offence is to the culture of modern teenagers. A. Phippen and J. Agate 'New social media offences under the Criminal Justice and Courts Act and Serious Crime Act: the cultural context' *Entertainment Law Review* (2015) 26(3) pp. 82–87.
45 The Obscene Publications Act 1959 would criminalize the "publication" of these materials and if they contained any indecent photographs possession would also be an offence and this is discussed further at Chapter 7.
46 *Sentencing Council, Sexual Offences Definitive Guideline* (2013) p. 28. Accessible at http://www.sentencingcouncil.org.uk/wp-content/uploads/Final_Sexual_Offences_Definitive_Guideline_content_web1.pdf.
47 'New sentencing guideline gives greater focus to impact of sex offences on victims', Sentencing Council, December 12, 2013. Accessible at https://www.sentencingcouncil.org.uk/news/item/new-sentencing-guideline-gives-greater-focus-to-impact-of-sex-offences-on-victims.
48 For factors identified by the Court of Appeal as relevant in these circumstances see *Attorney General's Reference (Nos 11 and 12 of 2012)* [2012] EWCA Crim 1119.
49 *Attorney General's References Nos 74 and 83 of 2007 (Keith Fenn and Simon James Foster)* [2007] EWCA Crim 2550.
50 *R. v Charles (Ashley Dwayne)* [2011] EWCA Crim 2153.
51 K. Stevenson 'It is What "Girls of Indifferent Character" '.

52 [2012] EWCA Crim 1119.
53 *Sentencing Council, Overarching Principles, Sentencing Youths* (2009). Accessible at https://www.sentencingcouncil.org.uk/wp-content/uploads/web_overarching_princi ples_sentencing_youths.pdf. Also see the *Sentencing Council Updated Note of Approach* (2014). Accessible at: https://www.sentencingcouncil.org.uk/wp-content/uploads/Sex ual_offences_-_note_of_approach_when_sentencing_offenders_under_18.pdf.
54 Para 3.3. See also the decision of the court in *R. v K* [2014] EWCA Crim 2907.
55 House of Commons, Home Affairs Committee *Child Sexual Exploitation and the Response to Localised Grooming* London: The Stationary Office (June 2013), para 57. Accessible at http://www.publications.parliament.uk/pa/cm201314/cmselect/cmhaff/68/ 68i.pdf.
56 CPS Guidelines on Prosecuting Cases of Child Sexual Abuse. Accessible at http://www. cps.gov.uk/legal/a_to_c/child_sexual_abuse.
57 HM Government *Working Together to Safeguard Children. A Guide to Inter-agency Working to Safeguard and Promote the Welfare of Children* London: HM Government (March 2013). Accessible at http://media.education.gov.uk/assets/files/pdf/w/working% 20together.pdf.
58 College of Policing *Responding to Child Sexual Exploitation* London: Authorised Professional Practice (2014). Accessible at https://www.app.college.police.uk/app-content/ major-investigation-and-public-protection/child-sexual-exploitation.
59 Established and regulated by the Children Act 2004.
60 See reports from the Local Government Association *Tackling Child Sexual Exploitation: A Resource Pack for Councils* London: LGA (2015). Accessible at http://www. local.gov.uk/documents/10180/6869714/Tackling+Child+Sexual+Exploitation+Resou rce+for+Councils+20+01+2015.pdf/336aee0a-22fc-4a88-bd92-b26a6118241c. House of Commons, Communities and Local Government Committee *Child Sexual Exploitation in Rotherham: Some Issues for Local Government* London: The Stationery Office (2014). Accessible at www.publications.parliament. uk/pa/cm201415/cmselect/cmcom loc/648/648.pdf.
61 Baroness Hale in *R. (on the application of D) v Camberwell Green Youth Court* [2005] UKHL 4.
62 *R. (on the application of OP) v Secretary of State for Justice* [2014] EWHC 1944 (Admin).
63 Youth Justice and Criminal Evidence Act 1999 s35 as amended by the Coroners and Justice Act 2009 s105.
64 Practice Direction (Crown Court: Young defendants) [2000] 1 WLR 659.

Chapter 5

Offences that Reflect an Imbalance of Power

Introduction

Despite the widely held belief that child sexual abuse is perpetrated by strangers, children are far more likely to be sexually abused by someone they know.[1] Some of this abuse takes place within families, often involving siblings but, as has become increasingly well reported and recorded, abuse also often involves individuals placed in a position of trust or care over individuals.

At the time of writing, hardly a week seems to go by without a fresh allegation of abuse in an institutional setting being reported by the media. It is tempting to think that there has been a huge increase in such abuse during recent years, whereas, in fact, the majority of reported allegations seem to relate to historical offences that were committed decades ago. It may be difficult for those who were not born in the 1970s to understand how different attitudes to sexual abuse were then. It seems that offences committed in care homes, hospitals or schools were often not reported or acted upon by the authorities in the way they might be now. Consequently, many victims did not speak out until many years after the offences took place, perhaps out of fear that they would not be believed, or that their complaint would not be acted upon. In response to this in March 2015 the Home Secretary established a statutory inquiry (the Goddard Inquiry) with the aim of conducting a national review to "examine the extent to which institutions have failed in their duty of care to protect children against sexual abuse, and to make recommendations to improve child protection for the future". Given the scale of the inquiry they do not expect to conclude until 2020, but will be publishing regular interim reports.[2]

The Goddard Inquiry has, in part, been driven by the revelations and the publicity generated in the last few years by the allegations made against Jimmy Savile, the former disc jockey and television presenter, who died in 2011. He was heavily involved in charitable work, such as fund raising for a number of hospitals, where he also volunteered. In October 2012, on a television programme, five women complained of abuse by Savile while they were pupils at Duncroft Approved School in the 1970s. Following the programme many more allegations were made by people who were abused by him whilst in hospitals, hospices or care homes. Savile had never been prosecuted during his lifetime, seemingly using his celebrity status and charitable work as a shield against allegations. However, as a result of these allegations of historic abuse a criminal investigation into sexual abuse claims against Savile was launched (Operation Yewtree) and this resulted in the publication in 2013 of a joint report by the Metropolitan Police Service and the National Society for the Prevention of Cruelty to Children (NSPCC).[3] As Savile had died, there could be no prospect of any criminal prosecutions, but the report did serve to point out weaknesses in the criminal justice system and to underline the importance of institutions having procedures to protect children and vulnerable people from abuse.

One of the issues which became apparent during the investigation was that there were a number of people working within the various organizations Savile frequented who had suspicions about his behaviour but either they did not speak out or were not listened to by their managers. On 3 March 2015 the Government announced plans to extend the offence of wilful neglect introduced by the Criminal Justice and Courts Act 2015 to cover teachers, medics, social workers and carers who fail to report sexual abuse of children.[4] Under the proposals someone who fails to protect children from sexual abuse by wilful neglect could face up to 5 years' imprisonment. Although the details were not clear, there was immediate criticism of this proposal, as it puts a very heavy burden on some professionals who may not be fully aware of the risk to a particular child but could be criminalized through inaction.

This chapter will consider three groups of offences that take place in settings or with individuals where there may be an imbalance of power between the parties involved: abuse of a position of trust, familial child sex offences and sexual offending against those with a mental disorder. For the abuse of a position of trust offences this imbalance in power comes about by virtue of a relationship established by 'looking after' children in particular settings, for the familial offences through defined familial relationships and for the offences against those with a mental disorder through a lack of victim capacity or by virtue of the caregiver relationship.

These offences have generated surprisingly little case law in the superior courts and, consequently, there is little in the way of academic commentary. Clearly there is an issue with under-reporting or proceeding with cases in this area, something the Goddard Inquiry will address. But equally, cases may be being successfully resolved in the Crown Court.

Sections 16–19 – Abuse of Position of Trust

The clear aim of this set of offences is to protect young people from being influenced by those who have power or control over them. Abusing a position of trust in order to sexually offend is often spoken about in very general terms, particularly since the Savile inquiry, but the statutory offences discussed here are actually very specific. Not all relationships amount to a 'position of trust' and, where offences are committed against children under 16-years-of-age, cases would normally be brought under the general child offences discussed at Chapter 4.

The offences of abuse of a position of trust were first introduced by the Sexual Offences (Amendment) Act 2000, which also equalised the age of consent for homosexual and heterosexual sex. The introduction of the offences seems to have been a reaction to concern about older men (such as teachers) persuading young men to engage in sexual behaviour but also reflected a genuine feeling that there was a gap in the law that did not adequately protect young people over the age of consent from the influence of older adults. The offences contained in that Act have now been replaced by sections 16–24 of the Sexual Offences Act 2003 (SOA 2003).

There are in fact four separate offences relating to the abuse of a position of trust in sections 16–19, which cover a range of behaviour. The behaviours covered are sexual activity with a child (s16), causing or inciting a child to engage in sexual activity (s17), sexual activity in the presence of a child (s18) and causing a child to watch a sexual act (s19). These closely mirror the child sex offences contained in sections 9–12 of the same Act but with some very important differences. As the type of sexual behaviour covered is so similar to the child sex offences discussed in Chapter 4 they will not be discussed in detail here. This chapter will concentrate on the specific elements of the offences that deal with the position of trust relationship.

The *actus reus* of all four offences have certain elements in common, not least that the offender must be in a position of trust over the child. It is sometimes assumed that anyone considered to be in a position of trust is covered by these offences but this is incorrect. Section 21 defines what a position of trust is, and it is very specific. Broadly, it covers people who look after children in an institutional setting. It does not apply to family members (a common misconception) as sexual activity with child family members is covered by a different set of offences. There are also some surprising omissions, which will be discussed below.

All the offences must be committed by someone aged 18 or over, and so are clearly aimed at adults who are deemed to be taking advantage of young people.

It is important to realize that consent is not a defence to a charge of abuse of a position of trust. In many cases it is clear that the young person has actively and enthusiastically consented to the sexual behaviour but this does not excuse the actions of the adult. It is the nature of the position of trust between the two people that gives rise to an imbalance of power that is the issue here, not the factual consent of the young person.

Sections 21 and 22 – What is a position of trust?

Section 21 defines what constitutes a position of trust. The definition is quite precise and detailed but a person will generally be in a position of trust where they 'look after' the young person in a specified number of institutions and settings. A person 'looks after' the child if he is regularly involved in caring for, training, supervising or being in sole charge of the child (s22(2)). It is clear that teachers are covered by this definition, as are doctors and nurses. However, it is important to note that not all employees of schools or hospitals would come within the definition. For example, school bus drivers or caretakers are probably not people who 'look after' the children. In a hospital context, those who provide catering services are probably not 'looking after' the child either. The Act does not define the meaning of the word 'regularly', which does raise questions about the position of temporary staff, for example supply teachers, who may have only had contact with a child on very limited occasions. There is a lack of case law on these definitions but perhaps this merely illustrates that in practice there does not appear to be a problem in identifying when an offence has been committed.

Not everyone who looks after a child will come within the ambit of the offences. Only those within the organizations listed in section 21 can be guilty of abuse of a position of trust.

The list covers a wide range of institutional settings in which young people are accommodated or cared for. It includes young offenders' institutions, care homes, children's homes, hospitals, foster care and educational institutions (schools and colleges). The institutions may be private, public or voluntary and the abuser does not need to be a paid member of staff, a volunteer could also be guilty of abuse of a position of trust. Section 21 also covers those who have unsupervised contact with children who have been provided with accommodation under the Children Act 1989, for example social workers who oversee the child's welfare, or personal advisers who support children aged 16–17 who have been placed in local authority care.

Although the list seems to be wide ranging, there are a number of people who would not be covered by the offences. For example, scout leaders, sports coaches (outside of a school/college context) or members of the clergy. Bearing in mind the publicity surrounding historic abuse in the Church, this last omission seems significant. Many young people who attend church are clearly influenced by their church leaders and it seems an obvious relationship to be covered. Also, bearing in mind the often close-knit relationships between sports coaches and their athletes, with coaches often controlling quite intimate aspects of the trainee's life, this seems to be quite an important omission.[5] The NSPCC have criticized the definition of a position of trust and suggested that the categories should be extended to cover others such as sports coaches, members of the clergy and youth and community workers.[6] Most reported offences have involved school teachers; this is unsurprising as they fall most clearly into the definition of a person in a position of trust and have regular contact with children. This is also one of the few sexual offences where women have been exposed as sexual offenders, with a number of high-profile cases reaching the media.[7]

For the offences to be made out, the *mens rea* requires the adult must know or could reasonably be expected to know that they are in a position of trust in relation to the child. The offences specifically state that the defendant is to be taken not to know or reasonably be expected to know of the circumstances by virtue of which he is in a position of trust unless sufficient evidence is adduced to raise an issue as to whether he knew or could reasonably be expected to know. In other words, it is *presumed* that the defendant did know or could be reasonably expected to know about the position of trust unless they can show evidence that there is an arguable case to show otherwise. In most cases, the adult would obviously be aware that they are in a position of trust but it is possible that someone who, for example, taught at a large school, might not know that a particular child is a pupil at that school.

Who is a child?

It is an essential element of these offences that the relevant activity involves a child. As was mentioned above, the offences closely mirror the child sex offences that are contained elsewhere in the SOA 2003. However, for the purpose of the offences contained in sections 16–19, a child is someone under the age of 18, not 16. This means that there is an overlap between these and other child sex offences but that the age of consent is effectively raised to 18 where the child is being looked after by the adult in the stated institutional setting. For example, if a teacher engaged in sexual activity with a pupil aged 15, they could be charged under section 9 (sexual activity with a child) or section 16 (abuse of a position of trust). However, since the maximum penalty under section 9 is higher than section 16 (14 years as opposed to 5 years), it is likely that he would be charged under section 9. However, if the teacher had sex with a pupil aged 16 or 17 he could only be charged under section 16, as for section 9 the child must be under 16 years old. These abuse of position of trust offences are therefore aimed principally at protecting 16- and 17-year-olds, who are above the general age of consent but are regarded as vulnerable because of the position of trust held by the adult.

The offences require that the child is under 18 and the adult does not reasonably believe that the child is over 18, or the child is under 13. The offences specifically state that the defendant is to be taken not to have reasonably believed that the child was 18 unless sufficient evidence is adduced to raise an issue as to whether he believed it. Bearing in mind the nature of the relationship of trust between the parties, it is rare that such evidence would be brought. In the vast majority of cases, teachers, medics, etc., would definitely be aware of the age of the child.

Section 23 – Marriage exception

Section 23 provides a defence to actions that would otherwise be an offence under sections 16–19. The Act calls this an 'exception' rather than a defence, but it is effectively a defence. Conduct by a person that would otherwise be an offence is not an offence if the adult and the child are legally married or in a civil partnership and the child is over 16. At first sight this seems a curious exception until it is remembered that it is legal to marry at the age of 16 (with parental consent). So, a doctor who is married to a 17-year-old being treated by him is not committing an offence by engaging in lawful sexual intercourse. Of course, most organizations do have internal disciplinary rules to deal with relationships in these circumstances, and it is suggested that most schools would not be happy about teachers teaching their husband or wife.

Section 24 – Relationships that pre-date the position of trust

Section 24 provides that conduct that would otherwise be an offence under sections 16–19 would not be an offence if, immediately before the position of trust arose, there was an existing sexual relationship between the parties. To give an example of how this would work, a teacher could quite legally engage in a sexual relationship with a 17-year-old at another school (not his own school). If he then took up employment at the same school as the 17-year-old, the previous existing sexual relationship would provide a defence to a charge under section 16. What amounts to a relationship is not defined; it may be assumed a one-off sexual encounter would not satisfy the definition, but whether a 'relationship' requires an association of days, weeks or months is unspecified.

What is clear is that the sexual relationship must have been a lawful one, so a pre-existing sexual relationship with a child under the age of 16 would not provide a defence, as such a relationship would have been illegal under section 9 of the SOA 2003.

Sentencing

The maximum penalty for abuse of a position of trust is 5 years' imprisonment. However, sentences are often far less than that, in many cases reflecting the fact that the young person is fully consenting in the sexual activity. For example in *R v Wilson (Daniel Rushton)* (2008)[8] a sentence of 10 months' imprisonment was reduced to 6 months on appeal. The appellant in the case was a trainee (married) teacher at a college and pleaded guilty to causing or inciting sexual activity with a girl aged 17 who was a pupil at the college. They developed an emotional relationship, which became a consensual sexual one. The defendant accepted full responsibility for what had happened and showed great remorse. His appeal against sentence was allowed. The court took into account the fact that he had paid a considerable penalty for his behaviour, in that his career in teaching was at an end and he would remain subject to the notification requirements of the sex offenders register for some years. He would not be able to work with children again. This case also illustrates the wide-ranging consequences of a conviction for abuse of position of trust – not just a possible prison sentence, but also the destruction of a future career.[9]

In January 2015, Stuart Kerner, a teacher, received an 18-month suspended sentence for two counts of sexual activity with a 16-year-old girl from his school. The case was reported widely in the press because the judge, Joanna Greenberg QC, said that the girl had effectively *groomed him*, rather than the other way round. The Attorney General's Office did at first announce that it was going to review the sentence for being too lenient, before announcing shortly afterwards that the offence is not included in the unduly lenient sentences scheme (whereby a sentence can be referred to the Court of Appeal for being too low).[10]

Criticisms

It has been noted above that there has been some criticism of the fact that the definition of a position of trust is too narrow and should be extended to cover a broader range of situations in which children may be influenced by others, such as in the Church. On the other hand the abuse of position of trust offences prohibit behaviour that is already criminalized in sections 9–12 of the SOA 2003, except that the age of a child is raised to 18 where there is a position of trust. The maximum penalty for abuse of position of trust is 5 years, substantially less than the offences in sections 9–12. There is therefore an argument that we do not need these specific offences at all. As Spencer points out "all that was really needed was a single section saying that in ss9–12, for '16' read '18' where the defendant was in a position of trust".[11]

Sections 25 and 26 – Familial Sexual Abuse of Children

As the NSPCC report highlighted, sexual abuse within the family is not unusual. The SOA 2003 introduced two new offences relating to sexual abuse of children within a family, which replaced various old offences relating to incest. In fact, there are two separate sets of offences relating to sex within a family, one set that relates only to children and one that relates to sexual relationships with adult family members. The latter category will be dealt with in Chapter 6 and is not primarily justified as an abuse of power; so here we will concentrate on offences involving child family members. Arguments for the existence of offences relating to incest are also considered in Chapter 6. Here the aim of protecting the vulnerable from abuse of power within a family is a convincing argument and can be regarded as the main justification for these offences.

Section 25 SOA 2003 (sexual activity with a child family member) makes it an offence for a person (A) to intentionally touch another person (B), where the touching is sexual and A and B are related to each other in the way set out in section 27. B must be under the age of 18. The *mens rea* requires that the touching be intentional and A must know (or could reasonably be expected to know) of his relationship to B. In most situations, the relationship would be known to the defendant as the essence of the offence is that the child is a family member. However, it could be possible that someone might not be aware of their relationship, especially where children have been adopted. Lack of knowledge would mean the offence was not made out; but once the relationship was known, then an offence would be committed if the relationship continued.

Section 26 (inciting a child family member to engage in sexual activity) has similar elements to section 25. Here it is an offence for a person (A) to intentionally incite another person (B) to touch, or to allow himself to be touched, by A. Again, the touching must be sexual, the relationship between A and B must come within the description at section 27 and B must be under the age of 18. Knowledge of the relationship also applies here.

Either offence can be committed by an adult or a child (who is over the age of criminal responsibility). Consent of the child (B) is irrelevant and is not a defence. The offences are completely gender neutral and so can cover homosexual as well as heterosexual contact between family members. The *actus reus* requires only 'sexual touching' (as defined in sections 78 and 79) and, as has been discussed above, is much wider than penetrative sexual intercourse.

The penalties for each offence depend on the age of the defendant and the type of sexual activity. Where the defendant is over 18 and the activity involved penetrative acts, the maximum penalty is 14 years' imprisonment, whereas a defendant under 18 years is liable to a maximum of 5 years' imprisonment.

As the actions prohibited by sections 25 and 26 are already covered by the general child sex offences in sections 5–13, it could be argued that there is no need for these two offences at all. However, the Home Office Report, *Setting the Boundaries*, stated that there was a need to express society's disapproval of certain behaviour within families and also to reflect the looser structure of modern families.[12] Once again, there is one very important difference between these offences and those contained in sections 5–13, i.e. the meaning of a 'child'.

Who is a child for the purposes of sections 25 and 26?

A child for the purpose of these sections is someone under the age of 18, not 16. So, in effect the sections raise the age of consent for a child to 18 where the child is engaging in sexual activity with a family member. Someone who did engage in sexual activity with a child under the age of 16 could be charged with an offence under sections 5–13 and so, as with the abuse of a position of trust offences, these sections are really meant to apply to 16–18-year-olds. Both sections provide that B must be under 18 and A must not reasonably believe that B is 18 or over, or B is under 13. There would usually be no difficulty in establishing the age of the child or the reasonableness of A's belief as the child is a family member.

Section 27 – Relevant family relationships

The description of the relevant family relationships is surprisingly wide. There are three main categories of relationships covered.

Firstly, close blood relatives are included (s27(2)). The relationships are that of parent, foster parent, grandparent, brother, sister, half-brother, half-sister, aunt or uncle. Aunt is defined to mean the sister, or half-sister of a person's parent, with uncle given the equivalent meaning. This effectively excludes aunts and uncles by marriage only. This could be criticized on the grounds that if the purpose of the legislation is to protect young people from abuse within a family, there is no logical reason why aunts and uncles by marriage should not be included. Most young people would not make a distinction between those aunts and uncles who are related by blood and those who are related by marriage. The position of influence within the family would probably be equally felt.

The second category of relationships relates to more distant relatives, who are living or have lived in the same household as the child, or have been regularly involved in caring for, training, supervising or being in sole charge of the child (s27(3)). The specific relatives included are step-parents, partners of step-parents, step-brothers or step-sisters and cousins. This category also includes the situation where the parent or present or former foster parent of one of them is or has been the other's foster parent.[13] There were concerns that individuals could enter into relationships for the purpose of having access to children and this category recognizes this by including these more distant members of an extended family.[14] Interestingly, this list includes people it would be legal to marry. It is legal to marry a cousin, and to have a sexual relationship with a cousin in most circumstances. However, if at least one of the parties is under 18 and they live (or have lived) in the same household then such a relationship would be a criminal offence. However, as we will see below, there is a defence of marriage.

The third group of relationships is even wider. Section 27(4) provides that the relation of A and B is within the definition of a relevant family relationship if A and B live in the same household and A is regularly involved in caring for, training, supervising or being in sole charge of B. This would include more distant family members who are not included in section 27(2) and (3) but also includes people who would not normally be regarded as family members at all. For example, au pairs or nannies could come within this definition, provided they were deemed to be regularly involved in caring for, training, supervising or being in sole charge of the child.

Section 27(1)(b) makes clear that the provisions also apply to adoptive family relationships. An amendment to the original section also now makes clear that an adopted child's biological family relationships are also prohibited.

Section 28 – Marriage exception

As has been noted above, it is legal to marry some of the family members contained in section 27, for example cousins and step-siblings. Therefore, similarly to section 23, section 28 provides that conduct that would otherwise be an offence under section 25 or 26 is not an offence if the child is over 16 and A and B are lawfully married or in a civil partnership.[15] It is for the defendant to prove that the marriage/civil partnership was lawful at the time. Thus, cousins living in the same household who are not married commit an offence if they engage in sexual activity before the age of 18; but cousins who are married do not, even if they were brought up together as children.

Section 29 – Sexual relationships that pre-date family relationships

Section 29 provides an exception to these two offences akin to that at section 24. Here it applies where A and B are not close relatives (as defined in section 27(2)) and a prior lawful sexual relationship existed between them immediately before they became related in the ways set out in the rest of section 27. This could happen, for example, where two unrelated 17-year-olds were having a legitimate sexual relationship but later became related as step-brother and sister due to the marriage of their parents. The relationship must have been lawful, so any sexual relationship engaged in before the couple were 16 would not count for this exception, though whether the Crown Prosecution Service would choose to prosecute in these circumstances is another issue.

Sexual Offending Against Those with a Mental Disorder

One of the aims of the SOA 2003 was to ensure that vulnerable people are protected from abuse and exploitation. However, one of the guiding principles was also stated to be that the criminal law should not intrude unnecessarily into the private lives of adults. The issue of adults with a mental disorder is an area where the law has a difficult balance to maintain. On the one hand, adults whose ability to consent is impaired do need to be protected from those who would take advantage of them; but on the other hand there is the issue of whether such a person has a right to a sex life and the enjoyment and fulfilment that they could achieve through their sexuality. Article 8 of the European Convention on Human Rights enshrines the right to a private life and this includes a sexual life.[16] However, this right must be balanced with the need to protect those whose ability to consent may be impaired through a mental disorder.

There are three different types of offences in the SOA 2003 in relation to those who have a mental disorder. One set of offences deals with persons whose mental disorder is severe enough to impede their ability to exercise a choice. The second set of offences relate to sexual activity that is the result of inducement, threat or deception. Finally, there are specific offences that can only be committed by care workers.

Sections 30–33 – Offences Against Persons with a Mental Disorder that Impedes Choice

There are four different offences relating to persons whose mental disorder impedes their choice. These are contained in sections 30–33 of the SOA 2003 and, as with the offences relating to abuse of position of trust, they mirror the child sex offences in sections 9–12 of the Act. Section 30 relates to sexual activity or, more accurately, sexual touching. Section 31 makes it an offence to cause or incite a person with a mental disorder impeding choice to engage in sexual activity. Section 32 makes it an offence to engage in sexual activity in the presence of a person with a mental disorder impeding choice, and section 33 deals with causing a person with a mental disorder to watch a sexual act. As the *actus reus* of these activities have been discussed in relation to the child sex offences in Chapter 4 this section will concentrate on the elements of the offences relating to the person with the mental disorder.

It is an essential element of all four offences that the victim is unable to refuse the particular activity because of, or for a reason related to, a mental disorder. It is also essential that the defendant knows or could reasonably be expected to know that the person has a mental disorder and that because of it is likely to be unable to refuse.

For the purpose of these offences "mental disorder" has the same meaning as the definition in section 1 of the Mental Health Act 1983, as amended by the Mental Health Act 2007, which is that mental disorder means any disorder or disability of the mind. This is a broad definition but it should be noted that just having a mental disorder is not sufficient for these offences. The mental disorder must also mean that the person is "unable to refuse" because of it. There may well be some disagreement amongst professionals about whether a particular person is unable to refuse because of a mental disorder. See for example, the case of *A Local Authority v TZ (by his litigation friend, the Official Solicitor)* (2013)[17] where an expert psychiatrist reported that TZ lacked capacity to consent to sexual relations, whereas the judge declared that TZ did have the capacity to consent to and engage in sexual relations. TZ suffered from learning disabilities, autism and hyperactivity disorder and had formed a problematic relationship with another man. TZ gave informal evidence to the judge, Justice Baker, who was satisfied that he did have the necessary understanding of the mechanics of sexual activity as well as the need to weigh up the emotional consequences of having sexual relations. He commented that "a person is not to be treated as unable to make a decision merely because he makes an unwise one".[18]

The Act does give further guidance on when a person is unable to refuse. He is unable to refuse if he lacks the capacity to choose whether to agree to the particular behaviour (whether because he lacks sufficient understanding of the nature or reasonably foreseeable consequences of what is being done, or for any other reason) or he is unable to communicate such a choice.[19]

These phrases were considered in the case of *Cooper* (2009).[20] The complainant in the case was a 28-year-old woman with schizo-affective disorder, an emotionally unstable personality disorder and a low IQ. As a result of her disorders she had a tendency to become upset without rational cause and to act impulsively. She met the defendant in the car park of the mental health resource centre she attended while in a distressed and agitated state. He invited her back to his friend's house, where she was given crack cocaine and engaged in oral sex with the defendant. Her evidence was that she was panicky and afraid at the time and gave evidence that she was saying to herself "these crack heads . . . they do worse to you". She did not therefore object to the oral sex. The defendant was charged and convicted with an offence under section 30 but the Court of Appeal allowed his appeal on the basis that the complainant's irrational fear due to her mental disorder did not mean that she lacked capacity to choose and there was no evidence that she was physically unable to communicate her choice. The Crown then appealed to the House of Lords. The House of Lords overturned the Court of Appeal decision and held that an irrational fear that prevented the exercise of choice could give rise to a lack of capacity to choose. In addition, the inability to communicate choice referred to in section 30(2) was not limited to a physical inability to communicate but could include an inability to communicate that was the result of, or associated with, a disorder of the mind, which was the case with the complainant. The Crown's appeal was therefore allowed and the conviction reinstated.

In *Tower Hamlets LBC v (1) TB (by her litigation friend, the Official Solicitor)* (2014)[21] the Court of Protection had to consider the question of capacity in relation to a 41-year-old woman with a learning disability. TB had been married to her husband for 18 years but had been subjected to domestic violence by him and, at the time of the case, was living separately from him in a flat where she received 24-hour care. During their marriage they had regular sexual intercourse and the husband maintained that, because of his culture and religion, he had the right to have sex with her and she had a duty to submit. The case was partly concerned with the question of her residence but also about her capacity to consent to sex with her husband. The court concluded that, for the purposes of determining capacity to consent to sex the person needed an awareness of the mechanics of the act, that there were health risks involved and that s/he had a choice and could refuse. TB failed to understand the last two matters; in fact, she did not even understand the link between sex and pregnancy. She had no idea that she had a choice and could refuse sex. The court declared that she did not have the capacity to consent to sex (and also that it was not in her best interests for her to return to live with her husband).

The *mens rea* of the offence requires that the defendant knows or could reasonably be expected to know that the person has a mental disorder and that, because of it, or for a reason related to it, is likely to be unable to refuse. This may be easy to show in some cases, but rather more difficult in others. Many people who suffer from a mental disorder do not show obvious signs of it and it may therefore be reasonable to assume that a particular person is fully consenting and able to do so.

There is an issue here, and for sections 34–37 also, that a denial of consent should open up liability for offences contrary to sections 1–4 of the Act. The Home Office envisaged that section 30 "should be an alternative to charging rape but should also provide an alternative verdict in the event of a rape charge not being proved".[22] This was an issue considered by Baroness Hale in *Cooper* (2009)[23] where she observed that rape had initially been charged but an offence of section 30 later substituted with the benefit that the prosecution "has only to prove the inability to refuse rather than that the complainant actually did not consent". She also commented that the *mens rea* for section 30 "puts a greater burden of restraint upon people who know or ought to know that a person's mental disorder is likely to affect her ability to choose".[24] Despite these clear benefits, this raises the prospect that offences under sections 30–33 may be charged because there is less of a burden on the prosecution, rather than because they accurately reflect the offending behaviour.[25]

The sentences for the offences at sections 30 and 31 do reflect the seriousness of this behaviour. However, the maximum sentences are different for penetrative and non-penetrative acts. If the behaviour involves penetration of the anus or vagina with anything or penetration of the mouth with a penis, then the maximum sentence is life imprisonment. Perhaps surprisingly, this includes penetration of the defendant by the person with the mental disorder as well as penetration of the person with the mental disorder by the defendant. In other cases, the maximum sentence is 14 years. For sections 32 and 33 there is a maximum sentence of 10 years.

Sections 34–37 – Offences Brought About by Inducements, Threats, or Deception

Sections 34–37 of the SOA 2003 broadly follow the type of behaviour covered in sections 30–33, but here the sexual behaviour is engaged in as a result of inducements, threats or deception. In each offence the agreement of the person who has the mental disorder is obtained by means of an inducement offered or given, a threat made or a deception practised. For the purposes of these offences, the person with the mental disorder is not incapable of consenting; rather their consent has been obtained by promises or threats that may not have influenced someone without a mental disorder. There is no definition of the words 'inducement', 'threat' or 'deception' in the Act. However the Explanatory Notes to the Act do mention that an inducement might be promising presents of anything from sweets to a holiday. A threat might be a threat of physical violence, perhaps to the person themselves or the person's family. A deception might be the suggestion that the person will get into trouble if they do not engage in sexual activity. Clearly, some types of threat may appear more serious to a person with a mental disorder and this is exactly what the offences provide for.

That said, again the offences at sections 1–4 may be better suited to the circumstances in some cases where consent has been obtained by threat or deception. As Chapter 3 has explored, what amounts to deception that removes an individual's freedom to choose for the purposes of section 74 is a developing area, and one that may well cover many situations that would also squarely fall under sections 34–37.

The maximum penalties for offences contrary to sections 34 and 35 depend on whether the acts involve penetration or not. The maximum penalty for penetrative acts is life imprisonment and is 14 years for other types of behaviour. Sections 36 and 37 have a maximum penalty of 10 years.

Sections 38–41 – Offences by Care Workers for Persons with a Mental Disorder

The objective of the offences relating to care workers is to ensure that such workers do not use their position to exploit or abuse the people they are caring for, similar to those offences at sections 16–19. As before, this section of the SOA 2003 contains four separate offences, all with the common requirement that the offence is committed by someone who is caring for the person with the mental disorder. The four types of behaviour covered are: sexual activity with a person with a mental disorder (s38), causing or inciting sexual activity (s39), sexual activity in the presence of a person with a mental disorder (s40) and causing a person with a mental disorder to watch a sexual act (s41). The common element in these offences is that the defendant is involved in the care of the person with a mental disorder. The lack of capacity to consent or inability to consent is not an issue for these offences. The emphasis here is that the defendant is a care worker and they are caring for someone with a mental disorder, whether they are in fact capable of consenting or not.

As with the other offences, the maximum penalties depend on whether there are penetrative acts or not. The maximum penalty for sections 38 and 39 offences is 14 years where penetration occurs, or 10 years for other acts. This is lower than the life sentence that could be imposed for offences under sections 30, 31, 34 and 35. This can be explained by the fact that there is an overlap so that if a care worker engages in sexual activity with someone whose mental disability actually impedes their choice, then they should be charged with the more serious offence under section 30. Whereas the care worker offences can be committed against people whose mental disorder is less severe, and who otherwise may well be capable of consenting to sex. So, it is the nature of the relationship between the two people that is the issue in the care worker offences, rather than the state of mind of the vulnerable person. This could be regarded as a reflection of society's disapproval of certain behaviour and the accepted limits on sexual behaviour between carers and those they care for.

In all the care worker offences, the *mens rea* requires that the care worker knows or could reasonably be expected to know that the person has a mental disorder. It is presumed that the care worker knows this, unless sufficient evidence is adduced to raise an issue as to whether they knew or could reasonably be expected to know. In most cases, the carer would have actual knowledge of the mental disorder, as that is why they are providing the service. However, it is possible that volunteers or those who provide more general services may not be aware and therefore not be guilty of an offence if they engage in a sexual relationship with the person who has the mental disorder.

Section 42 – Who is a care worker?

There are effectively three different situations in which someone is regarded as a care worker. Firstly, the care worker could be employed in a community home, voluntary home or children's home and has (or is likely to have) regular face-to-face contact with the person with the mental disorder, who is accommodated in that home. Secondly, a care worker in a hospital or clinic who has regular face-to-face contact with a patient with a mental disorder is covered. Finally, there is a wider category of care worker, those who whether in the course of employment *or not* are providers of care, assistance or services to the person with the mental disorder. However, these services have to be in connection with that mental disorder, so a person providing general services, say ironing or transport, or perhaps educational services would not be regarded as a care worker for the purpose of these offences. The first two categories are aimed at employees but the final one would also include volunteer workers in homes, hospitals, etc., provided they have the required face-to-face contact with the person with the mental disorder.

Sections 43–44 – Defences to the care worker offences

There are two defences to the care worker offences and these closely follow the defences to the abuse of position of trust offences and familial offences mentioned earlier in this chapter. They relate to marriage, civil partnership or a pre-existing sexual relationship (ss43–44). These defences are meant to apply in the situation where the carer of the person with the mental disorder is actually their spouse (or civil partner) or is in an existing relationship before they become their carer. These defences only apply in relation to the care worker offences contained in sections 38–41, not the other offences involving persons with a mental disorder. The explanation for this is that the care worker offences apply even when the person with the mental disorder does have the capacity to consent to sex and it is to be remembered that a carer does not have to be a paid carer. Many people become carers of their spouses or partners and it would be very harsh to deny them a sex life with their partner. The pre-existing relationship defence is really meant to cover the situation where someone has an existing relationship with someone who later develops a mental disorder that is not severe enough to impede their choice. These defences do seem to provide the correct balance in that they allow people with a mental disorder to continue to have an intimate relationship even after they have begun to need care because of a mental disability.

Conclusion

The offences discussed above go some way to protecting the vulnerable from abuse where there is an imbalance of power. There are some gaps in relation to those who are regarded as being in a position of trust that need to be addressed and the SOA 2003 does seem to have resulted in many individual offences that apply to different age groups, when perhaps one set of offences would have been sufficient. On the other hand, the care worker offences seem to have struck the right balance in allowing those with a mental disorder to continue to enjoy a sex life, while protecting them from exploitation by carers. It remains to be seen whether the proposed Government proposals on extending the wilful neglect offence for those who work with children are a step too far.

The familial offences do provide significant protection for those aged under 18, although perhaps criminalizing ostensibly consensual relationships between young teenagers who may only be tenuously considered to be part of the same family may be over zealous.

Undoubtedly the many inquiries concerning institutional abuse and child exploitation will have an impact on the law in the years to come. Whether this will be substantive resulting in new criminal offences or merely prompt practical changes to the management of institutions and agencies is yet to be seen.

Notes

1 S. Corral, et al *Child Abuse and Neglect in the UK Today* London: NSPCC (2011).
2 Independent Inquiry into Child Sexual Abuse. The website of the inquiry with details of the terms of reference. Accessible at https://www.csa-inquiry.independent.gov.uk.
3 D. Gray and P. Watt *Giving Victims a Voice – Joint Report into Sexual Allegations Made Against Jimmy Savile* London: MPS and NSPCC (January 2013).
4 It currently extends to care workers and care provider organizations.
5 See C. Brackenridge and Y. Williams 'Incest in the family of sport' *New Law Journal* (2004) 154 pp. 179–180 for an interesting discussion of the family like nature of the relationships in the sporting world.
6 S. Corral et al *Child Abuse and Neglect in the UK Today.*
7 Including the cases of Caron Lewty (see *MailOnline* July 16, 2015; *Daily Mirror* July 16, 2015), Kelly Burgess (see *Daily Mail* April 8, 2014; *BBC News* April 7, 2014 http://www.bbc.co.uk/news/uk-england-bristol-26927378; *Daily Mirror* (online) February 23, 2014 http://www.mirror.co.uk/news/uk-news/drama-teacher-kelly-burgess-charged-3175535) and teaching assistant Emma Webb (*The Express* March 16, 2015; *The Sun* March 15, 2015).
8 [2008]1 Cr App R (S) 90.
9 The loss of a teaching career is commonly treated as a mitigating factor. See *R. v Cornwall (Joseph Matthew)* [2012] EWCA Crim 1227.
10 *Independent* 'Groomed teacher's sentence cannot be reviewed' January 16, 2015.
11 J.R. Spencer 'The Sexual Offences Act 2003: (2) Child and family offences' *Criminal Law Review* (2004) 347 pp. 357–358.

12 Home Office *Setting the Boundaries: Reforming the Law on Sex Offences* London: Home Office (2000).
13 Even if they have left the foster parents care: *R. v Thomas (Robert John)* [2005] EWCA Crim 2343.
14 *Setting the Boundaries*, para 5.6.7.
15 For further discussion see J.R. Spencer 'The Sexual Offences Act 2003: (2)'.
16 *Dudgeon v UK* (1981) 4 EHRR 149.
17 [2013] All ER (D) 144.
18 Ibid. para 53.
19 Section 30(2).
20 [2009]4 All ER 1033.
21 [2014] EWCOP 53.
22 *Setting the Boundaries*, para 4.6.3.
23 [2009]4 All ER 1033.
24 Ibid. para 34.
25 Something explored by Saunders in her review of the reported cases: C. Saunders 'Making it count: sexual offences, evidential sufficiency, and the mentally disordered complainant' *Liverpool Law Review* (2010) 31(2) pp. 177–206.

Chapter 6

Regulating Sexual Behaviour

The regulation of sexual behaviour is the focus of this chapter, which addresses sexual offending in private and in public. Demonstrating the diversity of the offending behaviour examined here, a number of the offences discussed are brought together in the Sexual Offences Act 2003 (SOA 2003) under the rather vague heading of "other offences". These range from the non-contact offences of exposure and voyeurism to consensual sexual activity in public toilets, intercourse with an animal and sexual penetration of a corpse.

This chapter also considers those offences that are preparatory to committing a sexual offence and the offences of committing, or consenting to, sexual penetration of an adult relative. Many of these offences were new in 2003 but some were existing offences that were comprehensively overhauled to bring them into line with modern sensibilities.

One theme running through our discussion is the moral perspective to much of this modern regulation. A number of the offences discussed here are justifiable on moral grounds, yet clearly we do not forbid all sexual activities that are morally injurious. Numerous sexual activities, such as adultery, swinging and polyamory, are morally troublesome but the law does not intervene. Although we have a long history of justifying criminalization on the grounds of morality it is unusual that this is the chief justification and, when it is, the legitimacy of an offence can become disputed.

The "other offences" also demonstrate a clear disregard for bodily integrity. The sexual penetration of an animal or a corpse cannot be consented to by the 'victim' and the offences of sexual activity in public toilets, exposure and voyeurism draw strangers into the offender's sexual experience. Ensuring real consent is a theme of the Act and is clearly absent where these offences are made out.

In attempting to tread a careful line between intruding into private sexual activity and protecting the public from invasive or dangerous behaviours these offences are quite specific in their language. As can be seen from the discussion below, there are concerns that certain dangerous behaviours may not be criminalized because of this specificity. However, although the SOA 2003 swept away the old legislative regime, we retain common law offences that can also be used to regulate more esoteric behaviours that fail to meet the exacting *actus reus* requirements of these statutory offences.

The Common Law Offences – Corrupting Public Morals and Outraging Public Decency

A moralistic approach to criminalization is most visible in the common law offences that have developed as responses to contemporary concerns brought before the courts. Corrupting public morals and outraging public decency are capable of being committed by way of a conspiracy (an agreement between two or more persons to commit a crime) but also exist as offences in their own right.

In *Shaw* (1962)[1] it was established that an offence of conspiracy to corrupt public morals existed where an agreement was made between two or more people to do any act which, if completed, would be likely to have the effect of undermining morality. In *Shaw* the appellant had published a directory of prostitutes, the *Ladies' Directory* which included the services offered by sex workers and nude pictures.[2] Shaw was convicted of numerous offences including conspiracy to corrupt public morals and appealed on the ground no such offence existed. Rejecting this submission, Viscount Simonds stated:

> In the sphere of criminal law I entertain no doubt that there remains in the Courts of Law a residual power to enforce the supreme and fundamental purpose of the law, to conserve not only the safety and order but also the moral welfare of the State, and that it is their duty to guard it against attacks which may be the more insidious because they are novel and unprepared for.

This residual power was explored further in *Knuller* (1973)[3] where adverts for homosexual encounters had appeared in a magazine. The directors of the publishing company were charged and convicted of conspiracy to corrupt public morals and conspiracy to outrage public decency.[4] Appealing against the convictions, the appellants argued their actions did not constitute either of these offences. On appeal they were acquitted of outraging public decency (and the Lords were split over whether the offence existed) but upheld (and broadly approved) the conviction for conspiracy to corrupt public morals. Homosexual acts in private were, of course, by this point, legal but as Lord Morris of Borth-y-Gest argued:

> But that does not mean that it is not open to a jury to say that to assist or to encourage persons to take part in such acts may be to corrupt them. If by agreement it was arranged to insert advertisements by married people proclaiming themselves to be such and to be desirous of meeting someone of the opposite sex with a view to clandestine sexual association, would it be a justification to say that adultery is not of itself a criminal offence? A person who, as a result of perusing the "Ladies' Directory," decided to resort to a prostitute was committing no legal offence: but it was open to a jury to hold that those who conspired to insert the advertisements did so with the intention of corrupting the morals of those who read the advertisements.

This is an interesting argument in the modern day. There are of course a plethora of websites offering extra-marital sex and the idea their publishers would be charged with conspiracy to corrupt public morals is preposterous; this then illustrates the flexibility of these common law concepts.

Conspiracy to corrupt public morals has been a little used offence but its sister offence of outraging public decency has continued to hold sway. In *Gibson* (1990)[5] an artist had displayed a pair of earrings made out of a freeze-dried human foetus. The artist and the operator of the art gallery where they had been displayed were charged with outraging public decency and appealed on a number of grounds, including that the prosecutions were barred by section 2(4) of the Obscene Publications Act 1959 (see Chapter 7). Lord Chief Justice Lane held that outraging public decency was distinct from obscenity. Where a charge under the Obscene Publications Act 1959 involved the corruption of public morals, outraging public decency merely required that the decency of the public *may* be outraged. Similarly in *May* (1990),[6] where a schoolmaster instructed two male students to order him to simulate sexual intercourse on his classroom desk, Lord Chief Justice Lane gave an equally abstruse description of the *actus reus* of the offence as "an act of such a lewd, obscene or disgusting nature as to amount to an outrage on public decency". The courts have attempted to define these rather oblique terms. *Stanley*[7] confirmed that obscenity is something at the upper end of impropriety and in *Choi*[8] the Court of Appeal held a disgusting act is one "which fills the onlooker with loathing or extreme distaste or caused annoyance". These interpretations suggest the offence could be impossibly broad, but in *Knuller* Lord Simon outlined the malleable but narrow focus of the offence:

> It should be emphasised that "outrage," like "corrupt," is a very strong word. "Outraging public decency" goes considerably beyond offending the susceptibilities of, or even shocking, reasonable people. Moreover the offence is, in my view, concerned with recognised minimum standards of decency, which are likely to vary from time to time. Finally, notwithstanding that "public" in the offence is used in a locative sense, public decency must be viewed as a whole; and I think the jury should be invited, where appropriate, to remember that they live in a plural society, with a tradition of tolerance towards minorities, and that this atmosphere of toleration is itself part of public decency.[9]

The offence continues to catch obscene activities that may not amount to exposure (see the discussion below) such as in *May*, where the defendant appeared to be masturbating under his clothes,[10] or where people engage in sexual intercourse in public.[11] A crucial question for the jury is whether a member of the public has been outraged by the act, and cases such as *Rose* (2006)[12] had maintained that the offence required a public aspect. Consequently if there was no evidence of at least two people witnessing the act no offence was committed. This position has now been eroded, most explicitly in *Hamilton* (2007),[13] where it was held:

> There is in our view no reason to confine the requirement more restrictively and require actual sight or sound of the nature of the act. The public element in the offence is satisfied if the act is done where persons are present and the nature of what is being done is capable of being seen; the principle is that the public are to be protected from acts of a lewd, obscene or disgusting act which are of

a nature that outrages public decency and which are capable of being seen in public.[14]

It appears the 'two-person rule' has then been superseded by the 'hypothetical two-person rule', which does allow the offence to be charged in place of voyeurism. It is hard to say this is a corruption of the offence when its limits have never been clear. Whether the offence requires *mens rea* has also been disputed. In *Gibson* the offence was understood to be one of strict liability, but in *Rose* the *mens rea* for public nuisance – that the appellant knew or ought to have known that, as a result of his action, a public nuisance would be committed – was used.

While it is easy to deride the imprecision of these common law offences, they do provide flexible offences amenable to changes in social and moral standards; but what they do not establish are sexual offences. Morals and decency are broad terms encompassing acts that may be sexual, but may just be outrageous, such as exhibiting earrings made of freeze-dried foetuses or urinating on a war memorial. The SOA 2003 has then established explicit offences to specifically criminalize public and private outrages of a sexual nature, while the common law offences continue to provide a safety net for those novel activities Viscount Simonds warns the legislature may not have contemplated.

Sections 61–63 – The Preparatory Sexual Offences

There were three preparatory sexual offences introduced by the SOA 2003. All are intended to make it easier to convict those who take steps towards sexual offending. Previous to the SOA 2003 these offences were either governed as non-sexual offences such as burglary with intent to rape, or were charged under the very specific rules dealing with attempts. The SOA 2003 has then brought together the most serious and frequently executed forms of preparative acts under the ambit of sexual offending.

The first is the section 61 offence of "administering a substance with intent" where a person intentionally administers a substance, or causes a substance to be taken by another person (B) (s61(1)), knowing that person does not consent (s61(1)(a) with the intention of stupefying or overpowering B, so as to enable any person to engage in a sexual activity that involves B (s61(1)(b)). The offence is a response to the use of 'date rape drugs' in order to incapacitate victims and is an echo of s75(2)(f) which raises the presumption of non-consent. As with the evidential presumption, this includes where a drink is adulterated with alcohol. The offence only criminalizes those who are administering the substance without consent, so buying drinks for a prospective sexual partner in the hope of having sexual intercourse with them is not within the ambit of the offence.

The offence itself is a serious one, with a maximum sentence of 10 years' imprisonment. If the drugs do incapacitate the victim and a sexual offence takes place then the relevant offence(s) could also be charged.

The second preparatory offence at section 62 is "committing an offence with intent to commit a sexual offence" (s62(1)). This requires the commission of a criminal offence with the intention of going on to commit a sexual offence (any offence under Part 1 of the SOA 2003 – s62(2)) – for example the grabbing (a battery)[15] or chasing (an assault)[16] of a woman in order to commit rape, or locking a man in a room (a false imprisonment) in order to sexually assault him. As section 62(2) clarifies, this includes where an offender intends to aid, abet, counsel or procure an offence, so where the victim has been for example falsely imprisoned so another can commit a sexual offence against them.

Attempts were previously very difficult to successfully prosecute as the steps taken had to be more than preparatory. The most extreme example is that of *Geddes* (1996),[17] who was seen by a teacher in the boys' toilets of a school carrying a ruck-sack. This was later found in some bushes containing a large kitchen knife, some rope and masking tape. The Crown had evidence from a local authority housing officer who had spoken to Geddes that he had said he wanted to kidnap a child for sexual purposes. Geddes was convicted of attempted false imprisonment. Quashing the conviction the Court of Appeal grudgingly accepted:

> In the present case there was not much room for doubt about the appellant's intention, and the evidence was clearly capable of showing that he had made preparations, had equipped himself, had got ready, had put himself in a position to commit the offence charged. It was true that he had entered the school, but he had never had any contact or communication with, nor had confronted, any pupil at the school. The whole story was one which filled the court with the gravest unease, but on the facts of the case the court felt bound to conclude that the evidence was not sufficient in law to support a finding that the appellant had done an act which was more than merely preparatory to wrongfully imprisoning a person unknown.

Thus, the existing provisions were considered too exacting but section 62 now merely requires an intention to commit any of the sexual offences in Part 1 of the SOA 2003 and so Geddes would likely be liable under this new offence.

Again this is a serious offence, where the offence is committed by kidnapping or false imprisonment the maximum sentence is imprisonment for life (s62(3)). For other offences it is a maximum term of 10 years.

The final preparatory offence is section 63 "trespass with intent to commit a sexual offence". This offence has the longest history as a specific offence. Previous to its inclusion in the SOA 2003 it was, perhaps surprisingly, included in the offence of burglary contrary to section 9 of the Theft Act 1968. As an offence that involved trespass onto premises with an ulterior intent (an intention to do something other than trespass – specifically to commit rape, grievous bodily harm or theft) the section 9 offence was effective but, as a property offence, it did not properly reflect the sexual aspect. Section 63 is both sexual and broader, requiring that a person must be a trespasser on any premises (s63(1)(a)), knowing or being reckless as to whether he is a trespasser (s63(1)(c)) and must intend to commit a sexual offence on the premises (s63(1)(b)). Premises and structure bears the same meaning as under the Theft Act 1968 and the consequent case law. This would then include offenders who reach through a window to commit a sexual offence, whether that window was in a house or a tent.

It also allows for convictions where the evidence of what has transpired is unclear but clearly points to a sexual offence. In *R v H* (2011)[18] the appellant (H) was found in the toilet of an elderly woman's house. The woman was naked from the waist down and H was in her toilet pulling up his trousers. The victim had dementia and evidence suggested that she believed H, a frequent visitor to her home, was her husband. The Crown were unable to prove that there had been any penile penetration on the day H was apprehended. He was however liable for the section 63 offence.

This is again a serious offence with a maximum sentence of 10 years.

Sections 64 and 65 – Sex with an Adult Relative

While the common law offences are explicitly grounded in matters of morality and decency the offences in the SOA 2003 were not conceived to reflect a moral code but to protect society and the vulnerable from abuse and exploitation. This said, sex with an adult relative (the modern incarnation of incest) has been recognized as something with a strong moral foundation. As *Setting the Boundaries* outlined:

> The offence of incest sets out in law a fundamental social taboo about sexual relations within the family, reflecting widely held abhorrence. We regard the offence as one of a fundamental breach of trust by one family member against another.[19]

The section 64 offence prohibits the penetration of the vagina or anus with any part of another's body and the sexual penetration of the mouth with a penis where the parties are related. Section 65 similarly criminalizes allowing this penetration, making this a gender-neutral offence. The prohibited relationships are set out at sections 64(2) and 65(2) and include the lineal blood relations you would expect: so, parent, grandparent, child, grandchild, brother, sister, but also those half-blood relations of half-brother, half-sister, uncle, aunt, nephew or niece. Adoptive children and parents are also relatives by virtue of the offence.

This is a wider conception of family than was found in the Sexual Offences Act 1956 which was concerned only with vaginal intercourse between lineal blood relatives, prohibiting sexual intercourse between a man and his mother, granddaughter, daughter, sister, half-sister or mother. A woman over the age of 16 was prohibited from sexual intercourse with her son, father, grandfather, brother and half-brother. There was no prohibition under the old offence of sexual intercourse between a man and his grandmother or between family members of the same sex, so these offences were quite clearly structured to prevent pregnancy.

The offences at sections 64 and 65 can only be committed by persons over 16-years-of-age where the victim is aged 18 or over.[20] Consent to the penetration does not negate liability here, indeed section 65 ensures both parties are liable. Where there is no consent to the penetration then again the offence would fall under section 1, 2 or 3 of the Act.[21] Both offences have a maximum penalty of 2 years' imprisonment.

The *mens rea* requires the penetration to be intentional and also requires that A knows he is related to B or could "reasonably be expected to know" (s64(1)(e), s65(1)(e)). Sections 64(4) and 65(4) clarify:

> Where in proceedings for an offence under this section it is proved that the defendant was related to the other person in any of those ways, it is to be taken that the defendant knew or could reasonably have been expected to know that he was related in that way unless sufficient evidence is adduced to raise an issue as to whether he knew or could reasonably have been expected to know that he was.

The offence is gender neutral, embracing homosexual offences including the anus and mouth in the list of prohibited orifices and allowing penetration by any part of the body. Peter Bowsher QC argues broadening our law to include homosexual activity was a step too far,[22] one driven by the (otherwise laudable) desire to provide equality under the law.

Where previously under the Punishment of Incest Act 1908 the law had been concerned with genetic defects arising from close family members procreating, the gender-neutral ethos of the Act now criminalizes activity where there is no possibility of pregnancy. The eugenics argument was considered insignificant by *Setting the Boundaries*, which focussed its attention upon establishing an offence that would prevent abuse that may have begun in childhood:

> The dynamics and balance of power within a family require special recognition, and we were concerned to ensure that patterns of abuse established in childhood were not allowed to continue in adulthood.[23]

This is a difficult justification to support. If offences were committed when one or both of the parties were children then the child sexual offences should be charged. If that abuse meant any ostensible consent to sexual activity in adulthood was not real consent then charges should be brought under sections 1–4 SOA 2003. To charge someone with offences under sections 64 and 65 would surely fail to reflect the harm.

These offences are perhaps two of the most straightforward in the Act. They do not concern themselves with non-penetrative sexual touching and the relationships are undoubtedly those that are socially considered to be out of bounds for sexual relations. This said, the principal criticism here is in the limitation it imposes on the autonomy of consenting adults. The rationale for criminalization appears to be legal moralism. The offence cannot be one that seeks to prevent genetic defects from interbreeding between family members – the prohibited sexual acts are not all procreative, contraception is widely and freely available and we do not otherwise prohibit sexual intercourse between parties who may pass on genetic defects.

The continuing criminalization of these sexual relationships has been questioned on a number of occasions[24] and the current issue is whether our law is compatible with Article 8 rights.[25] Although the offences have yet to reach our superior courts the decision of the European Court of Human Rights in the case of *Stubing* is instructive in this respect. Patrick Stubing had met his sister Susan for the first time when she was 16 and he was in his 20s and the couple had entered into a sexual relationship that produced four children. Convicted of multiple counts of incest Stubing submitted to the ECHR that this criminal conviction had interfered with his right to respect for his family life by preventing him participating in the upbringing of his children and had interfered with his sexual life by preventing him from continuing his private sexual relations with Susan.[26] Noting that the applicants Article 8 rights could be engaged the court went on to state:

> . . . the Court observes that there is no consensus between the member States as to whether the consensual commitment of sexual acts between adult siblings should be criminally sanctioned. Still, a majority of altogether twenty-four out of the forty-four States reviewed provide for criminal liability. The Court further notes that all the legal systems, including those which do not impose criminal liability, prohibit siblings from getting married. Thus, a broad consensus transpires that sexual relationships between siblings are neither accepted by the legal order nor by society as a whole. Conversely, there is no sufficient empirical support for the assumption of a general trend towards a decriminalisation of such acts. The Court further considers that the instant case concerns a question about the requirements of morals. It follows from the above principles that the domestic authorities enjoy a wide margin of appreciation in determining how to confront incestuous relationships between consenting adults, notwithstanding the fact that this decision concerns an intimate aspect of an individual's private life.[27]

As the court stated, there is no consensus regarding criminalization, and in Spain and Portugal consensual incest is not a specific criminal offence. Obviously we would be afforded this same margin of appreciation, one we have exercised before in cases including *Brown* (1993).[28]

Section 66 – Exposure

Public nudity and public sex are not offences *per se*; engaging in sexual activity in public may be an outrage to public decency, or it may be caught (in limited circumstances) by section 4A of the Public Order Act 1986. However the public exposure of genitalia has long been recognized as a deviant sexual act and the SOA 2003 introduced the offence of exposure to provide an unambiguous provision to address this offending behaviour, commonly known as 'flashing'. Previous to this, offenders could be charged under the Vagrancy Act 1824, the Town Police Clauses Act 1847 or the common law offence of outraging public decency.[29] Section 66 sets out the offence in clear, if limited, terms making it an offence to intentionally expose your genitals (s66(1)(a)), intending that someone will see them, and be caused alarm or distress (s66(1)(b)). The maximum sentence is 2 years' imprisonment.

The terminology of genitals clearly embraces both male and female offenders, something the Vagrancy Act had failed to do by prescribing the 'person' (penis) had to be "willfully, openly, lewdly and obscenely" exposed with an intention to insult any female.[30] Surprisingly *Setting the Boundaries* had suggested that exposure by women was "a different kind of behaviour to that normally considered as indecent exposure" and "we think these kinds of behaviour should be dealt with as part of public nuisance/public order which would apply to men or women, rather than a sexual offence."[31] But with the Act's emphasis on gender neutrality the neutral term was used.

The offence usefully excludes the practice of baring ones buttocks ('mooning') – one assumes on the assumption this is a normalized and non-sexual practice. The breasts are also excluded, an interesting omission in light of their inclusion as a sexual body part at section 68(1)(a). Again it must be assumed that baring ones breasts is not usually seen as a sexual act, particularly as breast feeding can be performed in public and breasts are increasingly used for political protest.

If the *actus reus* of the offence had been more inclusive the *mens rea* could easily have been used to defeat any assertion that merely revealing any body part was exposure.[32] The offence requires an intention to be viewed intending to cause alarm or distress,[33] allowing naturists to continue to practice their lifestyle without criminal sanctions. Equally, streakers would not be criminalized – unless their motivation were to alarm. As a sexual offence this stated purpose is slightly out of step with the rest of the Act, as an offence of public disorder rendered sexual by the inclusion of genitals.[34]

The inclusion of the offence in the SOA 2003 is, in part, a recognition of the fact that this may be an offence that leads to contact offending, a gateway offence that allows the offender to be labelled and dealt with as a sexual offender – something explored further at Chapter 10.

Section 67 – Voyeurism

Once again this was an offence introduced by the SOA 2003. Unlike exposure, a fairly simple offence a layperson could understand, the voyeurism offence is littered with terms that have required judicial clarification, a situation that could easily have been avoided.

The offence itself is in actuality four offences with the overarching voyeurism offence set out at section 67(1) where, for the purpose of obtaining sexual gratification, A observes another person doing a private act knowing that B does not consent to being observed for his sexual gratification. Section 67(2) makes it an offence for A to install or operate equipment, record, construct or adapt a structure or part of a structure, with the intention of enabling himself or another person to commit voyeurism. Section 67(3) makes it an offence to record images for the sexual gratification of a third party and section 67(4) to install equipment, adapt or construct a structure or part of a structure intending to commit an offence under subsection (1) or to allow another to commit an offence under the same. The maximum sentence for all offences is 2 years' imprisonment.

This broad range of offences certainly provides for the internet age where images may be captured for the sexual gratification of others.[35] It is not the convoluted nature of section 67 that is problematic but the terms within it. Key to the offence is the observation of the victim, but this term is not defined in the Act and some clarification was offered in *B* (2012):[36]

> The verb *'observes'* is not further defined in the Sexual Offences Act but we think it must connote a deliberate decision on the part of the defendant to look at someone doing a *'private act'*, as opposed to an accidental perception of someone doing a *'private act'*. *'Observes'* must also exclude a careless and, we think, reckless perception.

The deliberate observation must be done simultaneously with the specific, subjective, purpose of obtaining sexual gratification. Sexual gratification need not be simultaneous or contemporaneous with the watching, the gratification could be deferred.[37] This element provides a purposive *mens rea* that excludes an observation where that observation causes a sexual thrill but was not done with that intention – for example glimpsing someone in a swimming pool changing room. Excluding consensual viewing from the offence allows activities such as dogging (sexual activity, usually in a car park or park with the intention of being observed) to continue.[38]

That the observed person must be doing a private act is central to the offence – so central that the Act goes on to define at section 68 that: "a person is doing a private act if the person is in a place which, in the circumstances, would reasonably be expected to provide privacy", and per section 68(1):

(a) the person's genitals, buttocks or breasts are exposed or covered only with underwear;
(b) the person is using a lavatory; or
(c) the person is doing a sexual act that is not of a kind ordinarily done in public.

Whether any place is one that would reasonably be expected to provide privacy is an objective test and whether there is or is not a reasonable expectation of privacy will be closely related to the nature of the observing in any given case.[39] For example, in *Swyer* (2007)[40] marathon runners who had left the course and had gone behind the bushes to urinate had had a reasonable expectation of privacy from individuals who loitered for the purpose of watching them relieve themselves, but not from any passer-by. As Gillespie highlights,[41] this could cause difficulty for successfully prosecuting incidences of voyeurism in shops and shopping centres. These locations could not – by any stretch of the imagination – be termed private places, and this was the scenario faced in *Hamilton* (2007)[42] where Hamilton had secretly filmed up the skirts of women and girls in a shopping centre. The offences took place before the SOA 2003 was enacted and Hamilton was convicted of various offences,[43] including outraging public decency. The case stretched the definition of that offence in a manner that suggests the justices recognized the limitations of section 67, which may not embrace this activity, being neither, as Gillespie points out, public nor featuring persons covered only with underwear.

The typical example of a voyeur peeping into the windows of a private house also illustrates the difficulty with the definitional elements of this offence. For example, where a householder has made an attempt to maintain privacy and an offender then peers around curtains or through a blind this should be no impediment to a successful prosecution,[44] but if the curtains are not drawn is there still a reasonable expectation of privacy?[45] Again, this would turn on the nature of the observing, a glimpse of a woman undressing that was innocent or accidental would not satisfy the offence whereas an offender hiding in the bushes waiting to 'peep' would; there is an unsatisfying lack of clarity here.

It is not just then that the individual has to be in a private place; they also have to be engaged in a particular act, or unclothed.[46] At first glance the requirements of section 68(1)(a) seem unproblematic – when one has their private body parts uncovered or is wearing only underwear they would not expect to be spied upon. But there are a number of problems with this very precise requirement. Firstly what are breasts? In *Bassett* (2008)[47] they were defined as exclusively female, as Hughes LJ stated:

> . . . since the purpose is to bring *prima facie* within the meaning of 'private act' those parts of the body for which people conventionally expect privacy, it is clear to us that the intention of Parliament was to mean female breasts and not the exposed male chest. The former are *prima facie* still private in 21st century Britain; the second is not. We also think that that construction is supported by the use of the plural 'breasts' which we do not think is in ordinary non-medical usage in the context of the male body.

As Selfe has suggested, this excludes not only the male chest, but that of prepubescent children and, we would assume, any women who have undergone a mastectomy.[48] This is an unsatisfactory and unnecessarily restrictive reading of breasts, one that could have been avoided if the section had not defined the bodily parts. Equally, more pedestrian issues in section 68(1)(a) have also proved problematic. In *MacRitchie* (2008)[49] the courts addressed the meaning of underwear, something necessitated by the, it appears, common practice of voyeurs frequenting swimming baths. In this case the complainant had been secretly filmed while changing in a cubicle. While it was accepted a cubicle offered a reasonable expectation of privacy the question of what was worn at the time the video was taken was in question. The complainant had been changing from a bikini into clothing and the justices decided that that swimwear cannot be treated as underwear unless it was being worn as such. Clearly this avoids pictures taken at swimming pools and the falling under the offence of voyeurism but it does impart new complexity into the law – as Selfe asks, what of the person covering themselves only with a small towel?

The inclusion of buttocks here is also surprising. Although sections 66 and 67 seek to tackle very different offending behaviours section 66 infers buttocks are not, by their omission from that section, inherently understood to be private and sexual. To include them here seems at odds with that, particularly when revealing ones buttocks can be fashionable.

Section 68(1)(b) seems fairly straightforward and has not been contentious but section 68(1)(c) is loosely defined. It may be assumed that the section has been drafted to allow for changes in social acceptability, but it is so oblique it is difficult to know what sexual activity may be caught.

The voyeurism offences are, without doubt, unnecessarily wordy and the terminology has caused some difficulty for the courts. As Spencer suggests, the offence could have been easily captured in a shorter sharper definition which sets out:

(1) It is an offence to spy, without consent, or lawful authority, on another person's private bodily parts or private bodily functions.

(2) To do so is punishable with two years' imprisonment on indictment, or six months' imprisonment and a fine not exceeding the statutory maximum on summary trial.[50]

Despite the fact that the offence has required clarification, there have been many successful prosecutions. A significant number of convictions for voyeurism have involved covert filming or attempted filming of victims in private locations including women's shower cubicles,[51] tanning booths,[52] private bathrooms[53], and toilets.[54] As images are often captured as part of the offence there is a likelihood that offenders will also be charged with pornography offences. Where the images include images of children (and the intention does not have to be to capture images of children) making indecent photographs of children will also be charged.[55] Where the images are of adults and are shared the offence of disclosing private sexual photographs and films with intent to cause distress[56] could also be charged, although this is not a sexual offence.

Section 69 – Intercourse with an Animal

As discussed at Chapter 2 intercourse with an animal, previously termed 'bestiality', has historically been considered a serious sexual offence commonly regulated together with other 'unnatural' sexual acts.

Intercourse with an animal has been rarely prosecuted, undoubtedly because it usually takes place in private and with a victim who cannot complain.[57] This also provide some justification for the offence, as *Setting the Boundaries* highlights animals cannot consent to sexual penetration and a parallel can be drawn here with the child sexual offences.[58] Not only is this behaviour associated with immoral sexual proclivities but intercourse with an animal:

. . . was primarily a sex offence reflecting some profoundly disturbed behaviour. These are not simply the acts of loneliness and propinquity. There is evidence of a linkage between abuse of animals and other forms of sexual offending.

This offence is then also understood to be a gateway offence, one that could lead to offending against other vulnerable victims. Although there is a moral perspective to the criminalization of this behaviour, the offence is so limited it fails to embrace sexual activities with animals many would find morally abhorrent.

The offence at section 69 prohibits a person intentionally penetrating with his penis (s69(1)(a)) the vagina or anus of a living animal (s69(1)(b)), knowing or being reckless as to it is that which he is penetrating (s69(1)(c)). The offence can also be committed by a person who causes or allows penetration of their vagina or anus by the penis (s69(2)(a)) of a living animal (s69(2)(b) and knows, or is reckless, that is what they are being penetrated by (s69(2)(c)).

This statutory definition raises a number of issues. Firstly, the body parts that must be penetrated for the offence to be made out exclude oral penetration. This is a significant omission when we look to other sections of the Act. For example oral penetration can be rape, sexual penetration of a corpse includes penetration of *any* part of the body and the extreme pornography offence brands an image of oral sexual activity with an animal an extreme image;[59] in the light of this section 69 begins to look inconsistent.

Questions had arisen historically over what amounted to bestiality, specifically whether anal intercourse satisfied the offence and whether an "animal" included birds, as birds do not, strictly speaking, have vaginas. These issues have been resolved by the SOA 2003 and for the purposes of this offence the terms vagina and anus include "references to any similar part" (s79(10)) so this would include the cloaca of an animal (an opening used for reproductive, intestinal and urinary purposes). The definition of the offence then seems very complete, embracing partial penetration of any body part that is equivalent to a vagina or anus. This does however exclude other forms of sexual touching, perhaps for good reason as legislative overkill would criminalize affectionate relations between humans and animals. However, restricting the offence to penetration by (or allowing the penetration of) a penis also significantly narrows the ambit of the offence. By excluding digital penetration or even penetration with objects the offence excludes a number of activities that are both immoral and may cause injuries to the animal. This exclusion is justifiable if we consider that veterinarians and those who work in farming regularly penetrate animals, but these penetrations are non-sexual and the requirement that any other penetration had to be sexual could easily have been included, as it is at section 70 below. The construction of the offence clearly suggests the approach taken by the legislature has been to criminalize only the behaviour we find most repellent.[60] The necessity for the animal to be alive is also incongruous. If the offence is predicated upon prohibiting morally repugnant behaviour that may lead to future offending then why exclude dead animals? Surely the penetration of a dead animal is just as morally reprehensible as the penetration of a live animal.

The *mens rea*, an intention to penetrate, is a high standard, but knowledge or reckless as to what is being penetrated does broaden the offence. There is currently no case law that has addressed the *mens rea*.

The maximum penalty (2 years) shows a softening in the legal response to the offence that perhaps better reflects the social stigma. Few people in society today would support a life sentence or a sentence of death for perpetrators who have sexually offended against animals.

Section 70 – Sexual Penetration of a Corpse

The justification for criminalizing sexual penetration of a corpse, an offence also known as necrophilia, can be justified on similar grounds to section 69. The sexual penetration of a corpse is clearly a morally abhorrent act and indicative of sexual predilections that pay no regard to consent.

Section 70 establishes a broad offence encompassing penetration with a body part, or anything else (s79(1)(a)) of the body of a dead person (s79(1)(b)). This offence criminalizes the typical example of sexual intercourse with a dead body but also any other penetrative acts, excluding those that are for the purposes of embalming or criminal investigation. The *mens rea* is exacting, requiring an intentional penetration (s79(1)a)) and knowledge or recklessness that a dead body is being penetrated (s79(1)(c)). This would exclude a sexual partner who continues to have penetrative sex with a partner who has died. The penetration must be sexual (s79(1)(d)) and this once again is defined at section 78. The maximum penalty is 2 years' imprisonment.

Prior to the SOA 2003 we did not have a necrophilia offence in our law and the introduction of this in the consultation paper suggested we may have a problem that required legal attention. However there was no real evidence of this and the requirement for the offence seems to be *a priori*. In the words of *Setting the Boundaries*:

> we thought that most people would expect necrophilia to be an offence and would be surprised that it was not. It is certainly associated with other very deviant behaviour and there is no present possibility, for example, of those who kill and then have sex with the bodies of their victims being formally recognised and treated as a sex offender.

Introducing an offence as everyone thought it was already an offence is self-defeating justification, it suggests no offence was required as any deterrence effect was already in place. In reality, as the consultation suggests, most incidences of necrophilia involve murder where that more serious offence takes precedence and the offender can still be treated as a sexual offender, as Chapter 10 discusses.[61]

It is interesting that we have chosen to single out corpses as sexually out of bounds. In civil law a corpse is not construed as property unless it has been subject to work and skill that turns it into property.[62] A corpse is then neither person nor property and to privilege a human corpse above, say, a dead animal is odd if the justification for the offence is moral disgust or sexual depravity. Justifying the offence on the grounds that the act is demeaning to the relatives of the deceased presupposes there are any relatives. Once again this is an offence that is grounded in moral disgust but that also may expose deviant predilections.

Section 71 – Sexual Activity in Public Toilets

As we know sexual activity in public is not a sexual offence *per se*, but this does not mean that there have not been attempts to introduce a general offence into the law. The fifteenth report of the Criminal Law Revision Committee (1984) had recommended an offence to regulate sexual activity in public but *Setting the Boundaries* roundly rejected a broad prohibition, recognizing a risk of incursion into the lives of "every courting couple who choose a secluded spot merely because the public have a right or the ability to access it".[63] Despite this they did consider the issue and considered two methods of prohibiting sexual activity in public:

> We identified two possible ways of achieving this approach. One would be to rest on a definition of a public place and to add in the likelihood of being seen. We thought

this was fraught with potential difficulty. Is any public park or open space out of bounds, even at 1 am? Would a couple have to go into the bushes, and if so how far? On the whole we felt that was too prescriptive and difficult. The alternative approach is, like the present Public Order Act offences, to rely on a third party to be offended. We thought that this was a useful concept, but it raised questions about the applications of differing standards of public morality to sexual behaviour in public. Some people find public displays of same sex affection such as kissing or handholding objectionable when the same behaviour by a boy and girl might be accepted.[64]

Despite these myriad difficulties the Sexual Offences Bill included a general offence of sexual behaviour in a public place. This was subject to significant criticism in the House of Lords[65] both as an illiberal provision and as an offence that failed to tackle the real nuisance – sexual activity in public toilets by homosexual men – known as 'cottaging'.[66]

This behaviour had previously been regulated by the offences of importuning[67] and gross indecency, and these were set to be abolished by the SOA 2003, to some creating a danger that cottaging could not be controlled. As the national newspaper the *Express* argued:

> . . . What individuals do in the privacy of their own home is not our concern and homosexuals should be allowed the same freedoms in this regard as heterosexuals. However, to allow gay men to have sex in public toilets simply because there is not a law to stop mixed sex couples from doing so is as preposterous as it is dangerous.[68]

Despite the fact that the offence of outraging public decency could have been used to police this area (more obviously since the erosion of the two-person rule) similar concerns were raised by both Houses of Parliament and a new offence conceived to combat this specific behaviour. Section 71 then limits the right to sexual activity in public where a person "is in a lavatory to which the public or a section of the public has or is permitted to have access, whether on payment or otherwise" (s71(1)(a)) and they intentionally engage in an activity (s71(1)(b)) that is sexual (s71(1)(c)). Here sexual has its own definition that "an activity is sexual if a reasonable person would, in all the circumstances but regardless of any person's purpose, consider it to be sexual" (s71(2)). In the spirit of the Act this is a gender-neutral offence.

Sexual activity is a broad term encompassing the mischief that concerned Parliament and the press, sexual intercourse in toilets and masturbation, but may also cover any lesser sexual activity such as kissing. It is highly unlikely such sexual touching would be prosecuted but the offence is wide enough to embrace such behaviour.

The *mens rea* requires only that a person intentionally engages in sexual activity. This is a minimal requirement given exposure requires an intention to expose and to cause alarm or distress. The maximum penalty of 6 months' imprisonment does reflect the less serious nature of this offence.

Conclusion

These offences are a mixed bag in every sense. From the overly specific voyeurism offence to the expansive offences of sexual penetration of a corpse and sexual activity in public toilets the legislature have obviously found it difficult to create offences that clearly pinpoint offensive sexual activities. This is perhaps because we cannot point to a specific rationale for criminalization. All these offences can be seen as socially or morally injurious but as morals may shift other justifications are evident in the crafting of the offences; from the public nuisance aspect of the offences of exposure and sexual activity in public toilets, to the protection of the family in the adult familial offence.

The preparatory sexual offences set the scene for criminalization in many cases. While the offences at sections 61–63 are explicitly preparatory, those at sections 66–71 also recognize deviancy that needs to be labelled, punished and monitored as sexual. The offences at sections 64–65 are slightly different, reflecting a moral embargo on sexual activity that is consensual.

Notes

1 *Shaw v DPP* [1961] 2 All ER 446, HL.
2 A modern incarnation of the *Ladies Directory, The Guide to the Working Ladies of London*, prompted similar outrage in the print press; *Daily Mirror* January 28, 2012; *The Sun* January 28, 2012; *Islington Gazette* January 19, 2012.
3 *Knuller (Publishing, Printing and Promotions) Ltd. v Director of Public Prosecutions* [1973] AC 435.
4 Ibid.
5 *R. v Gibson* (Richard Norman) [1990] 2 QB 619.
6 *R. v May (John)* (1990) 91 Cr App R 157.
7 [1965] 2 QB 327.
8 [1999] EWCA Crim 1279.
9 *Knuller.*
10 See also *R. v Welford* [2008] EWCA Crim 1947, or under a cloth *R v Lunderbech* [1991] Crim LR 784.
11 *R. v Vaiculevicius (Andrius)* [2013] EWCA Crim 185.
12 *R. (Rose) v DPP* [2006] EWHC 852 (Admin).
13 *R. v Hamilton* [2007] EWCA Crim 2026.
14 Para 39.
15 *R. v Wisniewski (Mariuzs)* [2004] EWCA Crim 3361.
16 *R. v Murray David Edward Fairweather* [2011] EWCA Crim 1783.
17 (1996) 160 JP 697; [1996] Crim LR 894.
18 [2011] EWCA Crim 682.
19 Home Office *Setting the Boundaries: Reforming the Law on Sex Offences* London: Home Office (2000), para 5.1.4.
20 Where the victim is less than 18 the appropriate offences are at ss25 and 26 SOA 2003.
21 *R. v NW* [2015] EWCA Crim 559.
22 P. Bowsher QC 'Incest – should incest between consenting adults be a crime?' *Criminal Law Review* (2015) 3 pp. 208–218.
23 *Setting the Boundaries,* para 5.8.3.
24 V. Bailey and S. Blackburn 'The Punishment of Incest Act 1908: a case study of law creation' *Criminal Law Review* (1979) pp. 708–718; J. Morton 'The Incest Act 190as it ever relevant?' *New Law Journal* (1988) 138(6341) pp. 59–60.
25 P. Bowsher 'Incest – should incest between consenting adults be a crime?'
26 For further discussion see J.R. Spencer 'Incest and article 8 of the European convention on human rights' *Cambridge Law Journal* (2013) 72(1) pp. 5–7.

27 *Stubing v Germany* (2012) 55 EHRR 24.

28 [1994] 1 AC 212.

29 It appears outraging public decency is still being used when it is unclear if the *mens re*a for exposure will be made out: see *R. v Hardy (James)* [2013] EWCA Crim 2125.

30 Likewise the Police Town Clauses Act 1847.

31 Para 8.2.8.

32 In an appeal against dismissal where a bus driver suffering from irritable bowel syndrome had defecated outside the business premises. One rationale for his dismissal, that this could would be exposure under s66, was roundly dismissed by the Employment Appeal Tribunal: *Metroline Travel Ltd v Lim* [2013] UKEAT 0317/13/BA.

33 While someone will usually have to have seen the exposure for it to be brought to the attention of the authorities the exposure does not have to be viewed or causes alarm or distress; this is solely a *mens rea* element.

34 Although exposure is usually an offence that takes place in public and this was clearly the nuisance that the legislature was seeking to regulate the behaviour there is nothing in the *actus reus* of the offence that prevents it being successfully used where the offence is in private – so by exposing genitalia over video chat for example: see *R. v Adam Storer* [2013] EWCA Crim 2700.

35 *R. v Turner* [2006] All ER (D) 95; *R. v McGill* [2008] EWCA Crim 2662; *R. v Hodgson* [2008] All ER (D) 64 (Jun).

36 [2012] EWCA Crim 770.

37 *R. v Abdullahi (Osmund Mohammed)* [2006] EWCA Crim 2060 (case authority on causing a child to watch a sex act contrary to Sexual Offences Act 2003 s12).

38 Unless they are captured under public law offences or exposure.

39 *R.v Kevin Bassett* [2008] EWCA Crim 1174.

40 *R. v Swyer (Christopher)* [2007] EWCA Crim 204.

41 A.A. Gillespie ' "Up-skirts" and "down blouses": voyeurism and the law' *Criminal Law Review* (2008) 5 pp. 370–382.

42 *R. v Hamilton* (Simon Austin) [2007] EWCA Crim 2062.

43 Including taking and possessing an indecent photograph of a child contrary to s1(1)(a) of the Protection of Children Act 1978.

44 *R. v Christopher John Moss* [2010] EWCA Crim 294.

45 See *Sippings* [2008] EWCA Crim 46.

46 If the expectation is that the person is unclothed, but they are dressed, then a charge for attempted voyeurism could be made: see *R. v Al-Sayed (Sultan)* [2009] EWCA Crim 1922.

47 *R. v Kevin Bassett* [2008] EWCA Crim 1174.

48 D. Selfe 'Case comment *R. v Bassett (Kevin)*: voyeurism – the meaning of "privacy" and "breasts" ' *Criminal Lawyer* (2009) 193 pp. 2–4.

49 *Police Service for Northern Ireland v MacRitchie* [2008] NICA 26; [2009] NI 84.

50 J.R. Spencer 'The drafting of criminal legislation: need it be so impenetrable?' *The Cambridge Law Journal* (2008) 67(3) pp. 585–605.

51 *R. v Turner* [2006] All ER (D) 95.

52 *R. v McGill* [2008] EWCA Crim 2662.

53 *R. v IP* [2005] 1 Cr App R (S) 102; *McCann* [2007] 1 Cr App R (S) 4.

54 *R. v Hodgson* [2008] All ER (D) 64 (Jun).

55 *R. v Adams (John)* [2014] EWCA Crim 1898; *R. v Phillip Michael Jackson* [2012] EWCA Crim 2602; *R. v Sturgess (David Alan)* [2010] EWCA Crim 2550.

56 Criminal Justice and Courts Act 2015 s33.

57 For example see the review of prosecutions in the late Victorian period A.D. Harvey 'Bestiality in late-Victorian England' *Journal of Legal History* (2000) 21(3) pp. 85–88.

58 *Setting the Boundaries,* para 8.5.3.
59 Like the provision at s69 this does not seek to protect animals, since it is not concerned with whether the animals or people involved are real or even exist (it merely has to be a realistic portrayal).
60 For further discussion see I. Jones 'A beastly provision: why the offence of "intercourse with an animal" must be butchered' *Journal of Criminal Law* (2011) 75(6) pp. 528–544.
61 Including the 2006 murder of Diane Edwards by David Summers in Blyth, Northumberland and the 2005 murder of Sally Anne Bowman by Mark Dixie in Croydon, South London.
62 *Doodeward v Spence* (1908) 6 CLR 406.
63 *Setting the Boundaries,* para 8.4.5.
64 *Setting the Boundaries,* para 8.4.7.
65 HL Deb, May 19, 2003, cols 85–588.
66 For further discussion of the history and policing of cottaging, see C. Ashford 'Sexuality, public space and the criminal law: the cottaging phenomenon' *Journal of Criminal Law* 71(6) pp. 506–519.
67 Sexual Offences Act 1956 s32.
68 *Express,* June 20, 2002.

Chapter 7

Pornography

Introduction

There is no settled definition of pornography. In seeking to define it, the oft-quoted Williams Committee stated "a pornographic representation is one that combines two features: it has a certain function or intention, to arouse its audience sexually, and also has a certain content, explicit representations of sexual material (organs, postures, activity, etc)".[1] Echoing this the Criminal Justice and Immigration Act 2008 identifies an image as pornographic if it is of such a nature that it must reasonably be assumed to have been produced solely or principally for the purpose of sexual arousal.[2] This said, there is no strict legal definition of pornography as pornography *per se* is not illegal. Materials that reach the thresholds of obscene, indecent or extreme may be criminalized; but we do not seek to ban pornography, rather to restrict it to socially acceptable forms and control its distribution. Hence our legal regulation has typically focused on criminalizing the dissemination of prohibited materials, targeting producers and distributors of pornography rather than those in possession – although it will become evident that this position has now shifted significantly. There has been a strong focus in academic literature and the media on the dangers posed by pornography, particularly in terms of children viewing it online. Despite this, a number of high-profile prosecutions have been unsuccessful in convincing juries that even quite extreme adult materials should be declared criminal.

The question of what amounts to pornography is a difficult one and whether an image is criminally pornographic or merely erotic and/or harmless entertainment is often in the eye of the beholder. Consider for example Page 3 (topless models in tabloid newspapers); are these images harmless titillating fun or obscene and harmful? When the law seeks to protect those who assert a right not to be offended and allows freedom of expression it requires a delicate balance. Historically our legal system has resolved this conflict by relying upon the good sense of magistrates and jurors to decide whether materials reach the criminal threshold.

First we must briefly consider why, or indeed whether, pornography should be regulated. In a jurisdiction that has a duty to respect freedom of expression and private and family life this is an important question, as to prohibit or restrict materials requires sound – and proportionate – justification. How do we decide which pornography is and is not fit for society? As we will see the law has taken a piecemeal approach as it has been forced to respond to emerging threats and in the modern day the main driver of legislative change has been the proliferation of images on the internet – something we will see has been responded to through the creation of targeted offences.

Pornography and Harm

As the internet has become widely accessible the rationale for viewing pornography as a threat to society has gained credence.[3] Previously home-grown pornography and strict customs controls[4] that forbade the importation of indecent or obscene articles gave the State some measure of control. By bringing cheap and free pornography into the home the internet has in many ways liberalized pornographic materials, but it has also caused significant difficulties in policing illegal material.[5] As researchers have pointed out, "for anyone who has ever been curious about illegal sexual behaviours, the Internet provides a private, anonymous and inexpensive way to explore them".[6] The problem is not only how we control what material is on the internet but how we can control access to this material. Numerous suggestions have been mooted, from the very basic home filters and registration of end users to internal regulation (e.g. the Internet Watch Foundation). Difficulties in regulating pornography through legal channels have shifted the focus to Internet Service Providers (ISP) to exercise a duty of care, and material that contravenes the law is typically removed by those providers. This has recently been taken a step further with the roll out of 'opt in porn' where ISPs are expected to automatically apply filters to screen out pornography. It remains to be seen how effective this will be and the law still needs to be able to react to criminal images on and offline.

Concern about viewing images online flows from the assumption that pornography is harmful. Who the victims of pornography are is a contested area as opinions differ *vis-à-vis* whether a threat exists, whether it is quantifiable and against whom that threat is directed. When the pornography in question is 'revenge porn', where a private sexual image is distributed without consent and with the intention of causing distress, the immediate victim is clear and this is a specific offence.[7]

The traditional feminist view dictates pornography causes harm to societal perceptions of women; specifically that pornography degrades women and undermines their status in society. From the 1970s an increasing number of feminists contended that pornography objectified women, sought to make them inferior in the eyes of men and was a tool of a patriarchal society.[8] The radical feminists were not only concerned with the impact of pornography on the status of women, but the impact on the performers.[9] But not all feminists share this opinion and many view the suppression of pornography as unjustified censorship.[10]

While traditional feminists see pornography as a method of subjugating women, social scientists have looked for a causal link between viewing pornography and sexual harm. To some theorists exposure to pornography could prompt or increase sexual offending, as Kingston and Malamuth suggest:

> Both the theoretical and empirical findings we have reviewed support the notion that, although the majority of men are not influenced by pornography exposure,

some who possess certain characteristics or underlying cognitive structures
are negatively impacted by such exposure.[11]

But do we have any evidence of a causal link, even in a small number of cases? We
have insufficient space to go into detail here, suffice it to say the evidence is inconsistent. As a 1990 report concluded "inconsistencies emerge between very similar
studies and many interpretations of these have reached almost opposite conclusions".[12] More recently the Government have stated there is "some evidence" that
viewing violent pornography "may have an effect on young peoples' attitudes to
sexual and violent behavior" and "some men can exhibit heightened aggression".[13]
All very oblique.

There has been more accord about the dangers of what has been termed
"extreme pornography". This is pornography considered to go far beyond the 'normal' and has been deemed harmful, although how harmful continues to be a matter of debate. A report conducted for the Home Office and Department of Health
asserts the evidence:

> . . . supports the existence of some harmful effects from extreme pornography
> on some who access it. These included increased risk of developing pro-rape
> attitudes, beliefs and behaviours, and committing sexual offences. Although
> this was also true of some pornography which did not meet the extreme por-
> nography threshold, it showed that the effects of extreme pornography were
> more serious.[14]

As we will discuss below, the dangers posed by extreme pornography have
prompted the development of new offences.

There is a more generic argument that pornography is harmful to society. Simply put pornography may have the capacity to corrupt; its portrayal of sex as a
functional rather than relational activity may degrade men and women and, more
importantly, family life. Those who consume pornography may become accustomed
to casual sexual encounters or use pornography as a substitute for 'normal' sexual
activity. Moralists would argue that statistical correlations between pornography
and harm are unnecessary and, as the moral majority finds pornography objectionable, community intolerance proscribes the need for legal censorship. We do see
this ethos expressed in the regulation of sex establishments, including shops, strip
and lap dancing clubs.[15] This argument presumes a shared social morality, something discussed at Chapter 1, and libertarians would argue the dangers of censorship outweigh the possible harm of pornography. Groups such as the campaigning
organization Liberty have questioned the need to censor on a moral basis, particularly when the law begins to impinge upon the possession of adult pornography.[16]

More recently, legal regulation has focused on the threat pornography poses to
children. Not only is pornography understood to strike at childhood innocence but
also there is the more tangible argument that children are more in danger of physical and psychological victimization in the creation of these images than adults. The
causal argument – that the proliferation of child abuse images may normalize children as sexual objects – is also more defensible when we consider children rather
than adults.[17] Furthermore there are concerns that access to pornography could

negatively influence children's perceptions of sexual relations and relationships. This exposure argument throws into sharp relief the difficulty in defining pornography, with sexual imagery such as magazine covers and music videos subsumed into these debates[18] and the focus of the Home Office *Sexualisation of Young People Review*.[19] This document drew attention to the influence of age inappropriate materials on the development of young people's cultural norms and examined the evidence for a link between sexualisation and violence. The conclusions reached were again general, suggesting "broad agreement . . . that sexualising children prematurely places them at risk of a variety of harms, ranging from body image disturbances to being victims of abuse and sexual violence". But the review once again failed to identify a clear causal link. Popular attention has recently shifted to the emotive subject of children mimicking sexual activities they may purposefully or accidently view.[20] Again research is inconclusive here as to whether exposure to pornography causes sexual experimentation or is merely a correlative factor.[21]

Legal Regulation

It is surprising and disappointing that the Sexual Offences Act 2003 (SOA 2003) did not overhaul the regulation of pornography. The law in this area continues to be governed by the common law and a number of Acts, many of which overlap. The SOA 2003 did introduce a number of child sex offences criminalizing instances where D caused, incited, arranged, or facilitated the exploitation of children at sections 48–50. These are not pornography offences *per se*, and are regulated as offences where pornography is incidental. These offences are discussed in more detail at Chapters 8 and 9.

The regulation of pornography falls under three broad themes: materials regulated as indecent, obscene and extreme. Indecency has been addressed in general terms at Chapter 6, here indecency is key to regulating child abuse photographs with obscenity the focus of the general offence. More dangerous materials are regulated as extreme pornography.

Indecency

Child abuse images

The term child abuse images will be used here as the term child pornography is widely considered to trivialize a serious crime, failing to reflect both the gravity of the offence and the exploitation of children in the production of such images. As Claire Lilley of the National Society for the Prevention of Cruelty to Children has stated:

> We need to educate people that these are not just images; that by looking at these images, they are committing an offence; that a child is being re-victimised every single time an image is looked at; and that they are potentially affecting their own sensitivity around the issue and escalating their own ability to go down that route and end up abusing in the physical sense themselves.[22]

As child abuse became recognized as a significant threat, child abuse images came to be recognized as part of the cycle of abuse. Initially, legal focus was upon the making and distribution of photographs of children; but as the scale of the problem, exacerbated by the internet, became clear attention has increasingly turned to criminalizing the possession and proliferation of images on the internet. Operation Ore[23] in 1999 further focused police resources and public attention on the accessibility of child abuse images online and its legacy is reflected in greater funding for specialist policing and the creation of the Child Exploitation and Online Protection Centre (CEOP), a multi-agency vehicle that investigates and seeks to prevent child abuse online. CEOP is now part of the National Crime Agency and has made significant headway in recent years, receiving 18,887 reports relating to child sexual exploitation with 790 children protected as a result of CEOP activities.[24] In 2014 its largest operation to date led to the arrest of 660 suspected child abusers by targeting offenders accessing child abuse images.[25]

One important change brought about by the SOA 2003 was the definition of a child for the purposes of these images. Previous to 2003 a child was one less than 16 years of age, an age in line with many other child sexual offences. This was raised in 2003 to a person younger than 18 (s45(2)) to reflect social change and bring the child abuse image offences in line with those child exploitation offences discussed at Chapter 5.

The offences

Simply put, section 1 of the Protection of Children Act 1978 (PCA 1978) makes it an offence to take or permit to be taken, and to show, make, distribute or advertise indecent photographs or pseudo-photographs of a child.[26] This broadly reflects those acts criminalized by the Obscene Publications Act 1959 discussed below and case law has, for both these offences, construed these terms widely. For example, providing another with a password to enable him to access pornographic data stored on a computer is showing the data[27] and downloading, saving and/or printing of images is capable of amounting to an offence of making the photograph.[28] Defendants who download an image will then make and possess that photograph, although as the Sentencing Council noted, downloads should more rightfully be treated (for sentencing) as a possession offence, as the making offence is more serious.[29]

The possession of images was criminalized by the Criminal Justice Act (CJA 1988). To have possession the defendant (D) must have custody or control of the image[30] and know he has, or had, the image in his possession.[31] Therefore if a photograph is stored in the cache of a computer without D's knowledge he cannot be said to have it in his possession. However downloaded and deleted photographs that are recoverable (where D has the knowledge to recover them) can be said to be in possession – conversely if D cannot recover them they cannot be in his possession.[32] Clearly this raises evidential difficulties and the matter of irretrievability should be countered by crafting a careful indictment.[33] You will notice the offences here may not cover one emerging method of viewing child abuse images online; liability for live-streamed images will depend upon whether viewing live streaming can be construed as possessing, an issue that will clearly cause evidential difficulties.[34]

As the photograph may not always be traceable – or in the case of a pseudo-photograph the 'child' may not exist – the actual age of the subject is not required, nor does it form part of the *mens rea* of the offence. The age of the child in the photograph is ultimately for the jury to determine[35] although if the age is known this can be taken into account in determining if the photograph is indecent.[36]

The focus on photographs reflected the problem faced at the time the legislation was drafted[37] – today a less precise term would undoubtedly be used. "Photograph" then carries its ordinary meaning (inclusive of the negative image) but also encompasses moving pictures, in the words of the Act, "an indecent film, a copy of an indecent photograph or film, and an indecent photograph comprised in a film".[38] Materials that are not photographs, such as drawings, may give rise to an offence under section 62 of the Coroners and Justice Act 2009.

Photographs now also include pseudo-photographs (an image that appears to be a photograph) and all references to photographs in our proceeding discussion are inclusive of pseudo-photographs.[39] An indecent pseudo-photograph of a child embraces those images that are clearly supposed to represent a child and those manipulated photographs where "the dominant impression conveyed is that the person shown is a child, notwithstanding that some of the physical characteristics shown are those of an adult" (s7(8) PCA 1978).[40] Where a photograph of a child is merged with that of an adult this will be criminalized where that image looks like a child.[41] Photograph also includes a tracing or other image, made electronically or by other means, for example, where the outline of a photograph is traced and transferred to a piece of paper, scanned or, by logical extension, created by any device with a camera.[42] Advancements in technology have made hard copy photographs almost defunct and the law has had to keep up. Thus, electronic files (for example JPEGs, GIFs) are also photographs for the purposes of the Act.[43]

The crux of these offences is that the photographs are indecent. Indecency is a malleable term and for the purposes of this offence, the PCA 1978 did not provide a definition; it is for the jury to decide whether a photograph is indecent[44] by looking at the evidence[45] objectively.[46] Although *mens rea* is required, the defendant's purpose in taking, making etc., the photograph is not part of the assessment of indecency.[47] Moreover an otherwise decent photograph may be rendered indecent if taken out of context. The case of *Murray* (2004)[48] demonstrates that where D manipulates a documentary film that is otherwise decent in order to focus on an indecent element – in this case the manipulation of a child's penis – it is for the jury to objectively decide if this is an indecent image, outside of the context of the film makers. Likewise an otherwise innocent image of, for example, a naked child on the beach, could become indecent if circulated as sexual imagery.

The *mens rea* here is less than clear, but where D has made, taken, or permitted to be taken, published, distributed or showed (or possessed them with a view to distribution or showing)[49] indecent photographs or pseudo-photographs he must do so deliberately.[50] In *Atkins* v *DPP* (2000)[51] the court held that both section 1 PCA 1978 and section 160 CJA 1988 require intention or knowledge that an indecent image has been made, distributed, etc. For possession, showing and distributing the image the only *mens rea* requirement is that the person knowingly possesses, etc., – and the defences discussed below explain when D may not 'know' for the purposes of the offence – they need not know the photograph was, or was likely to be, of a child. However for the taking or making of an image D must have the knowledge that the image portrays, or is likely to portray, a child. As Gillespie states "For a person to be convicted of taking or making an indecent photograph of a child, the prosecution must show two elements of *mens rea* whereas with the other offences only one element needs to be proven."[52]

Defences

It is a defence to the offences in the PCA 1978 for D to show he had a legitimate reason for having the photograph in his possession, or he had not seen the photograph and did not know, nor had any cause to suspect, it to be indecent. This defence also applies to the possession offence in section 160 of the CJA 1988. However, there is an additional defence to the possession offence in the CJA 1988, which is that the photograph was sent to him without any prior request made by him or on his behalf and that he did not keep it for an unreasonable amount of time. Once possession has been established the burden then shifts to D who must establish, on the balance of probabilities, that he has not seen the image and did not know nor did he have cause to suspect it to be a pornographic image.

A legitimate reason for possession encompasses any legitimate claim that the defendant can substantiate and could include legitimate research or business reasons. A claim by D that he had not seen the photograph and thus did not know or suspect it to be indecent provides a defence where, for example, the material was part of a larger set of downloaded adult pornographic images. Likewise if D received unsolicited images (so spam e-mail for example) and this included a child abuse image that D deleted (so it was unrecoverable for D) he would have a defence. How soon D would have to dispose of it is not established in the Act and has not been clarified by later legislation that has utilized the same defence.

The offence of taking or making an indecent photograph of a child in the PCA 1978 originally had no statutory defence. However, with the age of a child raised to 18 by the SOA 2003 a specific defence was required to protect close relationships where a child, aged 16 or over, consents to the taking of a picture, the parties were married or in an enduring family relationship and the photograph is of the child alone or the child and the defendant only (s45 SOA 2003 inserted by s1A PCA 1978). This provides a defence for D who takes, makes and/or possesses such an image. There are difficulties with this defence. Firstly, there is no definition in the Act of an 'enduring family relationship' and this omission is unfortunate. Concerns were raised during the passage of the Bill regarding this omission but it was felt it best to leave the definition to the good sense of the jury, although this does of course make it difficult to regulate behaviour. Secondly the image must only be of the child or the child and D. This underlines the fact this defence was created to protect private sexual relationships. This is understandable in terms of preventing the exploitation of 16- and 17-year-old persons but does perhaps deny a right to a less conventional sex life. The same defence also applies to section 160 of the CJA 1988.[53]

The SOA 2003 introduced a further defence to section 1(1)(a) PCA 1978, "making an indecent photograph". The defence provides an exception where it is necessary to make such a photograph for the purposes of the prevention, detection or investigation of crime or for the purposes of criminal proceedings.

Outstanding issues

There are concerns about the breadth of these child abuse image offences when images are created and communicated by young people. The phenomenon of what is colloquially termed 'sexting', sending sexually explicit e-mails and texts, may not be new but its proliferation amongst young people has been of some concern. Difficulties have arisen in defining sexting – studies tend to take a wide approach, considering all virtual and text sexual approaches as sexting.[54] In practicality the term has generally been used to reflect a narrower range of behaviours, specifically pictures sent as explicit methods of flirtation.

Under the expansive definitions given to the *actus reus* of the PCA 1978 and the Criminal Justice and Public Order Act 1994, photographs of the breasts or genitals of those aged under 18 are criminal when taken, sent, distributed and shown – all likely activities for teenagers.

Commentators such as Gillespie have questioned whether prosecuting teenagers is a proportionate response.[55] In practice, although creating and sharing these indecent photographs is a substantive criminal offence, the Association of Chief Police Officers has clarified that it does not support prosecution for self-taking or consensually sharing images.[56] It seems the emphasis will be upon secondary victimization – where photographs are distributed by others. This said, a schoolgirl in Nottingham reportedly received a caution for taking and sending an explicit photograph of herself.[57] The law will continue to develop in this area and, as Stone has suggested, we can draw on international examples to inform future policy.[58]

Obscenity

Obscenity is governed by the Obscene Publications Act 1959 (OPA 1959)[59] and, despite the long history of the offence, there have been few opportunities to contemporarily assess what society considers obscene. Prosecutions have remained fairly low; with 152 prosecutions in 2008–09 falling to 33 in 2013–14.[60] This small number of prosecutions, coupled with a sea-change in what society considers to be corrupting imagery, has led to calls for the abolition of the offence and recent prosecutions have not helped its reputation. In January 2012 the Crown Prosecution Service (CPS) took the decision to prosecute Michael Peacock who had been distributing gay pornography, featuring extreme sexual violence including sadomasochism, the insertion of needles, urolagnia and fisting.[61] These were activities the police and CPS had long considered contrary to modern standards of propriety – but a jury disagreed. The *Observer* newspaper lauded the acquittal of Peacock as a "victory for common sense" and evidence the OPA 1959 is now irrelevant.[62] A similar scenario had played out in 1960 when a jury had also disagreed with the Crown's contention that D.H. Lawrence's *Lady Chatterley's Lover* was obscene.[63]

The crux of the obscenity offence is that the article must (unsurprisingly) be obscene. There is a perceptible difference between indecency and obscenity. Indecency is at the lower end of the scale and obscenity at the upper end.[64] While the statutory offence of obscenity seeks to protect people from becoming depraved and corrupted the common law indecency offences merely ask whether decency *would* be outraged.

Proscribing illegality in this arena is difficult without careful consideration of the material in question, making this a tricky area for self-regulation and challenging for prosecutorial agencies to manage. As we will see, the substantive law offers little guidance on obscenity, however the CPS have sought to define what activities are suitable for prosecution, including:

- sexual acts with an animal;
- realistic portrayals of rape;
- sadomasochistic material that goes beyond trifling and transient infliction of injury;
- torture with instruments;
- bondage (especially where gags are used with no apparent means of withdrawing consent);
- dismemberment or graphic mutilation;
- activities involving perversion or degradation (such as drinking urine, urination or vomiting onto the body, or excretion or use of excreta); and
- fisting.[65]

Post-*Peacock* it is hard to be confident this list is an effective list of exemplars.

The Offence

To be obscene the article must have the capacity to deprave and corrupt – although there is no necessity to demonstrate it has actually depraved or corrupted. To modern ears 'deprave and corrupt' is an archaic phrase and it is indeed one drawn from the dicta of Chief Justice Cockburn in *Hicklin* (1868)[66] where a common law gloss was put upon the Obscene Publications Act 1857. Justice Byrne elaborated on the meanings of these terms in *Penguin Books Ltd*[67] and said:

> To deprave means to make morally bad, to pervert, to debase or corrupt morally. To corrupt means to render morally unsound or rotten, to destroy the moral purity or chastity, to pervert or ruin a good quality, to debase or defile.

In *DPP v Whyte* (1972)[68] Lord Wilberforce clarified that the Act "... is not merely concerned with the once for all corruption of the wholly innocent; it equally protects the less innocent from further corruption, the addict from feeding or increasing his addiction". Hence publication to unknown persons cannot negate liability on the grounds the publisher was unaware the material may deprave and corrupt those persons – in publishing to an unknown audience they are taking a risk it may.[69] Moreover as *Shaw* (1961)[70] established a man can be corrupted more than once.

The material must be capable of depraving and corrupting a significant number of persons who may be exposed to it.[71] The offence is then context-dependent and, as Lord Wilberforce has stated, "an article cannot be considered as obscene in itself: it can only be so in relation to its likely readers".[72] This was confirmed more recently in *Elliot* (1996)[73] where the Court of Appeal approved the direction of the trial judge:

> It is not a question of whether it is disgusting or offensive or shocking, nor whether it was made in good taste or bad taste, or whether it is trash or tat or not, or whether it is boring in places or not. The question you have to decide is whether it would have a defiling effect on those likely to see it. Will it debase the watchers or hearers; will it make them worse morally, will it make them more rotten, will it taint them and defile them?

As the Act makes clear, the material need only be *likely* (having regard to all relevant circumstances) to be seen by those it could deprave and corrupt – pornography that has been classified for adult viewing could then be classed as obscene if children can readily access it. You may expect this would have significant ramifications for the publishers of internet pornography; however, as the Culture, Media and Sport Committee point out, no prosecutions have been brought in this regard.[74]

The article in question, such as a magazine, may be comprised of both innocent and questionable items[75] and the correct approach to deciding whether this makes the article obscene was set out by Lord Chief Justice Widgery:

> Where you have an article such as this comprising a number of distinct items, the proper view of obscenity under section 1 is to apply the test to the individual items in question. It is equally clear that if, when so applied, the test shows one item to be obscene that is enough to make the whole article obscene.[76]

Obscenity is a publication offence, possession of obscene articles only becomes actionable where that article is an indecent photograph of a child or falls within the definitions of an extreme image discussed below. However publication is construed broadly – the Act clarifies publication includes distribution, circulation, sale, letting on hire, giving, or lending, offering it for sale or for letting on hire.[77] The Act was amended in 1964 to include those who have "an obscene article for publication for gain", unless "he had not examined the article and had no reasonable cause to suspect that it was such that his having it could make him liable to be convicted of an offence". Case law further explains:

> The forms of publication included in the definition in section 1(3)(a) fall into three distinct groups: in one group, comprising the words "sells, lets on hire, gives or lends," publication is to an individual; in the second group, comprising the words "distributes, circulates," publication is on a wider scale, involving more than one person; in the third group a mere offer for sale or letting on hire constitutes publication.[78]

Thus publication may be to an individual, the world at large or an attempt at either. Recent case law has confirmed publication can embrace private communications. In *Smith (Gavin)* (2012)[79] the defendant's computer contained records of an explicit conversation concerning fantasy sadistic sex against young children. He was using instant communication in a one-to-one context and at trial it had been accepted that transmitting comments to an individual was not publication; but on appeal it was held that publication need only be to one person. Gillespie has suggested this decision is unsound;[80] the Act had been amended in 1994[81] to include the transmission of data stored electronically and this allowed it to deal with data stored on computers, discs and servers; but it is this, Gillespie argues, that defeats the reasoning in *Smith*. The amendment sought to criminalize the transmission of "data stored" not real-time conversations where data is not usually saved when the programme is exited.

Jurisdictional issues are surmounted by our expansive view of publication. Although many internet pornographers are based abroad and therefore outside the reach of the law, not only is there a publication when images are uploaded but when they are downloaded, as Lord Justice Rose stated in *Waddon* (2000):

> . . . there can be further publication when those images are downloaded elsewhere. That approach is, as it seems to us, underlined by the provisions of s1(3) (b) as to what is capable of giving rise to publication where matter has been electronically transmitted.[82]

"Article" includes materials containing or embodying matter to be read or looked at or both, any sound record, and any film or record of a picture including file negatives. This definition includes video cassettes,[83] DVDs and other forms of electronic data storage.[84] Plays do not fall under this definition, but the Theatres Act 1968 makes it an offence to present or direct a public performance of a play that is obscene.

Hicklin (1868)[85] is usually cited as authority for the proposition that no *mens rea* is required for obscenity. This case pre-dates the 1959 Act and in the more contemporary judgement of *Penguin Books* Justice Byrne held that if a defendant publishes an obscene article the inference that he intends to deprave and corrupt is irrebuttable.

Defences

Section 2(5) of the OPA 1959 provides a defence for a person who proves they had not examined the article and had no reasonable cause to suspect that it was obscene.

It is also a defence that the publication is for the public good on the grounds it is in the interest of science, literature, art or learning, or of other objects of general concern (s4). "Public good" is a very generic phrase and requires a delicate balancing act to be performed by the jury, as the Court of Appeal has explained:

> the jury must consider on the one hand the number of readers they believe would tend to be depraved and corrupted by the book, the strength of the tendency to deprave and corrupt, and the nature of the depravity and corruption; on

the other hand, they should assess the strength of the literary, sociological or ethical merit which they consider the book to possess. They should then weigh up all these factors and decide whether on balance the publication is proved to be justified as being for the public good.[86]

Thus the jury may declare an article depraving but accept it has an inherent public benefit. Asking the jury to perform mental gymnastics is not unusual; but may suggest the offence is ripe for repeal or reform.

Extreme Pornography

2008 saw the enactment of the first new significant pornography offence for 30 years at section 63 of the Criminal Justice and Immigration Act 2008 (CJIA 2008). Termed "extreme pornography" the offence was established with the stated aims of protecting "those who participate in the creation of sexual material containing violence, cruelty or degradation, who may be the victims of crime in the making of the material, whether or not they notionally or genuinely consent to taking part" and "to protect society, particularly children, from exposure to such material, to which access can no longer be reliably controlled through legislation dealing with publication and distribution, and which may encourage interest in violent or aberrant sexual activity".[87] The offence is not intended to criminalize material beyond that which it is illegal to publish under the OPA 1959, but instead to make it an offence to possess these extreme forms of pornographic material. As a possession offence the law here is very prescriptive, criminalizing only those images within section 63(7). It is important to recognize this offence seeks to regulate the demand for extreme pornography. Where the law on obscenity sought to tackle creation and distribution, here we have an offence which focuses on consumers.

It is perhaps surprising that this new and highly specific offence has so quickly resulted in a glut of prosecutions. McGlynn and Rackey point to CPS figures revealing that 2,236 cases of possession of extreme pornography reached a hearing between July 2008 and November 2011.[88] As prosecutions for obscenity have fallen prosecutions for possession of extreme pornography have risen – placing the emphasis on possession has clearly been successful. This said, commentators have questioned the compatibility of the new extreme pornography offence with Articles 8 and 10 of the European Convention on Human Rights (ECHR).[89] A wide margin of appreciation is afforded to the State in regulating freedom of expression[90] but, as we have seen, Article 8 has been given greater weight by the ECHR and although *Smethurst* (2001)[91] held the offence of possession of indecent images of children was compatible with Article 8 rights, the newer offences at section 63 CJIA 2008 and section 62 of the Coroners and Justice Act 2009 have not yet been subject to challenge.

The offence

Possession bears its ordinary legal meaning in the sense that D must have custody and control of the item. However it also requires D to have knowledge of the 'thing' in question. For example in *Ping Chen Cheung* (2009)[92] D knew he had in his possession DVDs; that he did not know some contained extreme pornography is a matter that could be dealt with through the defences. Knowledge of the item in question is only important in so far as a serious mistake has been made as to the items – as Justice King put it in *Ping*: "A belief, for example, that something which is in fact a collection of DVDs is a collection of, say, floor tiles might well qualify." Possession once again appears to be the only *mens rea* that need be proven. It is a matter of defence if D argues he did not know that the image was, or was likely to be, an extreme image.

"Pornographic" is defined in section 63(3) CJIA 2008 as where the image is of "such a nature that it must reasonably be assumed to have been produced solely or principally for the purpose of sexual arousal". This is an objective test and the intention of those who have produced the image will be irrelevant. Not only will it include inherently sexual images but also violent or fetishistic images produced to cause sexual arousal. In addition, section 63(6)(b) sets out that the image must be extreme, namely grossly offensive, disgusting, or otherwise of an obscene character. The CPS has clarified these are not intended to be read as separate notions, so "grossly offensive" and "disgusting" are not alternatives to "an obscene character" but merely examples of it.

To reach the threshold of an extreme image the image must portray in an explicit and realistic way any of the acts set out in section 63(7):

[a] an act that threatens a person's life;
[b] an act that results, or is likely to result, in serious injury to a person's anus, breasts or genitals;
[c] an act that involves sexual interference with a human corpse; or
[d] a person performing an act of intercourse or oral sex with an animal (whether dead or alive).

In response to criticisms concerning the omission of rape pornography from this list, the Criminal Justice and Courts Act 2015 has now broadened the category of extreme images to include the possession of extreme pornographic images that depict non-consensual sexual penetration in an explicit and realistic way (s63(7)(a)).[93] The image must feature:

[a] an act that involves the non-consensual penetration of a person's vagina, anus or mouth by another with the other person's penis; or
[b] an act that involves the non-consensual sexual penetration of a person's vagina or anus by another with a part of the other person's body or anything else, and a reasonable person looking at the image would think that the persons were real.[94]

"Image" means a moving or still image or data that is capable of conversion into a moving or still image. "Explicit" and "realistic" carry their dictionary definitions – and convey that the images need not portray real activities. As a possession offence, the law has moved into the private realm here and the offence needs to be precise in order to allow people to regulate their behaviour. The specificity of those images that may be adjudged extreme is welcomed; however, these descriptions are rather oblique. For example, for section 63(7)(b) there is little guidance as to what constitutes "serious injury"; and why are the prohibited parts of the body only the anus, genitals and breasts? An image needs to be pornographic to satisfy section 63(3) and, by limiting the list to these body parts it appears overly specific – should sexual mutilation of thighs or buttocks fall outside the offence? It may however provide some relief for the bondage, domination and sadomasochism community who have heavily criticized the classification of sadomasochistic images within the definition of extreme pornography as effectively criminalizing a significant amount of existing material, particularly as the image only need be realistic and likely to result in serious injury. Thus, posed images that present no risk of harm could be brought under the ambit of the offence. This said, the CPS threshold for prosecution here is high[95] and the trial of Simon Walsh, a barrister and former aide to Boris Johnson, will perhaps tighten this even further. Walsh was charged with possession of six images attached to an e-mail including images of anal fisting and urethral sounding. The prosecution claimed that these images were pornographic and extreme; the defence that they were merely 'souvenirs'. In an echo of *Peacock*, and bringing into question the objective test once again, the jury unanimously acquitted Walsh.[96] Section 63(7)(b) will undoubtedly be the genesis of significant case law in the future.

Participants in sadomasochism may also find that images they record are criminalized under section 63(7)(a) if the acts depicted appear to threaten life. The Explanatory Notes to the Act suggest "depictions of hanging, suffocation, or sexual assault involving a threat with a weapon" could fall under this section. But again this seems remarkably broad, and the CPS have felt the need to add that "merely wearing a mask or other fetish wear would not in itself make an act life threatening".[97] Clearly many of the images criminalized here would not be criminal in practice. This is a worrying constraint on freedom of expression, and is discussed in some detail by Foster who concludes it may be "out of line with human rights jurisprudence".[98] There is some relief provided by the defences if D can prove he directly participated in the act or any of the acts portrayed, and the act or acts did not involve the infliction of any non-consensual harm on any person (s66). The Act clarifies non-consensual harm is where there was no consent or it was harm "of such a nature that the person cannot, in law, consent to it" (s66(3)). Thus, images of willing sadomasochism participants suffering injuries that amount to actual bodily harm are not protected under this defence, as a person cannot consent to such harm in law.

Section 67(3)(c) criminalizes images featuring sexual interference with a human corpse. This image need only be realistic (s63(7)), a provision that then conflicts with its own defence at section 66(2)(c), which provides it is a defence for D to prove it was not in fact a corpse. Providing that the image may only be realistic and then shifting the burden to D to prove it was not a corpse seems remarkably convoluted. Moreover, section 70 SOA 2003 prohibits sexual penetration of a corpse, not "sexual interference" – this possession offence is again broader than the offence at section 70.[99]

Section 63(7)(d) criminalizes an image in which a person is performing an act of intercourse or oral sex with an animal, whether that animal is dead or alive – there is no defence for possession of these images. Again this prohibits the possession of images that do not amount to sexual offences under section 69 SOA 2003. The overwhelming majority of prosecutions for extreme pornography (85.95 per cent) have concerned images of bestiality.[100] However, sham images of sex with animals are also common, so can the authorities sort the dangerous from the humorous? There have been some difficulties in this regard, for example the now infamous prosecution of Andrew Holland, prosecuted for possession of a video of a woman having sex with a man in a tiger costume, a tiger that turned to the camera and said "That beats doing Frosties ads for a living!", highlighted the need for caution in prosecutions – and the importance of police and prosecutors viewing films with the sound on.[101]

Despite prosecutorial successes it is a number of matters still need ironing out – for example whether images of genital piercing fall within extreme pornography. Although body piercing has become increasingly normalized – and ear piercing is recognized as a social utility exception under *Brown* (1993)[102] – what of a defendant who receives and keeps an image of a genital piercing for sexual gratification? Body modification is not clearly excluded by *Brown* and one would assume it falls under section 63(7)(b).

Defences

The general defences are set out at section 65 and mirror those we discussed when addressing child abuse images, including where there is a legitimate reason for possessing the image (s65(2)(a)), where the defendant had not seen the image and did not know it was extreme (s65(2)(b)) and where it was sent without request and not kept for an unreasonable period of time (s65(2)(c)).

The defence at section 66 of the Act applies where the person in possession of the extreme pornographic image proves that he was a participant in the act depicted and that no harm (other than harm that can be – and was – lawfully consented to) occurred to the participants. This defence does not apply where the images involve animals or a real corpse. In light of the inclusion of rape pornography the Criminal Justice and Courts Act 2015 also provide that it is a defence for D to prove "that what is portrayed as non-consensual penetration was in fact consensual" – this only applies where the participant could lawfully consent.

You will notice these defences suffer from the same lack of precision as noted before. Once again spam e-mails and sms are happily excluded (if the defendant does not keep the image for an unreasonable period of time). The realistic nature of images at section 65(2)(c) does deal with the concerns of filmmakers regarding scenes of necrophilia, but does not properly tackle the same issue where the sexual activity is with an animal. The defences also fail to address the concern raised by Liberty, that pornography could be sent to you by request (thus negating the defence at s65(1)(c)(i)) but you may not have realized it would fall under section 63(7).[103]

The extreme pornography offence coupled with changes in morality suggest the OPA 1959 may now be redundant. Publishers and distributors have possession of articles and there would be no real difficulty in prosecuting under section 63 CJIA 2008 where the prescriptive nature of the offence would make the law clearer and fetter jury discretion. The new extreme pornography offences have perhaps better captured the public mood, shifting responsibility to the consumers of abhorrent pornography.

Extreme Child Images

An offence of possession of a prohibited image of a child, punishable by up to 3 years' imprisonment was enacted in the Coroners and Justice Act 2009 (CJA 2009). This is targeted at non-photographic images and specifically excludes indecent photographs or pseudo-photographs of children.

Criminalizing the possession of fantasy images was an important step in preventing such images being used to groom children and in response to the fear these images were "reinforcing potential abusers' inappropriate feelings towards children".[104] The new offence has not been universally welcomed,[105] as may have been expected in the light of the criticism raised to the Government's initial consultation and the Joint Committee on Human Rights.[106] Disapproval has largely focused on the lack of empirical evidence linking the possession of these images with child sexual abuse – as recognized in the Government's own consultation. No 'real' children have been harmed and links between abusers using these materials to groom children have no evidential basis. The law has then responded to a potential threat, a rationale not uncommon in this area.

Mirroring section 63 of the CJIA 2008, three elements must be established: that the image possessed is pornographic, features a prohibited image and is grossly offensive, disgusting or otherwise of an obscene character (s62(2) CJA 2009). "Possession" bears the same meaning as discussed previously and "pornography" the definition at section 63(3) of the CJIA 2008. There is no offence of "making" a prohibited image; the focus is on the consumer, although it seems odd the offence does not attempt to tackle those who produce these images if they are considered dangerous.

"Image" includes moving and still images and stored data that can be converted into an image (s65(2)(a)(b)). As the offence excludes photographs and pseudo-photographs at section 65(3), the prohibited images here are cartoons (including manga), computer-generated images and drawings. These need not be representations of real children as section 65(7) and (8) makes clear images of an imaginary person or child are included. Images in classified films are excluded from the offence. Section 63 clarifies this means images that form part of a series of images contained in a "recording" (any device capable of storing data electronically) and that a classified work is one for which a classification certificate has been issued under section 4 of the Video Recordings Act 1984. However, reflecting *Murray* (2004),[107] the exclusion does not apply to extracts of images from classified films "which must reasonably be assumed to have been extracted solely or principally for the purpose of sexual arousal" (s63(3)).

In order to be a "prohibited image", the image must be pornographic, grossly offensive, disgusting, or otherwise of an obscene character and focus solely or principally on a child's genitals or anal region, or portray any acts set out at section 62(7). The obscenity test, with its higher threshold, differentiates this offence from the possession of indecent photographs of children and reflects we are not dealing here with 'real' images.

Child once again means a person under the age of 18, although it may be difficult to judge the age of a fictional 'child' in an artistic representation. The images here need only be partially representative of a child, as section 65(6)(a) and (b) set out the image can be treated as of a child if "the impression conveyed by the image is that the person shown is a child, or the predominant impression conveyed is that the person shown is a child despite the fact that some of the physical characteristics shown are not those of a child". It is difficult to discern from this which images would be "of a child" and which would not.

If the prohibited image is not one that focuses on child's genitals or anal region then it must satisfy section 62(7), which sets out, in fairly specific terms the prohibited acts:

(a)   the performance by a person of an act of intercourse or oral sex with or in the presence of a child;
(b)   an act of masturbation by, of, involving or in the presence of a child;
(c)   an act that involves penetration of the vagina or anus of a child with a part of a person's body or with anything else;
(d)   an act of penetration, in the presence of a child, of the vagina or anus of a person with a part of a person's body or with anything else;
(e)   the performance by a child of an act of intercourse or oral sex with an animal (whether dead or alive or imaginary);
(f)   the performance by a person of an act of intercourse or oral sex with an animal (whether dead or alive or imaginary) in the presence of a child.

While images detailing these acts are ostensibly those most would agree should be regulated, we must remember these are not photographs but drawings and cartoons. Moreover, the inclusion of imaginary animals, from which one assumes 'animals' such as unicorns, confuses the matter further. Cartoons and manga particularly do not make a ready distinction between animals and people and the specificity of these sections could cause difficulties if the character in question were neither animal nor person.[108] The use of the term "creature" would perhaps have been more inclusive.

Once again the *mens rea* looks only to possession – the defendant must know he has custody and control of the image. With offences now focused upon the consumers of pornography, one may expect section 62 CJA 2009 and section 63 CJIA 2008 would require a *mens rea* of intending to possess the *prohibited* images.

The defences at section 64 of the CJA also mirror those we have seen for the extreme pornography offence and carry the same meaning.

Conclusion

Much of our legislation was not crafted with the internet in mind and this has led to some creative interpretation of the *actus reus* of the offences. Where offences have been addressed in case law it is clear the judiciary have sought to give expansive definitions to the *actus reus*, leading to terms such as "publication" and "making" being divorced from their common sense meaning to tackle online offending. There are also a number of offences that overlap and the PCA 1978 and the CJA 1988 have been comprehensibly amended. With this in mind the Culture Media and Sport Committee have recommended the law concerning child abuses images be consolidated "with a view to providing even greater clarity for the purposes of law enforcement and deterrence".[109]

While there is broad consensus that child abuse images pose a threat, there is no consensus regarding what amounts to pornography or how significant a threat pornography poses. This explains why we have such a jumble of offences regulating this area – the exacting offences regulating child abuse and extreme pornography have demarcated these images as dangerous, while the OPA 1959 provides a safety net for articles that may contemporarily be viewed as damaging.

These responses, both statutory and judicial, are obviously set to tackle the perceived dangers of the internet and point to a need for a clear, reasoned and sensible prosecution policy. The CPS provides detailed guidance in this regard although, as the *Peacock* and *Walsh* prosecutions demonstrate, their confidence may sometimes be misplaced.

Notes

1 B. Williams *Report of the Committee on Obscenity and Film Censorship* London: Her Majesty's Stationery Office (1979).
2 Section 63(3).
3 For further discussion see Y. Arkdeniz. 'The regulation of pornography and child pornography on the Internet' *Journal of Information, Law and Technology* (1997) 1. Accessible at http://www2.warwick.ac.uk/fac/soc/law/elj/jilt/1997_1/akdeniz1/; C. Manchester 'Computer pornography' *Crim LR* (2005) p. 546; S. Dooley 'Obscene material on the Internet' *Solicitors Journal* September 8 (1995) pp. 866–868. D.S Wall 'The police and the virtual community: the Internet, Cyber-crimes and the policing of cyberspace' in P. Francis, P. Davies and V. Jupp (eds) *Policing Futures* London: Macmillan (1997) pp. 208–236.
4 At times these were perhaps too strict, taking too broad a view of corrupting materials, see *Conegate Ltd v Customs and Excise Commissioners* [1986] 2 All ER 688.
5 For example the Internet Watch Foundation found that child abuse images were usually hosted in countries outside the European Union. In the sample studied 51 per cent were hosted in the United States, 20 per cent in Russia and 5 per cent in Japan. Only 8.6 per cent of the sample were hosted in the European Union (United Kingdom and Spain), Press Release and Conference *'Remove Online Images of Child abuse'* Internet Watch Foundation, October 24 (2006).
6 A. de Almeida Neto, S. Eyland, J. Ware, J. Galouzis and M. Kevin 'Internet sexual offending: overview of potential contributing factors and intervention strategies' *Psychiatry, Psychology and Law* (2013) 20(2) pp. 168–181.
7 This is a criminal offence, but it is not a sexual offence: Criminal Justice and Courts Act 2015 s33.
8 A. Assiter *Pornography, Feminism, and the Individual* Winchester, MA: Pluto Press (1989); G. Dines, A. Russo and R. Jensen *Pornography: The Production and Consumption of Inequality* New York: Routledge (1998).
9 For further discussion of the testimony of performers see the commentary of MacKinnon and Dworkin in C. MacKinnon and A. Dworkin *In Harm's Way: The Pornography Civil Rights Hearings* Cambridge, MA: Harvard University Press (1998); A. Dworkin *Pornography: Men Possessing Women* New York: Plume (1989).
10 See G. Rodgerson and E. Wilson *Pornography and Feminism: The Case Against Censorship* London: Lawrence and Wishart (1991).
11 D. Kingston and N. Malamuth 'The importance of individual differences in pornography use: theoretical perspectives and implications for treating sexual offenders' *Journal of Sex Research* (2009) 46 pp. 216–232.

12 D. Howitt and G. Cumberpatch *Pornography: Impacts and Influences* London: Home Office Research and Planning Unit (1990).

13 Ministry of Justice 'Factsheet on the Criminal Justice and Courts Bill – Extension of the offence of Extreme Pornography (clause 16)' February 2014, p. 1.

14 C. Itzin, A. Taket, and L. Kelly *The Evidence of Harm to Adults Relating to Exposure to Extreme Pornographic Material: A Rapid Evidence Assessment (REA)* London: Ministry of Justice (2007).

15 Local Government (Miscellaneous Provisions) Act 1982 Schedule 3 amended by the Policing and Crime Act 2009 s27.

16 Liberty *Liberty Committee Stage Briefing on the Criminal Justice and Immigration* London: Liberty (October 2007) pp. 15–16. Accessible at https://www.liberty-human-rights.org.uk/sites/default/files/crimjust-immbill-committee.pdf.

17 Mitchell et al found almost 80 per cent of those arrested for child pornography charges admitted sex with children. However, a study by Seto and Eke conversely suggests there is not necessarily a link between child pornography offenders and their risk of committing contact sexual child offences: S. Mitchell, K. Finkelhor, et al 'Internet and family and acquaintance sexual abuse' *Child Maltreatment* (2005) 10(1) pp. 49–60; M.C. Seto and A.W. Eke 'The criminal histories and later offending of child pornography offenders' *Sexual Abuse: A Journal of Research and Treatment* (2005) 17 (2) pp. 201–210.

18 See M.A.H. Horvath, et al *Basically . . . Porn Is Everywhere: A Rapid Evidence Assessment on the Effects that Access and Exposure to Pornography Has on Children and Young People* Project Report. London: Office of the Children's Commissioner for England (2013).

19 L. Papadopoulos *Sexualisation of Young People Review* London: Home Office February (2010).

20 For example see the comments of District Judge James Prowse 'Judge blames online porn after boy rapes sister' *The Times*, March 4, 2014. Also reported in *The Independent*, March 3, 2014; *Daily Telegraph* March 4, 2014.

21 For a review of the studies see M.C. Seto and M.L. Lalumière 'What is so special about male adolescent sexual offending? A review and test of explanations through meta-analysis' *Psychological Bulletin* (2010) 136 pp. 526–575.

22 House of Commons Culture, Media and Sport Committee 'Online safety: Sixth Report of Session 2013–14: Volume I: Report, together with formal minutes, oral and written evidence' (2014) HC Paper No.729 (Session 2013–14) p. 9.

23 Launched after the Federal Bureau of Investigation shared the details of overseas subscribers with law enforcement agencies after investigating an online portal that provided subscriber access to child pornography.

24 Annual Review 2012–13 and Centre Plan 2013–14 Child Online Protection and Exploitation Centre. Accessible at http://ceop.police.uk/Documents/ceopdocs/AnnualReview CentrePlan2013.pdf.

25 'UK-wide operation snares suspected "paedophiles"' CEOP Command July 17, 2014. Accessible at http://ceop.police.uk/Media-Centre/Press-releases/2014/UK-WIDE-OPERATION-SNARES-660-PAEDOPHILES.

26 "Making" and "pseudo photographs" amendments per the Criminal Justice and Public Order Act 1994 s84(2).

27 *R. v Fellows & Arnold* [1996] Times LR Oct 3.

28 *R. v Bowden* Times November 19, 1999.

29 In *R. v Wild (No. 1)* [2002] 1 Cr App R (S) 157, the Court of Appeal had sought the views of the Sentencing Advisory Panel. *Report of the Sentencing Advisory Panel, Offences Involving Child Pornography* London: SAP (August 2002).

30 *R. v Porter* Times June 21, 2006.
31 *Atkins v DPP, Goodland v DPP* [2000] 2 All ER 425, [2000] 2 Cr App Rep 248, DC.
32 *R. v Porter; R. v Leonard (John)* [2012] EWCA Crim 277.
33 See the comments of Lord Chief Justice Judge in *R. v Leonard (John)* [2012] EWCA Crim 277.
34 For further discussion see F. Gerry 'UK laws on internet child abuse will struggle to cope with live streaming' *Criminal Law and Justice Weekly* (2014) 178(4) p 45.
35 *R. v Land* [1998] 1 Cr App R 301.
36 Ibid.
37 For discussion of the social backdrop see S. Ost *Child Pornography and Sexual Grooming: Legal and Societal Responses* Cambridge: Cambridge University Press (2009).
38 Section 7(2).
39 Criminal Justice and Public Order Act 1994 s84.
40 See C. Manchester 'Criminal Justice and Public Order Act 1994: obscenity, pornography and videos' *Criminal Law Review* February (1995) pp. 123–131, at p. 125.
41 No child may be harmed in the production of a pseudo-photograph and the inclusion of manipulated images is meant to recognize these images may desensitize offenders and/or child victims..
42 The Criminal Justice and Immigration Act 2008 s70.
43 *R. v Fellows and Arnold* (1996) and an amendment by the Criminal Justice and Public Order Act 1994. The amendment to s7(4) by the CJPOA 1994 states that a photograph includes "data stored on a computer disc or by other electronic means which is capable of conversion into a photograph".
44 *R. v Owen* [1988] 1 WLR 134.
45 *R. v Stamford* [1972] 2 QB 391.
46 *R. v Smethurst (John Russell)* [2001] EWCA Crim 772.
47 Ibid.; *R. v Owen (Charles William)* [1988] 1 WLR 134.
48 *R. v Arthur Alan Murray* [2004] EWCA Crim 2211.
49 "With a view to" means it is the defendant's intent to bring about the *actus reus* or it is one of a number of aims. For further discussion, see commentary on the case of *R. v Dooley (Michael)* [2005] EWCA Crim 3093 in S. Leake and D.C. Ormerod 'Indecent photographs of children: meaning of words "with a view to"' *Criminal Law Review* June (2006) pp. 544–546.
50 *R. v Graham-Kerr* [1988] 1 WLR 1098.
51 [2000] 2 All ER 425.
52 A.A. Gillespie 'Child Pornography: balancing substantive and evidential law to safeguard children effectively from abuse' *International Journal of Evidence & Proof* (2005) 9(1) pp. 29–49.
53 SOA 2003 s45 inserted s160A into the CJA 1988.
54 For a review of the literature and a small-scale study of teens in London see J. Ringrose, R. Gill, S. Livingstone, and L. Harvey *A Qualitative Study of Children, Young People and 'Sexting.'* A report prepared for the NSPCC (2012). Accessible at http://www.nspcc.org.uk/Inform/resourcesforprofessionals/sexualabuse/sexting-research-report_wdf89269.pdf.
55 A.A. Gillespie 'Adolescents, sexting and human rights' *Human Rights Law Review* (2013) 13(4) pp. 623–643.
56 CEOP 'ACPO CPAI lead's position on young people who post self-taken indecent images' (2009). Accessible at https://www.ceop.police.uk/Documents/ceopdocs/externaldocs/ACPO_Lead_position_on_Self_Taken_Images.pdf.
57 *The Telegraph* (online edition) July 22, 2014. Accessible at http://www.telegraph.co.uk/news/uknews/crime/10983055/Teenage-girl-given-police-caution-for-sexting-explicit-selfie-to-boyfriend.html.

58 N. Stone 'The "sexting" quagmire: criminal justice responses to adolescents' electronic transmission of indecent images in the UK and the USA' *Youth Justice* (2011) 11(3) pp. 266–281.

59 As amended by the Obscene Publications Act 1964.

60 Crown Prosecution Service *Violence Against Women and Girls Crime Report 2013–2014* London: CPS (2014).

61 *R. v Peacock* unreported January 6, 2011 (Crown Ct (Southwark)).

62 *The Observer* January 8, 2012.

63 *R. v Penguin Books* [1961] Crim LR 176.

64 *R. v Stanley* [1965] 1 All ER 1035.

65 CPS *Obscene Publication Legal Guidance* London: CPS. Accessible at http://www.cps. gov.uk/legal/l_to_o/obscene_publications.

66 (1868) LR 3 QB 360 at 371.

67 [1961] Crim LR 176.

68 (1972) 3 All ER 12.

69 See the comments of Ashworth J. in *R. v Barker* (1962) 46 Cr App R 227.

70 [1961] 1 All ER 330.

71 *Calder & Boyars Ltd* [1969] 3 All ER 644.

72 *DPP v Whyte* (1972) 3 All ER 12.

73 [1996] 1 Cr App R 432.

74 Department for Culture, Media and Sport *Connectivity, Content and Consumers. Britain's Digital Platform for Growth* (2013). The recommendation by the Committee is for websites to require proof of age to gain entrance to pornographic websites. Similar concerns have also been raised in relation to television pay-per-view services and the Department for Culture, Media and Sport have also recommended that access to these services is strengthened and the content of these channels more rigorously controlled.

75 *R. v Goring* [1999] Crim LR 670, CA.

76 *R. v Anderson (James)* (1972) 56 Cr App R 115.

77 It is also an offence to send obscene or indecent articles through the post. The Postal Services Act 2000 s85.

78 *Per* Ashworth J. *R. v Barker* (1962) 46 Cr App R 227 where the appellant had posted pornographic photographs, for payment, to four individuals and was charged with the publication of these photographs.

79 [2012] EWCA Crim 398.

80 A.A. Gillespie 'Obscene conversations, the internet and the criminal law' *Criminal Law Review* (2014) 5 pp. 350–363.

81 By virtue of the Criminal Justice and Public Order Act 1994 s168(1) and Schedule 9 para 3.

82 *R. v Waddon* unreported April 6, 2000, CA (Crim. Div.) See also *R. v Perrin* [2002] 4 Archbold News 2 which confirms the transmission of data (either uploading or downloading) constitutes publication.

83 The Video Recordings Act 1984 also requires all videos to be certified by the British Board of Film Classification. The BBFC is to have special regard to the likelihood of videos being viewed in the home.

84 The courts are prepared to accept emerging forms of technology as comprising articles. See *Attorney General's Reference No 5 of 1980* [1980] 3 All ER 816.

85 (1868) LR 3 QB 360.

86 *Calder and Boyars Ltd* [1968] 3 All ER 644.

87 Home Office/National Offender Management Service and Scottish Executive *Consultation on the Possession of Extreme Pornographic Material* London: Home Office (2005) p. 11 and Home Office *Consultation on the Possession of Extreme Pornographic Material: Summary of Responses and Next Steps* London: Home Office (2006).

88 C. McGlynn and E. Rackley *Criminalising Extreme Pornography: Lessons from England & Wales*, Durham Law School Briefing Document, Durham University (2013).

89 See S. Foster 'Possession of Extreme Pornographic Images, Public Protection and Human Rights' *Coventry Law Journal* (2010) 15(1) pp. 21–27.

90 *Handyside v United Kingdom* (1976) 1 EHRR 737.

91 *The Times* April 13, 2001.

92 *R. v Ping Chen Cheung* [2009] EWCA Crim 2965.

93 C. McGlynn and E. Rackley 'Criminalising extreme pornography: a lost opportunity' *Criminal Law Review* (2009) 4 pp. 245–260; Rape Crisis South London *'Closing the Loophole on Rape Pornography'* (undated). Accessible at http://www.endviolenceagainstwomen.org.uk/data/files/Closing_the_loophole_on_rape_pornography.pdf.

94 Criminal Justice and Courts Act 2015 s37 amending Criminal Justice and Immigration Act 2008 s63.

95 CPS *Extreme Pornography Legal Guidance* Accessible at http://www.cps.gov.uk/legal/d_to_g/extreme_pornography/#an06b.

96 *R. v Walsh (Simon)* unreported August 8, 2012 (Crown Ct (Kingston)).

97 Ibid.

98 S. Foster 'Possession of extreme pornographic images, public protection and human rights'.

99 The offence could conceivably cause problems for the broadcast media where sexual interference with vampires and other denizens of the undead are not uncommon in fiction and the BBC asked for clarification of what sexual interference meant here.

100 McGlynn and Rackley *Criminalising Extreme Pornography: Lessons from England & Wales.*

101 *The Telegraph* (online edition) December 31, 2009.

102 [1994] 1 AC 212.

103 Liberty *Response to the Home Office Consultation Paper on the Possession of Extreme Pornographic Material* London: Liberty (2005). Accessible at https://www.liberty-human-rights.org.uk/sites/default/files/extreme-pornographic-material-ho-consultation.pdf.

104 Home Office *Consultation on Possession of Non-photographic Visual Depictions of Child Sexual Abuse* Home Office: London (2007).

105 For example see the discussion in S. Ost 'Criminalising fabricated images of child pornography: a matter of harm or morality?' *Legal Studies* (2010) 30(2) pp. 230–256.

106 Ministry of Justice/Northern Ireland Office 'Consultation on the Possession of non-photographic visual depictions of child sexual abuse: summary of responses and next steps' (2008). Joint Committee on Human Rights, *Legislative Scrutiny: CAJB, Eight Report of Session 2008–9* London: The Stationary Office (2009) para 1.172.

107 *R. v Arthur Alan Murray* [2004] EWCA Crim 2211.

108 For further discussion see A. Antoniou 'Possession of prohibited images of children: three years on' *Journal of Criminal Law* (2013) 77(4) pp. 337–353.

109 *Connectivity, Content and Consumers. Britain's Digital Platform for Growth* (2013).

Chapter 8

Prostitution

Introduction

Prostitution is often referred to as "the oldest profession". This reflects the belief that it has always been with us and probably always will. However, despite its continuing presence the law has generally sought to control it, even if total eradication seems unattainable. Prostitution itself, i.e. selling sex, is not illegal in England and Wales. However, many activities associated with prostitution are controlled by the criminal law.

Although prostitutes may be male or female, the majority of street prostitutes are female and the majority of clients male. Therefore, throughout this chapter, prostitutes will sometimes be referred to as female and clients as male, though it is acknowledged that this does not reflect the whole picture and the law is now gender neutral. Sex workers will be referred to as prostitutes throughout the chapter as, although 'sex worker' is the preferred term in the industry, our legal system continues to use the term 'prostitute'.

There are many problems associated with prostitution that make control desirable. Firstly, there is often a deep moral objection to the idea of someone selling their body for sex. For many religions, selling sex is not acceptable and even those who profess no religion may have a deeply held view that the practice is immoral, as it devalues intimate relationships and reduces them to the level of a commercial transaction.

For many feminists, tolerance of prostitution undermines the position of women in society and serves to strengthen the control of men over women's bodies. For example, The Poppy Project, a project that aims to help women to leave prostitution, is managed by the feminist Eaves organization, which is concerned with the issues of domestic abuse, sexual violence and exploitation of women.[1] Their vision is to promote a society in which all women live free from violence, exploitation, objectification and discrimination. Their commitment to end trafficking and prostitution is based on the idea that these activities maintain gender inequality.

For members of the public, prostitution may be a question of nuisance. Prostitutes can cause a nuisance by being on the street late at night and their clients may increase traffic nuisance. Arguments involving prostitutes and their pimps may cause disturbance. Young women living in an area affected by prostitution may feel threatened and insulted by approaches from kerb crawlers. There may be issues of used condoms being left in the street and prostitutes visibly operating in residential areas may reduce the value of adjoining properties.

There is also concern amongst some about the effect on children and young people seeing prostitutes operate in the street. This may encourage children to think about sex in a way that society does not feel appropriate, or even encourage them to think about prostitution themselves as a viable financial option. Most seriously, the abuse of children through prostitution, often by gangs who groom vulnerable individuals for sex, has attracted growing attention as the scale of the problem has become clear from investigations in Rotherham, Peterborough and several other cities.[2]

There are links between prostitution and drug use and with other criminal activities. As many activities associated with prostitution are illegal, the trade attracts individuals who are also involved in other illegal activities, such as trafficking or drug dealing.[3]

There is also the issue of the spread of sexually transmitted diseases by prostitutes and their clients, who may not use adequate protection and the historical concerns with this issue have already been dealt with in Chapter 2.

Finally, there is the serious issue of violence against the prostitutes themselves. Working on the street can be dangerous. This is illustrated by the murder of five prostitutes around Ipswich in 2006 by Steve Wright, a fork-lift truck driver who was an habitual user of prostitutes in the area. He was found guilty of their murder and sentenced to life imprisonment in 2008.[4] Prostitutes may also be subjected to violence by their pimps, who may use violence to control them. Often these attacks go unreported, as prostitutes are understandably reluctant to contact the police. It is this element of exploitation of prostitutes that some of the offences considered below aim to address.

Why do People Become Involved in Prostitution?

There appear to be many reasons why someone becomes a prostitute and there have been numerous studies on this issue.[5] The most obvious reason is financial. Poverty, combined with a lack of education or skills, may make prostitution the only option for some. However, it was noted in the consultation document *Paying the Price*[6] (considered further below) that many prostitutes had difficult childhood histories, which may have included time in care, subjection to violence and sexual and other abuse. These experiences may not only make them more vulnerable to exploitation by others but also may affect their own self-worth and attitudes towards sex in general. Others may have drug and alcohol problems and sex work can be an immediate source of cash that helps feed their addiction.

Children who run away from home are particularly vulnerable to exploitation from others, as are children with difficult family backgrounds, or with learning disabilities. Often such young people are groomed by those who firstly pretend to help them, and perhaps persuade them that they are their 'boyfriend' before going on to force them into prostitution. For example, in January 2014 a gang of men and boys were convicted of sexually abusing teenage girls in Peterborough. They befriended vulnerable girls, giving them gifts of money, drugs and alcohol, initially acting as if they were their boyfriends but leading on to the use of violence and abuse and prostitution.[7]

There are those who say that they choose prostitution as a profession. There are no statistics to suggest what proportion of prostitutes fall into this category. These prostitutes tend to be those who work in the higher end of the trade (perhaps as escorts), operating alone without any control by a pimp and who may earn a good salary from their work. However, it seems that these are in the minority with the vast majority of women who become involved in prostitution being poor and disadvantaged.[8] The Crown Prosecution Service (CPS) acknowledges this, making charging decisions subject to additional considerations, with a strong focus on welfare:

- to encourage prostitutes to find routes out of prostitution and to deter those who create the demand for it;
- to keep prostitutes off the street to prevent annoyance to members of the public;
- to prevent people leading or forcing others into prostitution;
- to penalize those who organize prostitutes and make a living from their earnings;
- generally the more serious the incident the more likely that a prosecution will be required;
- the age of the prostitute and the position of those living off the earnings will clearly be relevant.[9]

Although we have a wealth of research on prostitutes there has been less research done on why those who control prostitutes go into the sex business. *Paying the Price* noted that the reasons for becoming a pimp included a deliberate choice for some, for financial reasons, with others who grew up in areas where prostitution was common believing that they had no choice. The majority had a history of drug abuse and they also tended to be involved in other criminal activity, including firearms offences. However, it was also noted that although the 'classic pimp' continues to exist, the boyfriend with a serious addiction who pimps his girlfriend to fund his habit is becoming more common.[10]

The diverse reasons for entering prostitution are a challenge for the legal system, which must find a balance between protecting and helping the vulnerable to leave prostitution and punishing those who exploit them.

Feminist Attitudes Towards Prostitution

Firstly, it must be said that there is no one feminist view on prostitution. There has been significant debate on the subject amongst feminist writers and so this section is a very brief overview and necessarily simplistic. There are broadly two schools of thought: those who oppose any acceptance of prostitution and those who are in favour of some legalization, though with adequate controls to protect women from abuse.[11]

More radical feminists such as Catherine MacKinnon and Andrea Dworkin[12] have viewed prostitution as a form of violence against women, arguing women are compelled by social and economic circumstances into prostitution and so it can never be regarded as consensual sex. Rather it is more a form of sexual slavery with the buying and selling of sex being linked to male power over women, reflecting the inherent patriarchal nature of society. The female body is treated as a commodity, further contributing to the objectification and devaluation of women in society.[13] Julie Bindel, writer and feminist campaigner, challenges the idea that prostitution should be accepted because it has been with us for a long time, pointing out that so have poverty and racism but we do not accept that they are here to stay. In addition, prostitution can never be safe for women and those who work in prostitution will always be stigmatized. Seen in this light, society should be working towards eradicating prostitution by targeting pimps, traffickers and customers and also by giving women proper alternatives to selling their bodies.[14]

On the other hand, there are those who approach the subject of prostitution from the point of view of a woman's right to do what she chooses with her own body and be paid for it. This view sees sex work as empowering for those women who are not controlled by others and who are able to make a living from their choice of work. The way the law targets women involved in prostitution is viewed as an attack on their autonomy, their freedom of choice and their economic and social equality. The emphasis here is on protecting such women from the effects of criminalization and from exploitation by others. This approach is perhaps best illustrated by the work of prostitutes' rights groups such as the English Collective of Prostitutes, a campaigning group that is part of the International Prostitutes Collective. Their stated aims include decriminalization of street prostitution and brothels, better protection from violence, self-determination (with sex workers deciding how they want to work) and employment rights for sex workers, such as the right to join a pension scheme, or the provision of childcare and the right to freedom of movement within and between countries. They are also opposed to the criminalizing of clients, as consenting sex between adults should not be criminal, but also support better resources for those who wish to leave the industry.[15]

Despite these fundamental differences in attitude amongst feminist groups, there does seem to be some agreement on two main issues, i.e. that legal sanctions against prostitutes themselves are disproportionately harsh (or even unnecessary) and that more needs to be done to protect sex workers from violence and exploitation.[16]

Development of the Law

The modern history of the law on prostitution really starts with the Wolfenden Report 1957.[17] As Chapter 2 outlined, the report came to the conclusion that prostitution could not and should not be completely eradicated through the agency of the criminal law as the law should not be concerned with private sexual morality. As a result the law has largely concentrated on managing the public nuisance caused by prostitutes and their clients. The offences of soliciting in the Street Offences Act 1959 and of managing a brothel in section 33 of the Sexual Offences Act 1956 were some of the resulting statutory provisions.

However, many of the laws relating to prostitution had become outdated and ineffective. The Sexual Offences Act 2003 (SOA 2003) therefore began a process of reform by addressing concerns about trafficking and by introducing new offences relating to children and harsher penalties for those who exploit anyone for the purposes of prostitution.

In 2004 the Government published a consultation document on prostitution called *Paying the Price*,[18] which considered a number of different options. The first option was to consider shifting the focus of the law onto users of prostitutes, rather than the prostitutes themselves. The Swedish model (discussed below) was examined, but it was pointed out that there were several problems with following this approach in England and Wales. For example, the scale of street-based prostitution is limited in Sweden and there is also less Class A drug abuse found among Swedish street prostitutes, an issue that is a significant problem in our jurisdiction.[19]

Next the idea of managed areas for prostitution was considered.[20] This would involve identifying particular areas where prostitutes and their clients are permitted to trade legally, whilst being monitored by the police and provided with health and other support facilities. The most well-known example of this approach is in the Netherlands, particularly the red light district of Amsterdam. However, it was noted that managing such areas could be highly resource intensive and contentious. One of the most difficult problems would be where such areas would be located in the England and Wales, bearing in mind the likely effect on the local business or residential communities.

As street-based prostitution was regarded as the most problematic part of the sex trade, the report also considered the possibility of licensing brothels.[21] A number of different schemes were examined, including those of the Netherlands, Austria and some of the Australian states. The arguments for and against the legalization and licensing of brothels are discussed further below in the section on brothels. However, the report stated that experience in some of these jurisdictions suggests that licensing schemes have failed to deliver the promised benefits, such as a safe working environment and lower organized crime associated with prostitution. In addition, in Australia the licensing of brothels did not reduce the amount of street prostitution.[22]

The final model considered was the registration of prostitutes (as happens in Austria, for example).[23] One of the objectives of a registration system is to ensure that sex workers are regularly checked for sexually transmitted diseases or drug use. However, experience in some countries (such as Greece and Germany) showed that most prostitutes simply did not register.

Following the consultation period, in 2006 the Home Office produced *A Coordinated Prostitution Strategy*, which concentrated on five main issues:

1. prevention – awareness raising, prevention and early intervention measures to stop individuals, particularly children and young people, from becoming involved in prostitution;
2. tackling demand – responding to community concerns by deterring those who create the demand and removing the opportunity for street prostitution to take place;
3. developing routes out – proactively engaging with those involved in prostitution to provide a range of support and advocacy services to help them leave prostitution;
4. ensuring justice – bringing to justice those who exploit individuals through prostitution, and those who commit violent and sexual offences against those involved in prostitution;
5. tackling off-street prostitution – targeting commercial sexual exploitation, in particular where victims are young or have been trafficked.

In addition, in 2008 the Home Office minister, Vernon Coaker, led a visit to Sweden (where buying sex is illegal but selling sex is not) and other countries to see how the problem was being tackled elsewhere. The resulting report, *Tackling Demand for Prostitution*,[24] led to the changes brought about by the Policing and Crime Act 2009.

The Swedish model

In 1999, Sweden criminalized the purchase of sex and de-criminalized the selling of sex, in an attempt to target demand and therefore reduce prostitution. Norway and Iceland also have similar systems. At first, it seemed that the law was effective, with fewer men reported purchasing sex and street prostitutes less visible in the main cities. In February 2014 the European Parliament approved a resolution by the British MEP, Mary Honeyball, calling for the Swedish model to be adopted throughout the continent. Though this is not legally binding, it was hoped by the European Parliament's Womens' Rights and Gender Equality Committee that it would influence other European states to follow the Swedish model and Northern Ireland has since criminalized the purchase of sex.[25] However, there have been some serious criticisms of the claim that the Swedish approach has reduced prostitution. For example, Jay Levy argues that there is no convincing evidence that overall levels of prostitution have declined since 1999. The apparent reduction in street prostitution merely reflects a change in the way sex is bought and sold, through the use of the internet and mobile phones. There are also concerns that the trade has simply gone further underground, with the consequence that prostitutes are even more at risk of violence and exploitation.[26] It was these concerns that persuaded the Government not to follow the Swedish model in our jurisdiction (though a new offence of "paying for the sexual services of a prostitute subjected to force" was introduced).

Despite the resolution of the European Parliament there does not appear to be a uniform policy across Europe in relation to prostitution at present. Some countries operate a system of licensed brothels, whereas others do not and some criminalize soliciting by prostitutes whereas others only penalize the purchase of sex.

In England and Wales, the culmination of all this activity was the Policing and Crime Act 2009, which amended existing legislation, and introduced the offence of paying for the sexual services of a prostitute subjected to force. The details of the legislation are considered below and reflect the overall aim of the Government, which was to seek to tighten up the law in relation to those controlling prostitution and to some extent to change the emphasis from the prostitute to the offender, in the belief that tackling demand for prostitution might lead to a reduction in the overall availability of sex for sale. It also illustrates a willingness to see prostitutes as victims of abuse and exploitation, rather than just offenders.

The Law

Prostitution, i.e. selling sex, is not in itself illegal. However, someone who is engaged in the sex industry could be guilty of a number of offences that are associated with it and that are considered below.

The meaning of "prostitute"

For the purposes of the SOA 2003, the word "prostitute" is defined in section 51(2). It means a person who, on at least one occasion and whether or not compelled do so, offers or provides sexual services to another person in return for payment. The payment could be to the prostitute themselves, or to another person, such as a pimp. "Payment" is widely defined to include the discharge of a debt or the provision of goods and services (including sexual services) gratuitously or at a discount (s54 SOA 2003). This could, for example, include providing drugs or alcohol to the prostitute or the person who manages her.

Soliciting in the street

The offence of soliciting is set out in section 1 of the Street Offences Act 1959, as amended by the SOA 2003 and the Policing and Crime Act 2009. Prior to those amendments, the 1959 Act made it an offence for a common prostitute to loiter or solicit in a street or public place for the purpose of prostitution. It might be thought the use of the word "common" in the 1959 Act was merely a moral judgement on the prostitute and there is some discussion of this in Chapter 2. However, the term did have a legal meaning. In *Morris-Lowe* (1985)[27] the court held that the word "common" meant that a single act of prostitution was not sufficient; there had to be an element of persistence for the offence to be committed. The word "prostitute" had also been considered in case law. In the case of *DPP v Bull* (1994)[28] the court concluded that only a woman could be guilty of soliciting in the street as the term "prostitute" was limited to females. The court's decision was based on the idea that the mischief the Street Offences Act 1959 intended to remedy was a mischief created by women. This judgement seemed to completely disregard the nuisance that may be caused by kerb crawlers, who it is suggested may cause at least at much nuisance to local residents and the general public as the prostitutes themselves. In addition, it completely disregarded the possibility of male prostitutes, who may be in the minority but do exist and should not be excluded from the possibility of conviction merely on grounds of their gender.

These issues resulted in a number of amendments to the offence of soliciting, firstly by the SOA 2003, which made clear that a prostitute could be male or female, and secondly by the Policing and Crime Act 2009, which removed the term "common prostitute" and replaced it with the term "persistently". The section now therefore reads:

> It shall be an offence for a person (whether male or female) persistently to loiter or solicit in a street or public place for the purposes of prostitution.

Conduct is persistent if it takes place on two or more occasions in any period of three months.[29] This definition of persistence has been criticized by the English Collective of Prostitutes as follows:

> Soliciting which takes place more than one in three months cannot be described as persistent and could more appropriately be called "occasional". To label it as

persistent shows an intention to criminalise. It makes a mockery of the abolition of the term common prostitute . . . as it will bring no reduction in the number of women arrested.[30]

It should be noted that the prostitute has merely to loiter, not actively solicit, to be guilty of the offence. The *mens rea* is in the purpose of the loitering, although as *Knight v Fryer* (1976)[31] made clear that purpose can be inferred from the circumstances.

The meaning of "street"

"Street" is widely defined and includes any bridge, road, lane, footway, subway, square, court, alley or passage which is open to the public. Doorways and entrances of premises that adjoin the street are also treated as part of the street.[32]

In *Behrendt v Burridge* (1976)[33] it was held that a woman who sat motionless in a window on a high stool illuminated by a red light was soliciting even though she was not physically in the street. She was soliciting in the sense that she was tempting or alluring passers-by to come in for the purposes of prostitution. However, putting adverts in shop windows is not soliciting. This was confirmed in *Weisz v Monahan* (1962)[34] where the court made clear that soliciting involves the physical presence of the prostitute. On the other hand, placing an advertisement relating to prostitution in or near a public phone box *is* an offence under the Criminal Justice and Police Act 2001, section 46.[35] There is no prohibition on placing adverts in the newspaper, although regulatory agencies caution against this.

Penalties for soliciting in the street

Until the Policing and Crime Act 2009 the penalty for soliciting was limited to a fine, not exceeding level 3 on the standard scale. This prompted the criticism that it made it more difficult for women to leave prostitution, in that the only way most of them could afford to pay the fine was to go back on to the street to earn the money. There is now an alternative penalty, which is a rehabilitative order designed to encourage prostitutes to find a way out of prostitution. The court is now able to make an order requiring the offender to attend a series of meetings with a named supervisor, to address the reasons for their prostitution and to explore ways of ending that involvement.[36] Breach of such an order is not a criminal offence, but if breached the Magistrates' Court can revoke the order and impose a fine instead. If the long-term goal is to reduce the number of women involved in prostitution, then the introduction of alternative penalties that seek to help, rather that punish, the offender, should be encouraged.

Kerb Crawling

Until the 1980s, the law on soliciting concentrated on the prostitute rather than the customer. However, it was becoming clear that the nuisance caused by those who were seeking prostitutes was as much of a problem as the prostitutes themselves.

The phrase "kerb crawling" is not used anywhere in the relevant legislation, which refers to "soliciting in a street or public place for the purposes of obtaining the sexual services of a prostitute". However, the term is used here to distinguish it from the offence of soliciting in section 1 of the Street Offences Act 1959 considered above. Again the *mens rea* for the offence looks to the purpose of the solicitation.

The original kerb-crawling offences contained in the Sexual Offences Act 1985 could only be committed by a man and prohibited soliciting another person for the purpose of prostitution in a public place (which could be from a vehicle or not). However, there were some problems with the offences. The main criticism was that to be guilty of the offence the man had to solicit persistently or in such manner as is likely to cause annoyance or nuisance. This was illustrated in the case of *Darroch v DPP* (1990),[37] which concerned an appeal from a man who was convicted after he was seen driving around a known red light district and beckoning a prostitute on one occasion. On appeal, his conviction was quashed because one invitation to a prostitute could not constitute persistent soliciting. This made the job of the police particularly difficult in that they would have to show persistence even if it was quite obvious what the intention of the kerb crawler was.

These offences have now been completely replaced by section 51A of the SOA 2003 (a section that was added by the Policing and Crime Act 2009). It is now an offence for any person in a street or public place to solicit another (B) for the purpose of obtaining B's sexual services as a prostitute. This includes soliciting from a vehicle but soliciting without a vehicle is equally an offence. "Street" has the same meaning as it does in section 1(4) of the Street Offences Act 1959, discussed above. There is now no need for persistence and no need to cause annoyance or nuisance. This means that someone who is soliciting for a prostitute can be found guilty even if it was the first occasion they had done this. It can be seen that this alters the emphasis from the prostitute to the customer. However, this may actually make the life of a prostitute more difficult in that she feels she has less time to make a judgement about a potential client and so may put herself in a risky situation in order to avoid the possibility of her client being arrested. It also encourages prostitutes to work in more secluded areas, which may also be more dangerous for them.

The penalty for this offence is a fine only, not exceeding level 3 on the standard scale. This may not be a sufficient deterrent for some and has led to some police forces experimenting with other solutions, such as publishing the pictures of men seen kerb crawling in local newspapers. It is also possible for a court to disqualify a kerb crawler from driving in appropriate cases.[38]

Causing or Inciting Prostitution and Controlling Prostitution for Gain

The SOA 2003 introduced two new offences relating to exploitation of prostitutes, which replaced some outdated offences originally enacted in 1956. These offences are clearly aimed at those who aim to gain financial reward from the exploitation of others. Section 52 provides that a person commits an offence if he intentionally causes or incites another person to become a prostitute in any part of the world and he does so for, or in the expectation of, gain for himself or a third person. The *mens rea* is quite is quite specific here in that there must be an intention to cause or incite and s/he must be doing this for gain. The maximum penalty is 7 years' imprisonment. The offence is intended to apply to those who recruit others into prostitution, whether by force or mere persuasion.

Section 53 provides that a person commits an offence if he intentionally controls any of the activities of another person relating to that person's prostitution in any part of the world and he does so for, or in the expectation of, gain for himself or a third person. The *mens rea* then requires an intention to control and make a gain. Again, the maximum penalty is 7 years' imprisonment. "Control" is not defined in the Act but the Explanatory Notes suggest that "requires or directs" would be caught by the term,[39] for example requiring a prostitute to charge a certain price or attend certain appointments.

Although the sections do not specify this, both are aimed at adult prostitutes as there are completely separate offences relating to children, which will be discussed below. The offences are gender neutral (unlike the old provisions they replaced) so both men and women can be guilty of these two offences.

The meaning of "gain"

It is an essential element of both the offences that the defendant intends to make some gain from the prostitute. Gain is defined quite widely in section 54 and covers any financial advantage, including the provision of goods or services (including sexual services) or the goodwill of any person that is likely to result in financial advantage in the future. It is therefore clear that gain does not only relate to monetary gain. Someone who received sexual favours from prostitutes he controls would be receiving gain. Providing sexual services to a third party who later supplies drugs at a discount would also be within the definition.

Paying for the Sexual Services of a Prostitute who is Subjected to Force

Section 53A was added to the SOA 2003 by the Policing and Crime Act 2009. Its aim is to target men who use prostitutes who have been trafficked or forced into prostitution and illustrates the change in attitude towards reducing the demand for prostitution rather than merely punishing the prostitute. A person commits an offence if they pay or promise to pay for the sexual services of a prostitute and a third person has engaged in exploitative conduct towards that prostitute in the expectation of gain. This is the first time we have had an offence that criminalizes paying for sexual services with an adult.

Although the heading of the section refers to force, the actual wording refers to "exploitative conduct" and this is defined as using force, threats (whether or not relating to violence) or any other form of coercion, or deception.[40] This is clearly wider than force and could cover the situation where a woman has been promised work in a bar, for example, but this work turns out to be prostitution. The sexual services can be provided anywhere in the world.

The offence is a strict liability offence with an absence of any *mens rea* require-ment. Section 53A(2) specifically states that it is irrelevant whether the defend-ant is, or ought to be, aware that the prostitute has been subjected to exploitative conduct. This raises the question of whether a customer would be able to tell if a prostitute had been subjected to exploitation, but lack of knowledge, even if reason-able, is not a defence. This subsection has received a lot of criticism as it effectively deprives the defendant of any defence to a charge under the section.[41] On the other hand, it has been criticized for not going far enough, in that a woman who is sub-jected to force cannot be truly consenting and there is an argument that the customer ought to be charged with rape or sexual assault, rather than under section 53A. The penalty for paying for the sexual services of a prostitute who is subjected to force is a fine only, whereas the penalty for rape could be up to life imprisonment.

Interestingly the CPS suggest that this offence should be used "most often" for off-street prostitution.[42] The CPS will then be largely reserving this offence to charge those frequenting brothels where the women are exploited – and most likely – trafficked. There is some evidence that the offence is hardly being used by the police.[43]

Brothels

The offence of keeping a brothel is contained in sections 33 and 33A of the Sexual Offences Act 1956 (as amended by the SOA 2003). It is an offence for a person to keep, or to manage, or act or assist in the management of a brothel to which people resort for practices involving prostitution. Although there are no explicit *mens rea* terms in the offence there must be knowledge that what is being managed etc. is a brothel.[44] Prostitution has the same meaning as that given in section 51(2) SOA 2003.

It has long been established that premises are not a brothel if used by only one prostitute,[45] though when a building has one common entrance but is divided into separate flats used by prostitutes, then the building as a whole can constitute a brothel.[46] This effectively means that it may be possible for a prostitute to act legally on her own, but she cannot work with other women, whether for mutual protection or convenience, without falling foul of this offence.

It appears that management of a brothel must involve taking an active part; menial or routine duties may not be enough.[47] This has resulted in some prostitutes employing 'maids' whose duties may not be sufficient for a prosecution. Whether a maid is prosecuted will depend on the nature of those duties. Minor assistance, such as cleaning and tidying and answering the door, may not be enough for the CPS to decide to prosecute; but someone who actively manages premises or is involved in taking telephone calls from customers and making appointments may well be prosecuted.

The maximum penalty for this offence is 7 years' imprisonment. However, the Policing and Crime Act 2009[48] introduced a new remedy into the SOA 2003, granting the courts power to close premises used for certain offences, which include causing or inciting prostitution for gain and controlling prostitution for gain. Ser-vice of a closure notice by the police prevents anyone from entering or remaining on the premises until a Magistrates' Court decides whether to make a closure order. The court can make a closure order for up to 3 months, though this can be extended to 6 months in total. The Association of Chief Police Officers welcomed this new power, as previously the police were powerless to close down establishments that were causing nuisance or harm to neighbours. However, this new power can be criticized as it effectively forces women in the sex trade to go back on to the street, the most dangerous environment for sex workers.

Arguments for the legalization of brothels

One approach to the problems associated with prostitution, especially street prostitution, is to consider the legalization of brothels. A licensing system for brothels is in operation in some European countries, most famously in the Netherlands, where the "red light" district of Amsterdam is a well-known tourist attraction. Legal brothels also operate in some parts of Australia, New Zealand and in the US state of Nevada.[49]

Supporters of legalization point to a number of advantages of such a system. Firstly, legal brothels would keep prostitution off the streets, thus minimizing the nuisance element of prostitution to local residents. They would provide a safer environment for prostitutes to work in, offering the opportunity to work with others, or with security staff who could protect the prostitutes from violence from customers. Prostitutes could be required to undergo regular health checks and customers to comply with health and safety requirements, such as using condoms. Those working in brothels would be required to prove that they are over a certain age, say 18 years, and would also pay tax and national insurance in the same way as other employees.[50] Paying tax may sound like a disadvantage to the prostitute, in that their income may decrease, but in some ways it is an advantage because a prostitute would be able to show proof of her income in order to get a mortgage loan, could pay into a pension scheme and receive sick pay when unable to work. A sex worker would therefore have a legal and acceptable way to earn a living. Another important argument for legalization is that a licensing system for brothels would take the control of the business away from criminals, thus breaking the link with other criminal activities, such as drug dealing. It is suggested that licensing would also free prostitutes from the violence and exploitation they experience from their own pimps.

Unfortunately, there is some evidence from the Netherlands that organized crime associated with prostitution may have actually increased following the legalization of brothels. In both Australia and Europe there are suggestions that while some licensed brothels do provide a safe, acceptable working environment, others do not, with some managers encouraging sex without condoms and threatening dismissal if a prostitute does not comply with a client's wishes.[51] There is also the issue that those with a drug or alcohol problem would not be employed in legal brothels and so would continue to work on the street. This would also apply to those who could not pass the required health examinations. The result would be a two-tier system, which would not solve the problems of street prostitution or exploitation of the vulnerable. On the other hand, it would allow the police to concentrate on the illegal side of the business, while leaving those who are operating legally to continue their profession. There is also the issue of where legal brothels would be situated. In Australia they are often in industrial estates or business parks, whereas in Amsterdam, the red light district is in the city centre. Most people in this country would probably not be happy living next to a brothel, so residential areas would not be appropriate. Finally, there is the question of whether we, as a society, should encourage people into prostitution. A legalized brothel system would send a strong message that sex work is morally and socially acceptable, encouraging young people to consider it as an appropriate career choice. To put it bluntly, should the State as a matter of policy become a legal pimp?[52]

Many of these arguments were considered by the Government in the consultation paper on sexual offences *Setting the Boundaries*, but it was concluded that there was no consensus about the legalization of brothels across a wide range of opinions.[53] However, in 2006, the Government did suggest that the law would be amended to allow two or three prostitutes to work together legally in small brothels.[54] This was an attempt to address the issue of women working together for reasons of safety but the suggestion was heavily criticized in the press and it was quietly dropped.

Children and Prostitution

According to the consultation document *Paying the Price*, around half of street prostitutes in Britain began their involvement in prostitution before their 18th birthday, with some studies suggesting as many as 75 per cent did so.[55] Originally, the offence of soliciting in the street for the purpose of prostitution was not restricted to adults; thus children who had reached the age of criminal capacity (10 years) could have been prosecuted for this offence, even though they may not have reached the age of consent. However, the emphasis for some years has been on treating a child involved in prostitution more as a victim rather than an offender. The CPS guidance on prosecuting the prostitution offences did make clear that children under 18 involved in prostitution should be treated as victims of abuse and that the focus should be on those who exploit and coerce children.[56] However, this did not mean that child prostitutes would never be charged as the policy went on to state:

> Only where there is a persistent and voluntary return to prostitution, and where there is a genuine choice, should a prosecution be considered. It will be need to be borne in mind whether there was a genuine choice available to the child. The police should not issue children involved in prostitution with a warning or caution but remove them to a place of safety.[57]

Bearing in mind the ways that children enter prostitution, often through exploitation, abuse or even financial need, this did beg the question of whether a child involved in prostitution should ever be considered to have a genuine choice, or whether instead they should always be treated as vulnerable victims of abuse. As a result of this concern, the Serious Crime Act 2015 made a number of changes to the law, the most important being that section 1 of the Street Offences Act 1959 has now been amended to make clear that an offender must be aged 18 or over. This came into force in May 2015 and so children can no longer be charged with soliciting for the purposes of prostitution. The aim was to recognize that children are victims rather than consenting participants.

There are a number of offences available to prosecute those who sexually exploit children. Some of them mirror the offences relating to adults discussed above, but the penalties are generally more severe, and there are some offences that relate specifically to children.

It is important to realize that a child for the purpose of these offences is someone under the age of 18, not 16. It is equally important to note that consent is not a defence to any of these offences. Although a young person may consent to sex at 16, they are not able to consent to sexual activity in the context of prostitution.

The offences explained below were amended by the Serious Crime Act 2015, mainly to remove any wording that referred to a child being involved in prostitution, substituting the wording "sexual exploitation" instead. It has become increasingly evident post the inquiries into grooming discussed in earlier chapters that children are being targeted and coerced into providing sexual services[58] and the amendment goes some way toward recognizing this.

Paying for the sexual services of a child

This offence was introduced for the first time by the SOA 2003. Section 47 makes it an offence to pay for or promise payment for the sexual services of a child. There is an excuse of reasonable belief that the child is over 18 but this does not apply where the child is under 13.

The offence relates to the *payment* for the sexual services, so no actual sexual activity needs to have taken place and, if it does, the offences at sections 5–12 are of course available. The payment does not need to be made to the child; it could be to a third person who, for example, is controlling or inciting the child into prostitution. It is sufficient that a promise to pay is made, so no proof that actual payment was made is necessary.

Payment is widely defined in section 47(2) and means any financial advantage, including the discharge of a debt or the provisions of goods and services (including sexual services) gratuitously or at a discount. This could, for example, be the provision of alcohol or drugs or other gifts. Although the section is aimed at protecting children involved in prostitution, the section does not mention the word "prostitute" but merely focusses on payment. It is therefore clear that someone could be guilty of this offence if the child is not actually a prostitute but is paid or offered money or gifts for sexual services on a one-off basis.

The penalty for this offence depends on the nature of the sexual activity and the age of the child. Where penetrative acts with a child under 13 are involved, the maximum penalty is life imprisonment. Whereas, if the child is between 13 and 16 years old and there are penetrative acts involved the maximum penalty is 14 years. Where the child is over 16 the maximum is 7 years' imprisonment.

Causing or inciting sexual exploitation of a child

Section 48 makes it an offence for a person to intentionally cause or incite a child to be sexually exploited in any part of the world. As at sections 8 and 10 SOA 2003, causing requires that the exploitation takes place and that a causal link is established; incitement only requires an encouragement to engage in a sexual activity. For example in *Khan* (2015) two 15-year-old girls were picked up in a car by Khan and his co-defendant and driven around while Khan suggested they came to work in his brothel; this was held to be incitement.[59] Again, to be guilty of the offence, it must be shown that the defendant did not reasonably believe that the child was 18 years or over, or that the child was under 13. The defendant must also intend to cause or incite the activity. Although this offence is similar to the one relating to adults in section 52 SOA 2003, in this case there is no requirement that the person who is inciting the child is motivated by gain. The mere action of causing or inciting the child is sufficient.

The penalty for this offence is a maximum of 14 years' imprisonment, which is significantly higher than the offence relating to adults (which has a maximum penalty of 7 years' imprisonment). This obviously reflects the seriousness of encouraging children and young people into prostitution.

Controlling a child in relation to sexual exploitation

The offence is contained in section 49 SOA 2003 and is similar to the offence relating to adults in section 53. A person commits this offence if he controls the activities of the child relating to the child's sexual exploitation anywhere in the world. "Control" is not defined in the Act but the Explanatory Notes suggest that "requires or directs" would be caught by the term – for example, requiring a child to charge a certain price or attend certain appointments. It is suggested though that the actions required to control a child may be less than those required to control an adult as children are more easily persuaded, so a wide definition of the word ought to be adopted in relation to children.

The excuse of reasonable belief that the child is over 18 again applies and the penalty is a maximum of 14 years' imprisonment.

Arranging or facilitating sexual exploitation of a child

Most of the elements of this offence are similar to those referred to above in relation to sections 48 and 49. Section 50 makes it an offence to intentionally arrange or facilitate the sexual exploitation of a child in any part of the world. This offence does not have an equivalent relating to adults. It is meant to cover people who have not gone as far as controlling a child but nevertheless have in some way aided the child's sexual exploitation. The sort of behaviour this could include would be to make arrangements for someone to meet the child, such as booking hotel rooms, or travel. The maximum penalty is 14 years' imprisonment.

The meaning of sexual exploitation

For the purposes of sections 48–50, a child is sexually exploited if:

(a) on at least one occasion and whether or not compelled to do so, they offer or provide sexual services to another person in return for payment or promise of payment (either to the child or to a third person); or
(b) an indecent image of the child is recorded.[60]

This definition acknowledges the connection between child prostitution and pornography and the issues relating to child pornography have been dealt with in Chapter 7.

Trafficking People for Sexual Exploitation

It is obvious that there is some connection between trafficking and sexual exploitation. The exact figures of people who are trafficked for sexual exploitation are extremely difficult to establish[61] but it is clear that children as well as adults are trafficked.[62] Victims may be brought into the country illegally, abused, threatened and kept isolated in order to provide sexual services for profit. Sometimes they enter the country legally but are deceived as to the nature of the work they will be expected to do by those who help them to relocate. The problems and issues relating to trafficking are considered fully in Chapter 9 and this chapter has already discussed the offence of paying for the sexual services of a prostitute who is subjected to force (s53A SOA 2003), which is intended to address the issue of those who are unwillingly involved in prostitution.

Specific trafficking offences were introduced in the SOA 2003 but these were repealed and replaced by the Modern Slavery Act 2015. It is now an offence to arrange or facilitate the travel of another person with a view to that person being exploited (which includes sexual exploitation).[63] This will be considered in more detail in Chapter 9. The maximum penalty for this offence is life imprisonment, though it will be seen in Chapter 9 that there are also other penalties the court can impose.

Conclusion

The law in relation to the 'oldest profession' has undergone great changes since the Wolfenden Report was published in 1957. Prostitutes themselves are no longer treated as a homogenous class and developments, in both substantive law and the criminal justice system, have reflected a change in attitude towards prostitutes themselves, with a willingness to see them as vulnerable people in need of help and support rather than merely offenders. The enactment of specific offences in relation to children was a particularly welcome development, as was the shift in emphasis towards treating child prostitutes as victims in the first instance. At the same time, there are now more severe punishments for those who exploit prostitutes, or for the users of prostitutes.

To avoid falling foul of the offences regulating street prostitution, sex workers are increasingly moving online and with this comes the dangers associated with meeting clients in private. Working alone, whether on the streets or in a private residence, is always going to be a risky activity and this is where regulated brothels are seen to be useful. However in this country we have not gone as far as legalizing brothels and there does not appear to be any political will to do so in the future. However, it could be argued that more needs to be done to provide alternatives to those who are trapped in the profession and find it difficult to see a way out.

Notes

1 See their website at www.eavesforwomen.org.uk for further information.

2 See for example A. Jay OBE *Independent Inquiry into Child Sexual Exploitation in Rotherham 1997–2013* (2014). Accessible at http://www.rotherham.gov.uk/downloads/file/1407/independent_inquiry_cse_in_rotherham.

3 G. Hunter, T. May and the Drug Strategy Directorate *Solutions and Strategies: Drug Problems and Street Sex Markets* London: Home Office (2004).

4 See for example, http://news.bbc.co.uk/1/hi/in_depth/uk/2008/suffolk_murders_trial/default.stm.

5 See R. Matthews, *Prostitution, Politics and Policy* Oxon: Routledge-Cavendish (2008) at Chapter 4 for a discussion of the issues and the studies.

6 Home Office *Paying the Price: A Consultation Paper on Prostitution* London: Home Office (2004) Chapter 2.

7 See, for example, J. Welch 'Peterborough sex gang's sophisticated grooming tactics' January 15, 2014. Accessible at www.bbc.co.uk/news/uk-england-cambridgehsire-25659042.

8 R. Matthews *Prostitution, Politics and Policy* Oxon: Routledge-Cavendish (2008) Chapter 4, p. 77.

9 Accessible at http://www.cps.gov.uk/legal/p_to_r/prostitution_and_exploitation_of_prostitution/#a15.

10 See *Paying the Price*, Chapter 2, 2.12.

11 M. O'Neill, *Prostitution and Feminism* Cambridge: Polity Press (2001) pp. 14–16.

12 See for example C. MacKinnnon, *Towards a Feminist Theory of the State* Cambridge, MA: Harvard University Press (1989) and A. Dworkin *Intercourse* New York: Free Press (1987).

13 J. Scoular 'The subject of prostitution. Interpreting the discursive, symbolic and material position of sex work in feminist theory' *Feminist Theory* (2004) 5 p. 343.

14 J. Bindel 'Eradicate the Oldest Profession' *The Guardian*, January 18, 2006. Accessible at http://www.guardian.co.uk/uk/2006/jan/18/ukcrime/prisonsandprobation.

15 http://prostitutescollective.net/1997/03/04//this-is-what-the-international-prostitutes-collective-stands-for.

16 J. Newman and L.A. White *Women Power and Public Policy* Oxford: Oxford University Press (2012) p. 247.

17 HMSO *Report of the Committee on Homosexual Offences and Prostitution* London: Her Majesty's Stationery Office (1957).

18 *Paying the Price*, Chapter 9.

19 *Paying the Price*, para 9.3.

20 *Paying the Price*, para 9.6.

21 *Paying the Price*, para 9.11.

22 *Paying the Price*, para 9.21.

23 *Paying the Price*, para 9.25.

24 Home Office *Tackling Demand for Prostitution: A Review* London: Home Office (2008).

25 Human Trafficking and Exploitation (Criminal Justice and Support for Victims) Act (Northern Ireland) 2015 s15.

26 J. Levy *Swedish Abolitionism as Violence against Women* (2013). Accessible at www.swou.org.

27 [1985] 1 All ER 400.

28 [1994] 4 All ER 411.

29 Street Offences Act 1959 s1(4)(a).

30 English Collective of Prostitutes 'Briefing on the Policing and Crime Bill' (June 2009). Accessible at http://prostitutescollective.net/2009/06/03/briefing-on-the-policing-and-crime-bill-2009–4.

31 [1976] Crim LR 322.

32 Street Offences Act 1959 s1(4)(c).

33 (1976) 63 Cr App R 202.

34 [1962] 1 All ER 664.

35 This section came about as a result of the problem of such advertisements in London, especially near to the Houses of Parliament, which apparently embarrassed and angered MPs and their visitors, as well as tourists.

36 Street Offences Act 1959 s1(2A)–(2D), introduced by the Policing and Crime Act 2009, s17.

37 (1990) 91 Cr App R 378.

38 Powers of Criminal Courts (Sentencing) Act 2000 s146.

39 See also *R. v Massey (Steven John)* [2007] EWCA Crim 2664.

40 Sexual Offences Act 2003 s53A(3).

41 For example see Editorial 'The Policing and Crime Act 2009' *Criminal Law Review* (2010) 2 pp. 91–92. Liberty *Liberty's Second Reading Briefing on the Policing and Crime Bill in the House of Commons* London: Liberty (January 2009). Accessible at https://www.liberty-human-rights.org.uk/sites/default/files/policing-and-crime-2nd-reading-commons.pdf.

42 CPS 'Legal guidance, prostitution and exploitation of prostitution' Accessible at http://www.cps.gov.uk/legal/p_to_r/prostitution_and_exploitation_of_prostitution/#a15.

43 S. Kingston and T. Thomas 'Sex workers and the Policing and Crime Act 2009' *Criminal Law and Justice Weekly* (2014) 178(14) pp. 207–208.

44 See *Sweet v Parsley* [1970] AC 132.

45 *Singleton v Ellison* [1895]1 QB 607.

46 *Durose v Wilson* (1907) 96 LT 645.

47 *Abbott v Smith* [1964] 3 All ER 762.

48 Section 21 and Schedule 2.

49 For an examination of the different models used in other countries, see Chapter 9, *Paying the Price.*

50 Income from prostitution is taxable at the moment, but being a cash business, the income is rarely declared to the tax authorities.

51 *Paying the Price,* para 9.17.

52 See 'A Licence for brothels', Editorial, *New Law Journal* (1996) August 9.

53 Home Office *Setting the Boundaries: Reforming the law on Sex Offences* London: Home Office (2000).

54 Home Office *A Coordinated Prostitution Strategy and a summary of responses to Paying the Price* London: Home Office (2006) Section 5.

55 *Paying the Price,* para 3.1.

56 Accessible at www.cps.gov.uk/legal/p_to_r/prostitution_and_exploitation_of_prostitution/index.html#a18.

57 Accessible at www.cps.gov.uk/legal/p_to_r/prostitution_and_exploitation_of_prostitution/index.html#a18.

58 For example see *R. v Hawthorn* [2015] EWCA Crim 721, where a vulnerable 15-year-old boy was sexually exploited by Hawthorn for gain.

59 *R. v Arslan Khan* [2015] EWCA Crim 831.

60 Sexual Offences Act 2003 s51, as amended by the Serious Crime Act 2015.

61 A. di Nicola 'Researching human trafficking: issues and problems' in M. Lee (ed.) *Human Trafficking* London: Routledge (2012) pp. 49–72; G. Tyldum 'Limitations in research on human trafficking' *International Migration* (2010) 48(5) pp. 1–13.

62 The Trafficking of Children for Sexual Exploitation, ECPAT UK, 2009, www.ecpat.org.uk.

63 Modern Slavery Act 2015 s2.

Chapter 9

The International Perspective

In a global environment it is insufficient to treat sexual offending as something that takes place purely within the limits of our home jurisdiction. Sex offenders may travel to commit offences or offend against citizens in other jurisdictions whilst at home. Not only do we have a duty to protect people in other countries, particularly children, but we also need to discourage dangerous behaviours that could be replicated at home. We also have duties as a signatory to international conventions, including the United Nations Convention on the Rights of the Child and the Protocol to Prevent, Suppress and Punish Trafficking in Persons, Especially Women and Children, to protect children from exploitation and abuse.

Our response to these duties has been to develop offences that have an inherent extra-jurisdictional aspect; to enact offences that allow us to exercise our legal authority beyond our normal boundaries; and to prevent persons becoming victims of crime by virtue of being brought into, or taken out of, the country. As well as these specific offences we also have a number of orders which are preventative in nature and can be used to stop offenders travelling to commit offences.

This chapter then highlights the international aspect to our governance of sexual offending. Most of the offences touched upon below are discussed in depth at other chapters.

Section 72 – Sexual Offences Against Children Committed Outside the United Kingdom

It will come as no surprise that offences concerning children are subject to stringent regulation. Case law has already ensured that legislation that is older than the Sexual Offences Act 2003 (SOA 2003) has been brought up to date to capture offences that have an extra-jurisdictional aspect. For example, offenders can be guilty of child pornography offences even if they view child abuse images that are stored on servers outside our jurisdiction, as this will amount to the making or possession of indecent images of children (see Chapter 7). Equally, sharing such images with persons outside our jurisdiction will amount to an offence.

An extra-jurisdictional offence existed prior to the SOA 2003 at section 1 of the Sexual Offences (Conspiracy and Incitement) Act 1996 which made it an offence to conspire to commit, or incite another person to commit, certain sexual acts against children abroad. There was a serious limitation to this offence, in that the offence had to be one of "dual criminality", so it had to be an offence both in our jurisdiction and in the country where the relevant act took place. Section 72 SOA 2003, as amended by the Criminal Justice and Immigration Act 2008 (CJIA 2008), now makes it possible to prosecute a British citizen for child sex offences committed overseas, regardless of whether the acts are legal in the country in question. It also allows prosecution of a UK *resident* where the act done abroad constitutes an offence in the United Kingdom and is also an offence in that country. The aim is to ensure that those citizens or residents who travel abroad to exploit children will not be able to evade prosecution by travelling to countries whose laws offer less protection to children than our law.

The provisions of section 72 only apply to certain sexual offences, which are mainly those against children, but also some offences that it is possible to commit against adults, but for the purposes of section 72 are committed against persons under the age of 18. A list of these offences is contained in Schedule 2 SOA 2003 (as amended by the CJIA 2008).

The following are the offences to which section 72 applies:

(a) offences under sections 5 to 15 of the SOA 2003 (i.e. the child sex offences that have been discussed in Chapter 4), abuse of position of trust (ss16–19 SOA 2003), the familial child sex offences discussed in Chapter 5 and child exploitation (ss47–50 SOA 2003);

(b) any offence under sections 1–4, 30–41 and 61 (e.g. rape, sexual assault, offences against persons with a mental disorder, or administering a substance with intent) *provided that* the victim of the offence was under 18 at the time of the offence;

(c) an offence under sections 62 or 63 (committing an offence with intent to commit a sexual offence and trespass with intent to commit a sexual offence) *provided that* the intended offence was an offence against a person under 18;

(d) an offence relating to indecent photographs of children under section 1 of the Protection of Children Act 1978 or section 160 Criminal Justice Act 1988 (see Chapter 7).

An attempt, conspiracy or incitement to commit any of these offences would also be an offence, as is aiding, abetting, counselling or procuring such an offence. Note, however, that there is a general defence under section 73 SOA 2003, which provides that a person is not guilty of aiding, abetting or counselling one of these offences where he is acting for one of the following purposes, rather than for sexual gratification:

(a) protecting the child from sexually transmitted infection;
(b) protecting the physical safety of the child;
(c) preventing the child from becoming pregnant; or
(d) promoting the child's emotional well-being by the giving of advice.

As noted above, a UK national can be prosecuted under section 72 if the act done outside the United Kingdom would constitute any of the sexual offences listed in Schedule 2 in England and Wales, even if that act is not an offence in the country in which it is done. A UK national is defined in section 72 and includes someone who is a British citizen, a British overseas citizen, a British overseas territories citizen or a British subject.

A "United Kingdom resident" is simply defined as an individual who is resident in the United Kingdom. In the case of a resident they can only be prosecuted under section 72 if they do something abroad that constitutes an offence under the law in force in that country and would also constitute one of the offences listed in the Schedule if done in England and Wales. A person who becomes a UK national or resident after having committed a relevant offence abroad can also be prosecuted if they are a national or resident at the time the proceedings are brought.

Prosecution problems

Just because it is possible to prosecute for crimes committed abroad it does not mean that it is easy to do so. There needs to be effective co-operation between authorities from different jurisdictions, which may have very different resources, languages and investigative methods. The evidence acquired from the foreign jurisdiction must be admissible and appropriate for our courts and must stand up to the criminal standard of proof in England and Wales. As a result of these difficulties successful convictions under section 72 are rare. An example of a successful prosecution was David Andrew Graham, aged 47, who was sentenced to serve 21 months in prison in 2013 after admitting offences against a boy in Cambodia. He pleaded guilty to offences of sexual activity with a child (s9 SOA 2003) following an investigation that involved a number of Cambodian agencies and the UK's Child Exploitation and Online Protection Centre (CEOP).[1] This was only the second time a successful prosecution had been achieved using section 72.

Although it is the only explicitly extra-jurisdictional offence in the SOA 2003, section 72 is not the only way to effectively criminalize those who commit, or seek to commit, offences against individuals outside of our jurisdiction. There are a number of other provisions that seek to prevent offences taking place globally.

Offences Committed by Offenders in the United Kingdom

Those offences criminalizing sexual activity with children that do not involve physical contact are phrased in such a way that offenders can commit offences against children who are not in the same jurisdiction. The law has been careful to be responsive to changes in technology and communications that allow offenders 'access' to children at a global level. So the offences at section 8 and sections 10–12 of the SOA 2003 are capable of being committed by electronic means, whether by text message, instant messaging or via a webcam. The section 14 offence of arranging or facilitating a child sexual offence makes clear that this could be "in any part of the world" and the section 15 grooming offence only requires D to "travel" to meet the child, and this can include travel to an airport. Likewise, for the offence at section 15A of sexual communication with a child for sexual gratification, there is no requirement that the child is in England or Wales.

Trafficking

Human trafficking is a global problem with many millions of people trafficked by organized criminal gangs for profit. The difficulties of quantifying the amount of trafficking are well known.[2] It is difficult to use traditional forms of data collection when dealing with traffickers and estimates of numbers cannot be assumed to be accurate. However, the lack of accurate information does not mean that we should ignore the problem. Here we are concerned with trafficking for sexual exploitation but – aside from the provisions in the SOA 2003 – much of the modern governance deals with *all* forms of trafficking and modern slavery. Trafficking may not only victimize those persons brought into or out of England and Wales by compelling them to engage in criminal activities, but can leave victims adrift in a country where they may not speak the language and are too scared to approach the authorities. Therefore when offences are committed by these victims you may expect that our legal system would take a measured approach in line with our international obligations.

Our drive to combat trafficking has not merely been driven by national concern but is our obligation as a signatory to the Protocol to Prevent, Suppress and Punish Trafficking in Persons, Especially Women and Children under the UN Convention against Transnational Organised Crime (2000), which is known as the "Palermo Protocol".[3] On a more local level the European Union has taken a lead in ensuring consistency in approach across the member states with the EU Strategy towards the Eradication of Trafficking in Human Beings 2012–16 being the current policy document.[4]

The SOA 2003 had already introduced specific offences of trafficking for sexual exploitation[5] as trafficking was already an issue we had engaged with through the EU Joint Action on Trafficking in Human Beings and the Sexual Exploitation of Children (2006). We have since become a signatory to the Council of Europe's Convention on Action against Trafficking in Human Beings and directive 2011/36/EU on Preventing and Combating Trafficking in Human Beings came into force in April 2013.

Our response to this is now contained in the Modern Slavery Act 2015.[6] The offence of human trafficking is set out in section 2, which provides that a person commits an offence if they arrange or facilitate the travel of another person 'V' with a view to V being exploited. This offence covers exploitation for sexual and non-sexual purposes but this chapter will only deal with sexual exploitation. It was thought that it would be simpler for prosecutors to deal with one offence that covered all types of trafficking, rather than having separate offences that dealt with different types of trafficking. The maximum sentence for the offence is life imprisonment.

In case there is any doubt about the meaning of the words "arranges" or "facilitates" section 2(3) gives some specific examples of what would be covered. The examples given are recruiting V, transporting or transferring V, harbouring or receiving V and transferring or exchanging control over V. These examples reflect the definitions of trafficking set out in the Council of Europe's Convention on Action against Trafficking. This is not an exhaustive list and it should be remembered that facilitating such actions is an offence, as well as actually arranging them. Thus, helping to arrange travel documents could be seen as facilitating human trafficking. "Travel" means arriving in or entering any country, departing from any country, or travelling within any country. The offence is therefore truly international and does include moving people around the United Kingdom for sexual exploitation.

Section 2(2) makes clear that it is irrelevant whether V consents to the travel or whether V is a child or an adult. Therefore, someone can be guilty of human trafficking even where V was complicit or even actively enthusiastic about the travel.

It is an essential element of the offence that it is intended that V would be exploited. Section 2(4) provides that a person arranges or facilitates V's travel with a view to V being exploited only if:

(a) the person intends to exploit V (in any part of the world) during or after the travel; or
(b) the person knows or ought to know that another person is likely to exploit V (in any part of the world) during or after the travel.

Note that it is irrelevant where in the world the actual exploitation might take place.

It is unfortunate that the offence uses the *mens rea* phrase "with a view to". Intending that V would be exploited would certainly satisfy the offence and it would also seem to include where exploitation was merely one of a number of aims.[7] It does not seem to embrace where D has recklessly exposed D to the possibility of exploitation.

Jurisdictional issues

It is obvious that there are limitations in prosecuting persons who are not based in the United Kingdom or who commit offences abroad. The Modern Slavery Act 2015 deals with these by making clear that a UK national commits the offence of human trafficking regardless of where the arranging or facilitating takes place or where the travel takes place.[8] A UK national could therefore be convicted for arranging travel abroad, including when it is anticipated that the exploitation will also take place abroad. However, a person who is not a UK national only commits an offence if any part of the arranging or facilitating takes place in the United Kingdom or if the United Kingdom is the country of arrival, entry, travel or departure.

The meaning of "exploitation"

The meaning of "exploitation" in the Modern Slavery Act 2015 is wide and covers a number of different types of exploitation including sexual exploitation. Section 3(3) provides that a person is sexually exploited if something is done that involves the commission of an offence under section 1 of the Protection of Children Act 1978 (indecent photographs of children) or Part 1 of the SOA 2003. Thus, intending to involve children in pornography would constitute sexual exploitation, but so would any conduct that constitutes an offence such as rape, sexual assault, sexual activity with a child, or controlling a prostitute for gain. However, the definition does not only cover offences committed in England and Wales. Section 3(3)(b) provides that any such conduct done outside England and Wales that would constitute an offence if it were done in England and Wales is also sexual exploitation.

There is an overlap between sexual exploitation and other types of exploitation, such as securing services by force, threats or deception or securing services from children and vulnerable persons.[9] It may be that more than one of these types of exploitation is present when a person is trafficked for sexual purposes.

Penalties

The penalty for an offence under section 2 of the Modern Slavery Act 2015 is, on conviction on indictment, imprisonment for life, or on summary conviction, to imprisonment for a term not exceeding 12 months or a fine or both.[10] However, there are other penalties the court can impose. Firstly, the court may make an asset confiscation order against someone convicted of slavery or trafficking.[11] In addition, section 8 enables the court to order the defendant to provide reparation to the victim. The point of this is to ensure the victim is compensated for the exploitation they have suffered but this will only be imposed where it is clear the defendant is able to pay. The court may also impose a Slavery and Trafficking Prevention Order or a Slavery and Trafficking Risk Order to restrict the activities of individuals who pose a risk of physical or psychological harm to others by their actions.[12]

Protections for victims of trafficking

One of the problems in securing a conviction for trafficking is that victims may be too frightened to come forward, or may be worried about the fact that they themselves have been involved in criminal activities whilst being exploited. Article 8 of the EU Directive[13] and Article 26 of the Convention[14] provides that victims of trafficking are not to be prosecuted or have penalties imposed upon them for their involvement in crimes they have committed as a direct consequence of having been trafficked (children need only have been "compelled" to have committed the offence). This is an important provision as there are examples of trafficking victims being re-victimized by our criminal justice system. For example in *R v O* (2008)[15] a 17-year-old Nigerian girl had been trafficked to the United Kingdom to work in a brothel. After escaping the brothel she was apprehended on board a coach at Dover Docks and was charged with possessing a false identity document. On appeal against conviction Lord Justice Laws, allowing the appeal, made the following comments:

> No steps were taken by the defence to investigate the history. No consideration was given by the defence as to whether she might have a defence of duress. The possibility that she might have been trafficked was ignored. There is nothing in the transcript to suggest that any thought had been given to the State's possible duty to protect her as a young victim. Nobody considered that if she was 17 or less, she should not have been in the Crown Court at all.

This was an example of negligent practice by the agents of the criminal justice system but in other cases, such as *R v C, E, I, F* (where the defendants were also convicted of offences relating to the possession of false identity documents) the fact the appellants had been trafficked (some for sexual exploitation) did not come to light until after conviction.[16]

The Modern Slavery Act 2015 therefore introduced a number of protections for victims, which are set out in Part 5 of the Act. These include the availability of special measures for victims giving evidence in court but also include a specific defence for victims of trafficking. Section 45(1) provides that slavery or trafficking victims who are over 18 are not guilty of an offence if they are compelled to do something as a result of their exploitation that would constitute an offence and a reasonable person in the same situation and having the person's relevant characteristics would have no realistic alternative to doing that act. This is intended to encourage victims to come forward and give evidence without being in fear of being convicted of offences they may have been involved in. "Relevant characteristics" means age, sex and any physical or mental illness or disability.

Section 45(4) contains a similar defence for victims who are under the age of 18. In that case, there is no requirement of compulsion. The defence merely provides that someone under the age of 18 who does the act as a direct consequence of being or having been a victim of slavery or relevant exploitation does not commit an offence where a reasonable person in the same situation and having the person's relevant characteristics would do that act. The lack of the compulsion requirement and the lower threshold for meeting the reasonable person test is a reflection of the particular vulnerability of children. Of course, the relevant characteristics will include the age of the child.

It is hoped that these provisions will encourage all agencies of the criminal justice system to be more proactive in looking at the background of accused persons when they are charged with crimes associated with trafficking.

Female Genital Mutilation

As Chapter 2 has discussed, we have well-established offences that try to prevent the practice of female genital mutilation (FGM) taking place on UK nationals overseas. The Female Genital Mutilation Act 2003 introduced offences of assisting a non-UK national to carry out FGM outside the United Kingdom on a UK national or permanent UK resident and an extra-territorial offence at section 4. The Serious Crime Act 2015 (ss70–72) amended the extra-territorial aspect of the 2003 Act by enabling the conviction under sections 1–3 of a defendant who is not a UK national where he is habitually resident in the United Kingdom, rather than "permanently" resident. The section 3 complicity offence also now extends to cases where the victim is only habitually resident in the United Kingdom.

The difficulty has been, and will continue to be, that we cannot prevent all children and women from travelling to undergo this procedure, although FGM Protection Orders will hopefully go some way toward tackling this. Rarely has criminalization been as unsuccessful as it has been here. As there have been no convictions to date the efficacy of the offence has to fall into question, but the substantive law here appears sound. A different approach is clearly required. It is rare for the legislature to accept that the threat of criminal sanctions is insufficient – but this is a case in point and now educational approaches have been employed under the Violence Against Women and Girls policy.

The reality is that the countries in which FGM is prevalent need to act to change cultural perceptions, whether by wider community interventions or through the threat of criminal sanctions, in order to eradicate the practice. In 2015 the Nigerian senate passed a general prohibition on FGM, but other African countries including Liberia and Sudan, have yet to ban FGM. International bodies such as the International Centre for Research on Women and Plan UK are working toward eradicating the practice by working with communities and it may be that changing cultural perceptions may be more successful here.

Controlling and Prohibiting Travel

One of the most straightforward ways of preventing sexual offenders committing offences in other countries is to regulate their travel. There are a number of orders in Part 2 of the SOA 2003 that can be used to track, restrict and prohibit travel, as well as controls that can be imposed as part of the sentencing process. So, for example, if an offender needs to travel outside the United Kingdom while on licence, they need to seek permission from their probation officer. Although these requests are considered on a case-by-case basis, permission is usually only granted in exceptional circumstances such as the serious illness of a family member.

The Sex Offenders' Register and civil orders

The notification requirements of the Sex Offenders' Register are considered in detail in Chapter 10, as are the various civil orders available to control sex offenders or those who are a risk to the vulnerable. This chapter will concentrate on the ways in which the various provisions can be used to control or prohibit travel.

The Sex Offenders' Register

Under Part 2 of the SOA 2003 registered sex offenders are required to notify the police of various details within 3 days of release from prison and annually thereafter, including details of their passports. They must also notify any changes to those details.

The notification requirements provided for in section 86(1) SOA 2003 have, since 2012, required registered sexual offenders to notify the prescribed police station of all foreign travel outside the United Kingdom (previously to this only travel of 3 days or more was subject to notification). This allows the police to remain aware of the whereabouts of offenders and allows the police to inform other jurisdictions that a sex offender is intending to visit their country where this is appropriate.

The Sexual Offences Act 2003 (Travel Notification Requirements) Regulations 2004[17] set out that an offender must notify the police of the following details when travelling abroad:

- date of departure;
- destination country;
- the point of arrival in that country and any other countries being visited;
- dates of intended stay in any country being visited;
- the identity of the carrier or carriers he intends to use to leave/return/or to travel to any other point(s);

- accommodation arrangements;
- date and point of arrival on return to the United Kingdom.

The offender must ensure that they give notification of the intended travel no less than 7 days prior to departure, though there is provision for emergency travel, which must be notified to the police at least 12 hours before departure.[18]

The offender must report in person to the police station within 3 days of his return to the United Kingdom.

Failure to notify or giving false information is subject to the normal penalties under section 91 SOA 2003, with a maximum of 5 years' imprisonment.

The notifications requirements do not prevent travel abroad. However, they do give the police the option to apply for a Sexual Harm Prevention Order, which can prevent an offender travelling abroad if necessary. This order is explained briefly below and in more detail in Chapter 10.

Sexual harm prevention orders and sexual risk orders

The SOA 2003 introduced foreign travel orders in sections 117–122. These were civil orders that aimed to prevent individuals convicted of sex offences against children from travelling abroad where there was a high risk of sexual harm. The orders were available on application by a chief officer of police to a Magistrates' Court where the offender had offended against a child and had acted in such a way as to give reasonable cause to believe that it was necessary for the order to be made and the order was necessary to protect a specific child or children in general. The orders lasted a maximum of 5 years[19] and the offender had to surrender their passport for the duration of the order.[20] The use of these orders was rare. From 2005 to 2012 only 50 orders were issues by the courts[21] and these orders have now been replaced with sexual harm prevention orders (SHPOs) and sexual risk orders (SROs).[22]

These new orders are also civil orders that allow a court to control the activities of sex offenders, or those considered to be at risk of causing sexual harm to the public, not just children. They can contain a ban on foreign travel where this is necessary for the purpose of protecting children or vulnerable adults abroad.[23] A child for the purposes of these orders is someone under the age of 18, irrespective of who is considered a child in the particular country concerned. It is also important to note that any activity that is deemed to constitute harm to a child or vulnerable person does not have to be illegal in the foreign country. It is therefore possible for the court to impose an order banning someone from travelling to a country where they intend to engage in sexual activity with someone we would consider a child but who is over the age of consent in that country. An order could restrict travel to a specific country, or even ban travelling to any country outside the United Kingdom. In the latter case, an offender will be required to surrender their passport.

Travel restrictions under SHPOs or SROs can be imposed for a maximum of 5 years, though they can be renewed for further 5-year periods.[24]

Notification orders

Notification orders may be made to protect the public from those who have been convicted, cautioned, or found not guilty by reason of insanity or disability, in relation to sexual offences committed outside the United Kingdom. Section 97 SOA 2003 provides that a chief officer of police can apply to the Magistrates' Court for an order that effectively makes the person subject to the notification requirements of Part 2 of the Act (the Sex Offenders' Register) as if they had been convicted in our courts. The defendant must have been convicted, cautioned etc., of a relevant offence outside the United Kingdom but the act must also have constituted an offence under Schedule 3 SOA 2003 if it had been done in the United Kingdom. This can apply to British citizens or foreign nationals who come to the United Kingdom and could result from the police being notified by foreign authorities or by the police's own enquiries. Once an order is made, defendants are treated in the same way as offenders required to comply with the notification requirements of Part 2 of the SOA 2003.

Conclusion

Although enforcing the law in the context of actions committed abroad is not easy, our obligations to the vulnerable, both in this country and abroad, have been taken seriously by the legislature. It is now the case that British citizens and residents can be prosecuted for actions that took place elsewhere in the world and many offences in the SOA 2003 have been specifically worded to allow the protection of children abroad as well as in England and Wales. The international problem of trafficking is difficult to quantify and control but the Modern Slavery Act 2015 attempts to address it by dealing with traffickers in a robust way, while incorporating some safeguards against prosecution for victims. The extension of the notification requirements of the SOA 2003 to travel abroad and the availability of civil orders to prohibit travel further strengthens the regime of control over sex offenders.

Notes

1 Accessible at http://ceop.police.uk/Media-Centre/Press-releases/2013/UK-man-sentenced-for-abusing-boy-in-Cambodia-.
2 See A. di Nicola 'Researching human trafficking: issues and problems' in M. Lee (ed.) *Human Trafficking* London: Routledge (2012) pp. 49–72. G. Tyldum 'Limitations in research on human trafficking' *International Migration* (2010) 48(5) pp. 1–13.
3 United Nations *Protocol to Prevent, Suppress and Punish Trafficking in Persons, Especially Women and Children, Supplementing the United Nations Convention against Transnational Organised Crime* United Nations, New York (2000). https://www.gov.uk/government/uploads/system/uploads/attachment_data/file/273193/5815.pdf
4 European Commission *Strategy Towards the Eradication of Trafficking in Human Beings* Brussels: European Commission (2012). For further information see http://ec.europa.eu/anti-trafficking/eu-policy/new-european-strategy-2012–2016_en.
5 At s59A of the Sexual Offences Act 2003 inserted by s109 of the Protection of Freedoms Act 2012. Section 59A replaced ss57–59 of the Sexual Offences Act 2003.

6 The background and research documents that shaped this act are available in the Explanatory Notes to the Act at http://www.legislation.gov.uk/ukpga/2015/30/notes/division/3.

7 See the discussion of the meaning of "with a view to" in *R. v Dooley (Michael)* [2005] EWCA Crim 3093.

8 Modern Slavery Act 2015 s2(6).

9 Modern Slavery Act 2015 s3 (5) and (6).

10 Modern Slavery Act 2015 s5.

11 Modern Slavery Act 2015 s7, which amends Schedule 2 of the Proceeds of Crime Act 2002.

12 See Modern Slavery Act 2015 ss14 and 23.

13 Directive 2011/36/EU on Preventing and Combating Trafficking in Human Beings.

14 United Nations *UN Convention against Transnational Organised Crime* New York: United Nations (2000). Accessible at http://www.unodc.org/documents/treaties/UNTOC/Publications/TOC%20Convention/TOCebook-e.pdf.

15 [2008] EWCA Crim 2835.

16 [2014] EWCA Crim 1483. See also *R. v LM* [2010] EWCA Crim 2327.

17 As amended by Sexual Offences Act 2003 (Notification Requirements) (England and Wales) Regulations 2012 No 1876.

18 Sexual Offences Act 2003 (Travel Notification Requirements) Regulations 2004, reg 5(3).

19 Policing and Crime Act 2009 s24 in conjunction with the Magistrates' Courts (Foreign Travel Orders) (Amendment) Rules 2010.

20 Policing and Crime Act 2009 s25.

21 Hansard, September 3, 2012, col. 193W.

22 SHPOs are governed by ss103A–103D SOA 2003 and SROs by ss122A–122K SOA 2003: see Chapter 10 for further details.

23 SOA 2003 ss103D and 122C.

24 SOA 2003 ss103D(1) and 122C(1).

Chapter 10

Protecting the Public

Introduction

The criminal justice system has a difficult balancing act to maintain. On the one hand the public, and especially the vulnerable, need to be protected from those who pose a continuing threat. However, on the other hand, even sexual offenders have a right to be treated fairly and in such a way that they are given a chance to change their lives in a positive way so that they become a contributing member of society.

Labelling people as sex offenders can result not only in specific sentencing regimes but also in continuing control over their future lives, even once they have left prison. Where they can work or live and with whom, and even their social life, may be monitored in such a way as would give rise to concerns about privacy in any other context.

Conviction for most of the sexual offences considered in this book will give rise to continuing monitoring through the Sex Offenders' Register, or through a variety of orders that are available to control those who commit sexual offences. However, it is not always the case that people who commit offences we may think of as sexual are subject to the same controls. The schedules of the Sexual Offences Act 2003 (SOA 2003) list a variety of offences, which can give rise to different controls. Some give rise to the notification requirements explained below and others to the likelihood of the imposition of a civil order. Some offences, for example actual bodily harm or grievous bodily harm, are not regarded as sexual offences *per se* but may still be taken into account when a court is considering the imposition of a civil order, even though they do not give rise to the notification requirements.

This chapter will consider the various methods of controlling sex offenders, concentrating on the registration and management of sex offenders in the community, through notification requirements, court orders and restrictions on employment. The treatment of sex offenders, rehabilitation and the use of chemical castration will also be briefly considered.

Sexual Offenders and Risk

Before we address the specific forms of management for sexual offenders it is important to understand how we identify sexual offenders, the risk they pose and how that risk is managed.

Although this textbook has considered those offences that are explicitly regulated and labelled as sexual many other offences may have a sexual component. For example a murder may be sexually motivated or a campaign of harassment may be sexually driven. Where sexual motivation is the cause of the offending behaviour this will be taken into account in sentencing as an aggravating factor but the offender may also be subject to treatment in prison or management in the community as a sexual offender.

The conviction and sentencing of offenders is only the beginning of the story. Once a sentence begins, whether that is custodial or within the community, the agencies dealing with that individual need to be cognisant to the specific needs of an offender and how to keep the community safe. This ethos is reflected in the Multi-Agency Public Protection Arrangements discussed below, but to successfully manage sexual offenders it is first necessary to understand the risk they pose. Risk of harm assessments are performed in a number of ways and for all offenders the Offender Assessment System collects data on past and current offending behaviour, social and economic factors and personal factors. The system then produces reports detailing the likelihood of reoffending, the level of risk and the offender's needs. For sexual offenders the more specific Risk Matrix 2000 tool is usually used by all agencies of the criminal justice system to identify the risk posed by each sexual offender, with offenders placed in a category of low, medium, high or very high.[1] This category will dictate how the offender is managed. There does not appear to be an equivalent statistical tool to assess female offenders, as they comprise such a small group of offenders. For young offenders the "Asset" tool is used by Youth Offending Teams to assess all young offenders who come into contact with the criminal justice system to develop intervention plans to divert them from offending. The National Offender Management Service is the agency of the Ministry of Justice that oversees this and provides offender management.

Numerous studies have demonstrated that it is very difficult to predict dangerousness[2] and therefore whether an offender will continue to be a danger to the public. However, the court will need to consider this risk, as far as it is able to, when sentencing and especially when it imposes a custodial sentence.

Custodial Sentences

Custodial sentences can be justified on a number of grounds. Firstly, there is the obvious need to protect the vulnerable from abuse but also sentencing is used to punish the offender or to act as a deterrent. Custodial sentences may also be used to show society's collective disapproval or to allay public concerns about sex offenders.

Issues regarding sentencing have already been dealt with in a number of chapters when dealing with offences and so will not be dealt with in detail here. It is worth reiterating that new guidelines, published by the Sentencing Council in the wake of the Savile inquiry,[3] came into force on 1 April 2014. These provide detailed guidance on specific offences and there are separate guidelines to deal with young offenders, as discussed at Chapter 4. Judges must consider the offender's culpability and the harm caused to the victim before considering a list of aggravating and miti-gating factors. Courts should look at the full context of the offender's behaviour and motivation in committing the offence, as well as giving greater emphasis to the impact of sex offences on victims. Particular attention should be given to the long-term harm the offence may have had on the victim's psychological wellbeing. This is especially true in relation to children who should not be treated as responsible for what has happened to them.

In light of the numerous cases of historical sexual abuse that have come to light in recent years the courts have had to consider how to approach the sentencing of these offenders. The Court of Appeal has confirmed that while an offender cannot be sentenced to more than the maximum term for an offence than was available at the time the offence(s) took place the sentence had to reflect modern attitudes, and the court could then take account of modern sentencing guidelines.[4]

Although sex offenders may serve a custodial sentence at any institution there are prisons that specifically or primarily house sexual offenders, including HMP Whatton in Nottinghamshire, HMP Bure in Norfolk and HMP Ashfield in Glouces-tershire. Dedicating estate to sexual offenders allows provision to be made for the appropriate levels of security (for both the community and the prisoners) and the provision of Sex Offender Treatment Programmes (SOTPs).

Medical Intervention

Although our treatment of sexual offenders favours containment and psychological treatment, anti-libidinal drugs can also be used to control sexual urges. Popularly known as 'chemical castration' these drugs can only be used where the offender consents to taking the medication and are used alongside treatment programmes. In some countries, including Poland and some states in America, the treatment is mandatory for those who pose a serious risk, but in most European countries the treatment is voluntary. In some jurisdictions physical castration can also be performed to prevent offending, although obviously it only prevents offences that involve penile penetration.

Medical treatment is not the definitive answer to preventing sexual offending. Firstly, not all offenders are motivated by a sexual urge; for example, rape can of course be an act of violence. Secondly, the use of drugs needs to be consistent, an easy variable to control when the offender is imprisoned but less easy to track when they are in the community. An intolerance to medication will also pose a problem for some.

Rehabilitation

Although there are serious concerns about the rates of recidivism for sexual offend-ers these rates are not (as far as they can be assessed) particularly high. For exam-ple, a study in 2002 found only 10 per cent of sexual offenders who were adjudged to have a high risk of reoffending had actually reoffended after 6 years, although the offences committed by that group of recidivists were serious.[5] Figures typically suggest that for criminal offences one in four offenders reoffend within a year, but for sexual offences these numbers are usually lower. This means very little. Reoffending is very difficult to track, sexual offences are under-recorded, many go unreported and this poses difficulties for the court when sentencing. Reoffending rates are also difficult to analyse as they are not so nuanced as to provide detailed breakdowns of particular offences. Thus it is difficult to know whether offenders have been rehabilitated.

Despite these shortcomings it is obviously important that we attempt rehabilitation and SOTPs, available both in custody and in the community, seek to rehabilitate offenders. Within prisons and Young Offenders Institutions a number of SOTPs are available for imprisoned sexual offenders and these are offered according to the level of risk and needs of the offender. The core SOTP aims to help offenders develop understanding of how and why they have committed sexual offences and to understand the harm caused to victims. There are also more targeted programmes such as the Internet Sex Offender Treatment Programme and the Healthy Sexual Functioning Programme, which seeks to modify offenders' sexual behaviour where the offending behaviour is related to their sexual interests. No-one can force offenders to engage in programmes and to be involved they must be motivated and willing to address their offending behaviour.[6]

Outside the formalized responses to offending there have been a number of initiatives to rehabilitate and reintegrate sex offenders into the community. For example Circles UK[7] has been building on a model established in Canada by providing a support network of volunteers for sex offenders in the community. The emphasis here is on practical support, help with finding work, managing money etc., but the consequence is that sexual offenders feel part of a community and may then be less likely to offend. There are also informal forms of community support when offenders have the support of friends or an organization such as, for example, a community group, a church or mosque.

Release from Custody – Preventative Measures

Sexual offenders are subject to special considerations in sentencing after their release from custody. There are a number of provisions contained in Part 2 SOA 2003 (as amended by the Anti-social Behaviour, Crime and Policing Act 2014) that can be used to control sex offenders. In terms of managing offenders in the community there is now a more joined-up approach that falls under the general heading of Multi-Agency Public Protection Arrangements (MAPPAs).

Multi-Agency Public Protection Arrangements

Multi-Agency Public Protection Arrangements (MAPPAs) were first introduced as arrangements for managing sexual and violent offenders in 2001[8] as a way of improving the assessment and management of the risk posed. It has been recognized that preventing reoffending is not something that can be achieved by one agency or through one form of intervention, as the 2010 Probation and Police inspection report summarizes:

> Successful work with sexual offenders requires the right mix of restrictive interventions to control the offender and help prevent reoffending and constructive interventions to change their behaviour and contribute to their safe rehabilitation into the community. Effective engagement, good communication and defensible multi-agency decision making are all fundamental ingredients to this difficult mix, essential for the protection of the public.[9]

Registered sexual offenders, i.e. those who are subject to the notification requirements, are one of the categories of offenders subject to the MAPPA framework. The police, probation service and prisons service have a statutory duty to work together to establish arrangements for the purpose of assessing and managing the risks posed in their area by sexual offenders. Information about offenders' histories and risk profile are shared across the relevant agencies with a view to prevent further offending. There are three categories of offenders and each offender will be allocated to a particular group. The MAPPA categories are:

- Category 1 – Registered sexual offenders as specified under Part 2 of the SOA 2003.
- Category 2 – This category is mostly for violent offenders but includes sexual offenders who do not qualify for the notification requirements discussed below and offenders disqualified from working with children.
- Category 3 – Other dangerous offenders. Those who have been cautioned, reprimanded, warned or convicted of an offence that indicates that he or she is capable of causing serious harm.

Most convicted sexual offenders will fall under category 1. After the offender has been allotted to a category the level of supervision is then decided in order to best manage the risk posed by the offender. The type of management will depend on the offender's risk assessment and general profile and may vary from the normal probation arrangements, to the use of Multi-agency Public Protection meetings, more specific involvement such as police surveillance (e.g. electronic tagging) or a requirement to live in specialized accommodation. The three levels (which do not relate directly to the categories) are:

- Level 1 – Ordinary Agency Management. These offenders are subject to the usual arrangements applied by whichever agency has the lead in supervising them. Management entails one or two agencies such as the police and probation service working together and they may share information about the offender with other agencies where necessary and appropriate.
- Level 2 – Active Multi-agency Management. The risk management plans for these offenders require the ongoing involvement of several agencies to manage the offender and there will be regular Multi-agency Public Protection meetings about that offender.
- Level 3 – Active Multi-agency Management. In this case the involvement of several agencies is required and this may involve senior staff and additional

resources. These may apply to offenders who have attracted particular media attention for the severity of their crimes and/or are in need of very careful management, which may include surveillance or emergency accommodation.

The level of management is not static and offenders may be moved up or down the levels dependent upon the risk they pose. This joined-up approach to community supervision must be considered in the light of the statutory provisions discussed below. There is a common misconception that offenders are largely unsupervised once in the community, aside from the need to fulfil notification requirements, but the level of MAPPA supervision should be responsive to the risk the offender presents.

Part 2 of the Sexual Offences Act 2003

Part 2 of the SOA 2003 deals with the notifications and orders that can be imposed upon sexual offenders as part of the sentencing process or where an application has been made to a Magistrates' Court. It is this part of the Act that has been subject to the most significant change since the inception of the SOA 2003 as the legislature has sought to update the law in line with social concerns.

The Sex Offenders' Register – the notification requirements

The Sex Offender's Register[10] is a national database containing details of records of those required to register with the police under Part 2 of the SOA 2003. The Register can be accessed by the police, National Probation Service, and HM Prison Service. The register was first introduced by the Sexual Offences Act 1997, which has now been replaced by the SOA 2003, and so does not include offenders who were convicted, cautioned or completed their sentences prior to 1997. Therefore the idea that all offenders are "on the register" is a misnomer.

The basic requirement is that offenders convicted or cautioned for specific sexual offences must notify certain details to the police within 3 days of their conviction or release from prison and annually thereafter. The process is generally known as registration and requires that offenders must also notify the police of any changes to these details and of any intention to travel abroad. There is also a requirement to notify the police when residing or staying in a household with a child for a period of at least 12 hours. The system is monitored by the police, who receive notification from the courts following conviction, and from the prisons and probation service following an offender's release into the community. The notification requirements are automatic if the offender falls within section 80 SOA 2003 and do not depend on an order of the court.

The categories of person who are subject to the notification requirements under section 80 are:

(a)   someone convicted of an offence listed in Schedule 3;
(b)   someone found not guilty of such an offence by reason of insanity;
(c)   someone found to be under a disability and to have done the act charged; or
(d)   someone cautioned for such an offence.

Most of the offences contained in Part 1 of the SOA 2003 are included in Schedule 3, but not all. For example, an offence under section 71 (sexual activity in a public lavatory) is not included. Many offences only give rise to the notification requirements if certain conditions are met. For example, someone convicted under section 13 of the SOA 2003 (child sex offences committed by children or young persons), must have been sentenced to imprisonment for a term of at least 12 months.[11] This is intended to ensure that only serious offending will give rise to the notification requirements. The schedule also includes a long list of sexual offences in other Acts, for example child pornography offences under the Protection of Children Act 1978.

The period when a relevant offender remains subject to the notification requirements depends on the sentence and age of the offender. The following table shows the notification periods set out in section 82:

Relevant Offender	Notification Period	Where Relevant Offender is under 18
Sentenced to at least 30 months and up to life imprisonment	Indefinite period (now subject to review – see below)	
Admitted to hospital subject to a restriction order	Indefinite period (now subject to review)	
Sentenced to at least 6 months but less than 30 months	10 years	Half
Sentenced to 6 months or less	7 years	Half
Admitted to hospital but not subject to a restriction order	7 years	Half
Cautioned	2 years	Half
Conditional discharge	Period of conditional discharge	
Person of any other description	5 years	Half

The details that relevant offenders must supply to the police include:

- name and address;
- date of birth;
- National Insurance number;
- e-mail address;
- passport, bank account and credit card details;
- details of any residence with a child.

Breach of the notification requirements without a reasonable excuse is a criminal offence under section 91 SOA 2003, subject to a maximum penalty of 5 years' imprisonment. What is a reasonable excuse will depend on the circumstances, but one example could be where the offender has had an emergency admission to hospital. Although 5 years is the maximum sentence for breach, the actual sentence imposed may be significantly shorter. In *B (David)*[12] a man who had been convicted of attempted rape and sentenced to 5 years' imprisonment had been released from prison on licence after 3 years. He failed to notify the police of his name and address within 3 days of his release and was sentenced to 3 months' imprisonment; whereas, in *Norton (Joseph)*[13] 18 months' imprisonment was appropriate for an offender who had failed to comply with the notification requirements on 11 previous occasions. In *Simmonds* a 3-year sentence of imprisonment for four breaches of a sexual offences prevention order was upheld by the Court of Appeal as the defendant posed a very high risk to children.[14]

Being made subject to the notifications requirements will have a significant effect on an offender's life, including what kind of job they can take, and so challenges have been made to the fairness of the requirements.

Ibbotson v UK (1999)[15] concerned an application to the European Commission of Human Rights claiming that the notification requirements under the SOA 1997 were a breach of Article 7 of the European Convention on Human Rights. Article 7 prohibits the imposition of a penalty heavier than the one applicable at the time the criminal offence was committed. Ibbotson had been convicted of child pornography offences in 1996 and on release became subject to the notification requirements of the 1997 Act. The First Chamber of the European Commission declared his application inadmissible on the grounds that the registration requirements did not amount to a penalty within the meaning of Article 7. The requirements were seen as preventative rather than punitive in the sense that they would help to dissuade an individual from reoffending.

There has also been a challenge to the indefinite period of notification required for offenders who are sentenced to 30 months' or more imprisonment, in this case successfully. In *R (on the application of F (by his litigation friend F)) and Thompson (FC) v Secretary of State for the Home Department* (2010),[16] the Supreme Court declared that the indefinite notification requirements were incompatible with Article 8 of the European Convention on Human Rights (right to a family and private life) because they do not contain any provision for review in individual cases. As a result of this ruling the SOA 2003 was amended by the Sexual Offences Act 2003 (Remedial) Order (2012)[17] so as to introduce a mechanism through which individuals could seek review of their indefinite notification requirements. The order inserted sections 91A–91F into the SOA 2003. These sections now provide that offenders who have been subject to the notifications requirements for at least 15 years can make an application to the police for review. The police can either amend the period for notification or decide that the indefinite period will continue if they consider that the offender remains a risk. Young offenders (i.e. those who were under 18 on the date of conviction/caution) can apply for a review after a period of 8 years. It is important to note that the right to apply for a review does not mean that the offender is automatically released from the notification requirements. The police must be satisfied that the offender no longer poses a risk after considering a number of factors, including representations from responsible bodies within the MAPPA framework and victims. The decision made by the police is also subject to a right of appeal to the Magistrates' Court. This was addressed in *R (NM & NE) v*

Birmingham Magistrates' Court (2015) where it was confirmed that a review of the notification requirements is to address whether continuing notification is required to protect the public, not to address its impact on the offender.[18]

Disclosure of information

There has been much debate about whether the information on the Sex Offenders' Register should be made public. As Chapter 1 has discussed, the drive for public access came about as a result of the murder of Sarah Payne, the 8-year-old girl abducted and murdered in 2000 by a sex offender who lived within her community, which, drawing on the exemplar of "Megan's Law" in the United States,[19] prompted the campaign for public access to information on sex offenders, which became known as "Sarah's Law". Concerns about making such information public centred on the risk of vigilante attacks on suspected offenders but also on the view that making the register public would discourage offenders from notifying the police of their whereabouts, driving known offenders underground where they could not be monitored. On the other hand, many supported the idea of Sarah's Law, arguing that the public has a right to know.[20]

Under section 327A of the Criminal Justice Act 2003, as amended by section 140 of the Criminal Justice and Immigration Act 2008, the authorities responsible for MAPPA arrangements in each area must consider whether to disclose information in their possession about the convictions of any child sex offender managed by them to any particular member of the public.[21] This would, for example, allow a police force to give information to schools, children's clubs or parents. There is a presumption that such information should be disclosed where the authority has reasonable cause to believe that a child sex offender managed by it poses a risk of causing serious harm to a child and the disclosure is necessary for the purpose of protecting the child.[22] The authority may impose conditions for preventing the member of the public concerned from disclosing the information to another person. This does not mean that the information on the Sex Offenders' Register is entirely public, as disclosure is at the discretion of the relevant authority. However, a pilot disclosure scheme, which originally ran in four areas, was implemented across England and Wales in 2011 and is known as the Child Sex Offender Disclosure Scheme.[23] Under the scheme a parent, carer, guardian or another interested party, can ask the police to check whether someone who has access to their children has a record of committing child sexual offences. Applications are made direct to the local police force and the disclosure is at the discretion of that force, which may impose conditions on the person who is given the information.

Pre-emptive measures – civil orders

The High Court can exercise a general power to protect children by issuing injunctions to prevent particular individuals from approaching children who have been identified as vulnerable to exploitation. In *Birmingham City Council v Riaz* (2014) a local authority was granted injunctions to prevent ten male respondents having contact with a vulnerable 17-year-old girl.[24] There was insufficient evidence (and willingness by the victim) to pursue criminal cases against the men. The terms of the injunction were very broad prohibiting the men from making contact with the girl by any means, approaching, following or being in her company or encouraging any other men to do the same. A general prohibition on them approaching any female under the age of 18 years, previously unknown to them, was also granted. Breach of the orders would be dealt with as a contempt of court. Acknowledged by the judge as a "bold and novel step" by the local authority, this application demonstrates that there are methods of protecting vulnerable children, although to date this is the only modern example of a local authority taking this action.

There are a range of other civil orders available to control the behaviour of sex offenders, with the aim of ensuring public protection. The intention is to prevent a sexual offence taking place, though these orders are often used after the commission of an offence as well. Their purpose is therefore meant to be preventative rather than punitive. These kinds of restraining orders were first introduced in 1998 and then enhanced in the SOA 2003. The original provisions have now been amended by the Anti-Social Behaviour, Crime and Policing Act 2014, to repeal some of the existing orders and replace them with new orders in England and Wales. There are now three civil orders available under Part 2 of the SOA 2003, sexual harm prevention orders, sexual risk orders and notification orders.

When imposing such an order the court acts in its civil capacity, so the civil rules of evidence apply and hearsay is admissible. However, the case of *R (on the application of McCann) v Manchester Crown Court* (2002)[25] (which was a case on anti-social behaviour orders) made clear while proceedings for these kinds of orders are civil in nature, it is the criminal standard of proof that applies when a court is deciding whether the defendant has carried out the relevant acts. This is because of the serious consequences of such an order and in particular the consequences of breaching an order. Although they are civil orders, breach of an order without reasonable excuse is a criminal offence with a maximum penalty of 5 years' imprisonment,[26] though community sentences might be appropriate where there is no real risk to the public.[27]

The making of an order is not a criminal conviction and so will not result in a criminal record. However, in most cases an order will be made following a conviction for a sexual offence and the orders will require the offender to register and comply with the notification requirements in sections 80–91 SOA 2003, outlined above.

It is possible for these orders to be made in relation to defendants who are under 18, provided they are over the age of criminal responsibility (10 years), though they would normally be dealt with in a youth court and the identity of the young person would not be published[28] unless the court decides that it is in the public interest.

In all cases it is possible for an interim order to be granted once the initial application is made but before the full order is granted.

Sexual harm prevention orders

Sexual harm prevention orders (SHPOs) replace sex offences prevention orders (SOPOs). The effect of an SHPO is to prohibit the defendant from doing anything described in the order. Examples could include restricting unsupervised access to children, limiting internet use, prohibiting contact with a particular person, or any activities that could be seen as preliminary to encouraging the exploitation of young people through prostitution or pornography.

Section 103A of the SOA 2003 provides that a court may make an SHPO when sentencing a defendant for certain relevant offences. The court can also impose an order if a defendant is found not guilty by reason of insanity, or is under a disability but found to have done the act charged. The relevant offences are listed in Schedules 3 and 5 of the SOA 2003 and are quite wide ranging, comprising statutory and common law sexual offences but also offences that are not specifically sexual, such as murder or kidnapping. However, as the orders are intended to relate to sex offenders, the court must be satisfied before imposing one that it is necessary for the purpose of protecting the public (or a particular individual) from *sexual* harm, or for protecting children or vulnerable adults from sexual harm outside the United Kingdom. This represents a significant change from the provisions relating to the old SOPOs as the requirement for them was that there had to be a risk of *serious* sexual harm, whereas now there need only be a risk of sexual harm, whether serious or not. It is recognized in the provisions that sexual harm need not be physical, as "sexual harm" is defined in section 103B(1) as physical or psychological harm caused by the offender. The offender's previous convictions and the assessment of risk provided in any pre-sentence report will be important factors when the court is making the decision whether to impose an SHPO.

Where a court has not imposed an SHPO, a chief officer of police or the Director General of the National Crime Agency may apply direct to a Magistrates' Court for an order.[29] This may be as a result of their own observations, or reports from others. In this case the offender must have been convicted, cautioned or found not guilty by reason of insanity or because they are under a disability in relation to a relevant offence as described above and must have acted in such a way as to give reasonable cause to believe that it is necessary for such an order to be made. People who have been convicted, cautioned, etc., of relevant offences committed abroad may also have an order made against them, provided that the offence would also be an offence if done in the United Kingdom. The application by a chief office of police must apply to anyone who resides within that particular police area, or someone whom the chief of police believes is intending to come into it. This could apply where someone is returning to the United Kingdom from abroad, or is released from prison in another area and intending to move home.

The order lasts for a fixed period (which will be specified in the order) of at least 5 years or until a further order is made.[30]

Section 103D now also specifically provides for prohibitions on foreign travel to be contained in SHPOs.[31] The purpose of this is to protect vulnerable people abroad from sex offenders who may think their activities are less likely to be noticed or investigated if they take place in another country. In this case the prohibition must be for a fixed term of not more than 5 years, though this can be extended by further 5-year periods. The order could prohibit travel to a particular country, or generally to any country outside the United Kingdom (other than one specifically exempted by the order). An order prohibiting travel to any country outside the United Kingdom must also require the defendant to surrender their passport to the police for the duration of the order.

There are provisions for variation, renewal or discharge of orders either by application of the offender or the police.[32]

It is important that orders are carefully drafted so that they are workable and do not cause practical problems in the future.[33] The Court of Appeal considered this is the case of *Smith (Steven), Clarke (Wayne), Hall (Bryan) and Dodd (Jonathan)* (2011),[34] which was a case on the old SOPOs but did raise some important issues that will also be relevant to the new orders. The case dealt with a number of appellants, all of whom had been convicted of sex offences, mainly in relation to child abuse images, and all of whom had been subject to SOPOs. The court emphasized that such orders offer a lot of flexibility but must be tailored to the requirements of the particular case. Therefore a blanket ban on computer use or internet access was not acceptable. Such a ban would be disproportionate because it restricts the defendant in the use of what is now an essential part of most people's lives and especially their employment. The most effective way to deal with computer and internet use was to require the offender to preserve their internet access history and to submit this to inspection by the police on request and some cases a prohibition on communicating with young people under the age of 16 via chat rooms or social media might be appropriate. The court also considered orders that prohibited contact with children under the age of 16. In that case, there had to be an identifiable risk of contact offences taking place before the court would impose a prohibition on unsupervised contact with children or a ban on the offender staying or living in any house where children were present. Such conditions might be necessary in cases involving predatory paedophiles where there was a genuine risk to a child but even then there needs to be a provision excluding incidental contact, such as occurs in everyday life, e.g. when dealing with a 15-year-old serving in a shop. Such restrictions on contact would normally only apply to children under the age of 16, unless the defendant was in a position of trust over 16–17-year-olds. One of the defendants in the case was prohibited from working as a DJ at events attended by children under 16 and this was held to be acceptable in the circumstances as it was the sort of activity that would be likely to present him with significant temptations, given his sexual interest in pre-teenage girls.

Sexual risk orders

Sexual risk orders (SROs) replace the former risk of sexual harm orders (RSHOs) and are governed by sections 122A–122K of the SOA 2003. The original orders only applied to persons who posed a risk to children, while the new orders are much wider.

A sexual risk order can be applied for by the police against someone even if they have not been convicted or cautioned for a sexual offence and so are much wider than the requirements for an SHPO considered above. Other requirements are similar to those for SHPOs. A chief officer of police or the Director General of the National Crime Agency can apply to a Magistrates' Court for an order if certain conditions are met. The conditions are that the person has done an act of a sexual nature as a result of which there is reasonable cause to believe that it is necessary for an SRO to be made. The court may make an order if it is satisfied that the defendant (the Act calls the person "the defendant" even though they may not have committed a criminal offence) has done an act of a sexual nature as a result of which it is necessary to make such an order for the purpose of protecting the public, or a particular member of the public from harm from the defendant, or protecting children or vulnerable adults from harm from the defendant outside the United Kingdom. Note that one act of a sexual nature is sufficient (previously at least two were required).

"Act of a sexual nature" is not defined in Part 2 SOA 2003 and the definition of "sexual" in section 78 SOA 2003 only technically applies to Part 1 of the Act. However, the Home Office guidance on Part 2 suggests that they might include similar examples of behaviour as were previously covered by the old RSHOs, such as giving a child anything that relates to sexual activity, or communicating with a child where any part of the communication is sexual, or acts that may be suggestive of grooming or exploitation of young people.[35] However, note that this new order does not just relate to children and therefore can include acts of a sexual nature involving adults.

Where the defendant actually commits a sexual offence (e.g. causing a child to watch a sexual act contrary to section 12 of the SOA 2003), then they would be charged with that offence. These orders are meant to apply where the behaviour of the defendant suggests that someone is at risk and so early intervention is appropriate to protect that victim from the actual sexual offence. In this case, the order has effect for a fixed period (not less than 2 years) as specified in the order.

Harm is defined in section 122B(1) as physical or psychological harm caused by the defendant doing an act of a sexual nature. Again, it is possible for the defendant to be a child and again an order could prohibit foreign travel (for a maximum of 5 years, but with the ability to extend for further 5-year periods).

There are provisions for variation, renewal or discharge of an order.[36] As for SHPOs, the maximum penalty for breach of an order is 5 years' imprisonment.[37]

Notification orders

Notification orders are made to protect the public from those who have been convicted, cautioned, or found not guilty by reason of insanity or disability, in relation to sexual offences committed outside the United Kingdom. These orders have already been mentioned in Chapter 9 but the details are repeated here for the sake of completeness. Section 97 SOA 2003 provides that a chief officer of police can apply to the Magistrates' Court for an order that effectively makes the person subject to the notification requirements of Part 2 of the Act (the Sex Offenders' Register) as if they had been convicted in the United Kingdom. The defendant must have been convicted, cautioned etc., of a relevant offence outside the United Kingdom but the act must also have constituted an offence under Schedule 3 SOA 2003 if it had been done in the United Kingdom. This can apply to British citizens or foreign nationals who come to the United Kingdom and could result from the police being notified by foreign authorities or by the police's own enquiries. Once an order is made, defendants are effectively treated in the same way as offenders required to comply with the notification requirements of sections 80–91 of the SOA 2003.

The Disclosure and Barring Service and disqualification orders

The Criminal Justice and Courts Services Act 2000 (CJCSA) introduced a power allowing courts to make a disqualification order by which a person convicted of an offence against a child can, and in some cases *must*, be disqualified indefinitely from working with children. The types of work offenders are prevented from doing are quite broad and include paid or unpaid positions. These "regulated positions" are set out in section 36 CJCSA and include work in schools, children's hospitals, care homes or social services departments, as well as any position where normal duties include caring for, training, supervising or being in sole charge of children, for example children's clubs. They also include positions where the person has unsupervised contact with children under arrangements made by a responsible person such as a parent, which is wide enough to cover babysitters. A person who is subject to a disqualification order commits an offence if they knowingly apply for or accept any work with children[38] with a maximum penalty of 5 years' imprisonment.

Disqualification orders are gradually being replaced by the barring provisions contained in the Safeguarding Vulnerable Groups Act 2006 (SVGA), as amended by the Protection of Freedoms Act 2012. They have not been completely replaced as yet and so it is still possible for a disqualification order to be made in some circumstances.

The SVGA established a central body that is responsible for a vetting and barring scheme called the Independent Safeguarding Authority, which has now been merged with the Criminal Records Bureau to form the Disclosure and Barring Service (DBS). This scheme applies to those who may work with children and vulnerable adults.

The scheme works by a system of referrals to the DBS from employers or organizations who have concerns that a person has caused harm or poses a future risk of harm to vulnerable groups including children. In addition, a person who is convicted or cautioned of certain offences will be automatically barred from working with children and/or vulnerable adults. Automatic barring offences include most of the offences in Part 1 of the SOA 2003, such as rape, sexual assault or sexual offences committed against children. It is an offence for someone who is on the barred list to seek or to engage in the activity from which they are barred, with a maximum penalty of 5 years' imprisonment.[39] It is also an offence for an employer to employ someone in an activity from which they are barred.[40] Employers are able to undertake a DBS check, which searches police records and in specific cases the barred list enables them to make an informed decision about recruitment of staff.

Conclusion

There is now a much larger range of control measures available, in addition to the traditional solution of locking offenders away. Even if an offender is subject to a custodial order, there are at least some schemes available to provide treatment and encourage rehabilitation, though these will depend very much on the willingness of the offender to engage with them. The civil orders have been extended to cover situations they did not apply to before and there is a limited but workable scheme to allow members of the public to check the background of someone they may suspect is a risk to their children. Though there have been some delays in fully implementing the Disclosure and Barring Service, it is hoped that it will eventually provide a comprehensive way of preventing access to vulnerable groups by those who might seek to take advantage of them.

Notes

1 For further discussion see A.R. Beech, L.A Craig, and K.D. Browne (eds) *Assessment and Treatment of Sex Offender: A Handbook* John Chichester: Wiley-Blackwell (2009). The Active Risk Management System (a dynamic risk assessment tool) has now been piloted and is expected to be rolled out alongside Risk Matrix 2000.

2 A meta study of the various risk assessment tools by Tully et al suggests these have an "at least moderate ability" to predict sexual recidivism in predicting sexual recidivism of adult male offenders: R.J. Tully, S. Chou, K.D. Browne 'A systematic review on the effectiveness of sex offender risk assessment tools in predicting sexual recidivism of adult male sex offenders' *Clinical Psychology Review* (2013) 33(2) pp. 287–316. A study by Helmus et al that looked at the ability of Risk Matrix to predict recidivism similarly found that the tool "has moderate to large predictive accuracy among sex offenders". L. Helmus, K.M. Babchishin, and R.K. Hanson 'The predictive accuracy of the Risk Matrix 2000: A meta-analysis' *Sexual Offender Treatment* (2013) 8(2) pp. 1–20.

3 See the Introduction to Chapters 4 and 5.

4 *R. v Clifford (Frank Maxwell)* [2014] EWCA Crim 2245. For critical discussion see the case commentary for this case at A. Ashworth *Criminal Law Review* (2015) 2 pp. 167–170.

5 R. Hood, S. Shute, M. Feilzer and A. Wilcox *Reconviction Rates of Serious Sex Offenders and Assessments of Their Risk* London: Home Office Research Development and Statistics Directorate Home Office (2002).

6 Brown provides a valuable review of the programmes and their efficacy. S.J. Brown 'An Introduction to sex offender treatment programmes and their risk reduction efficacy' in K. Harrison (ed.) *Managing High Risk Sex-offenders in the Community* Cullompton, Devon: Willan (2010) pp.81–104. Also see A Craig, L. Dixon, and T.A. Gannon *What Works in Offender Rehabilitation: An Evidenced Based Approach to Assessment and Treatment* Chichester: Wiley-Blackwell (2013).

7 http://www.circles-uk.org.uk.

8 Now governed by ss325–327 Criminal Justice Act 2003, as amended by the Criminal Justice and Immigration Act 2008.

9 HMI Probation and HMI Constabulary 'Restriction and Rehabilitation: Getting the Right Mix' An inspection of the management of sexual offenders in the community, A Joint Inspection by HMI Probation and HMI Constabulary London: HMIC and HMIP (2010).

10 Actually the Violent and Sex Offender Register, known as ViSOR, managed by the National Crime Agency.

11 Sexual Offences Act 2003 Schedule 3, para 22.

12 [2005] EWCA Crim 158.

13 [2014] EWCA Crim 1275.

14 *R. v Simmonds (Phillip Anthony)* [2015] EWCA Crim 1068.

15 [1999] Crim LR 153.

16 [2010] UKSC 17.

17 (2012) No 1883.

18 [2015] EWHC 688 (Admin).

19 The Jacob Wetterling Crimes Against Children and Sexually Violent Offender Registration Act 1994 (popularly, and in conjunction with other Acts, known as Megan's Law) required States to track sexual offenders and allowed for the release of information concerning their whereabouts. The release of information is handled differently by each State, for example, some notify communities that an offender is in the area and others have searchable websites.

20 See R. Scorer 'Sarah's Law – the debate' *New Law Journal* (2006) 156 1907.

21 Criminal Justice Act 2003 s327A, as amended by s140 Criminal Justice and Immigration Act 2008.

22 Criminal Justice Act 2003 s327A(3), as amended.

23 See https://www.gov.uk/government/news/national-rollout-of-scheme-to-protect-children.

24 [2014] EWHC 4247.

25 [2002] 1 AC 787.

26 SOA 2003 ss91,103I and 122H.

27 *Fenton* (2007) 1 Cr App R (S) 97.

28 Children and Young Persons Act 1933 s39.

29 SOA 2003 s103A(4).

30 SOA 2003 s103C(2).

31 This replaces foreign travel orders which were originally contained in the SOA 2003 and is discussed further at Chapter 10.

32 SOA 2003 s103E.

33 The proportionality of these orders has been addressed in numerous cases: see *R. v Mortimer (Jason Christopher)* [2010] EWCA Crim 1303; *R. v Lea (Nicholas)* [2011] EWCA Crim 487; *R. v Hemsley (Daniel Mark)* [2010] EWCA Crim 225.

34 [2011] EWCA Crim 1772.

35 Home Office, *Guidance on Part 2 of the Sexual Offences Act 2003,* March 2015 https://www.gov.uk/government/publications/guidance-on-part-2-of-the-sexual-offences-act-2003.

36 SOA 2003 s122D.

37 SOA 2003 s122H.

38 Criminal Justice and Court Services Act 2000 s35.

39 Safeguarding Vulnerable Groups Act 2006 s7(1).

40 Safeguarding Vulnerable Groups Act 2006 s9.

The Way Forward

We began this book with the assertion that in the regulation of sexual offending the law intrudes into sexual relations in order to protect the vulnerable, to reflect, reinforce and protect morality and social norms, and to protect the family unit. Whether the law goes too far or not far enough in achieving these goals is dependent upon your school of thought. There can be little doubt that the law is comprehensive in this area but following the numerous inquiries into child sexual abuse there will be many who believe the law is not strong enough or that the criminal justice system has failed to take the claims of victims seriously.

This chapter then reflects on the current state of the substantive law and the criminal justice system. Firstly, we will address whether the aims expressed in the *Setting the Boundaries* review[1] have been met by the Sexual Offences Act 2003 (SOA 2003), later legislative measures and criminal justice system responses. Secondly, we will briefly consider where we should go from here in terms of improving the substantive law and the processes that support it.

The Sexual Offences Act 2003

The Sexual Offences Act 2003 (SOA 2003) is still a relatively new piece of legislation and amendments were being made at the time of writing (July 2015), which have been incorporated as far as possible into this book. It is however timely to comment on whether the SOA 2003 has managed to meet its terms of reference set out in *Setting the Boundaries*, specifically:

> To review the sex offences in the common and statute law of England and Wales, and make recommendations that will: provide coherent and clear sex offences which protect individuals, especially children and the more vulnerable, from abuse and exploitation; enable abusers to be appropriately punished; and be fair and non-discriminatory in accordance with the ECHR and Human Rights Act.[2]

It is worth reiterating that there was a careful balancing act here. Not only was the review and the resultant SOA 2003 seeking to fulfil this brief but there was also a need to respond to societal perceptions of which kinds of sexual behaviours should be criminal and to stay, as far as possible, out of private consensual sexual relations.

Although not all the offences we have addressed in this textbook were established by the SOA 2003, those that came later, such as the amendments and new offences in the law regulating prostitution and pornography, were built on these same foundations of fairness, clarity, protection of the vulnerable and non-discrimination.

Coherent, clear offences

Bringing sexual offences under one Act has had the benefit of clarity, as sexual offences are, broadly speaking, those offences within the Act. This is of course slightly misleading as a number of offences can still be found in other pieces of legislation. Equally, as Chapter 10 has discussed, not all those convicted of sexual offences are regulated as sexual offenders despite being convicted of a sexual offence.

But for the first time in history our jurisdiction has an Act that brings most sexual offences under its auspices. The SOA 2003 is not necessarily accessible to the lay person, but the Explanatory Notes are commendably clear. The Act also contains a number of definitions to clarify the meaning of terms used within the Act such as "sexual", "penetration" and "touching". This said, the ongoing development of the *actus reus* and *mens rea* of the offences – particularly the development of conditional consent – is not something that could have been predicted from a reading of the Act. Rape and sexual assault, two common and widely known sexual offences, rely upon a lack of consent to transform otherwise legal acts into sexual offences. Consequently one would hope that consent was reasonably straightforward, but it has proved a significant problem since the enactment of the SOA 2003. Although the Act provided the first 'definition' of consent this has been heavily criticized and has proven difficult to apply in delineating the boundaries of consent. Defining consent was always going to be problematic. The history of rape and associated offences shows us that what has been meant by consent has always been disputed – so providing a perfect regime was perhaps an insurmountable task. The evolution of conditional consent has been the inevitable by-product of drawing tight parameters at sections 75–76 and it will be interesting to see how this concept continues to develop in case law.

There is general understanding, interest and cohesion on societal views about sexual offending. For example, undoubtedly we all agree an offence of rape is necessary and that the inclusion of oral and anal penetration in the offence reflects our modern conception. But there are ongoing debates about the *mens rea* of rape, although the general public usually do not appreciate they are engaging in debates about *mens rea* and evidence when they talk about an ability to give consent when drunk and whether "no always means no". Of course the public do not usually gain their knowledge about criminal offences from reading statutes and case law. Resultantly the Government, the police and the Crown Prosecution Service (CPS) have been at pains to try and explain the law in plain language, but the media also needs to take a lead. Debates about the efficacy of the law in dealing with sexual offending are, as Chapter 1 has explored, often only loosely related to reality. We will not reiterate here the misuse and misunderstanding of statistics by some sections of the media, but persistent misreporting continues to cause difficulties. The most obvious example is in the area of rape and consent. The issue was raised again in 2014 when the CPS issued new guidance to the police in assessing consent in rape cases. This was clearly communicated in a press release[3] but reported inaccurately in many newspapers – including the quality press – as (we paraphrase) "men must prove a woman said 'yes'".[4] Reporting a clear reiteration of the evidential presumptions as a significant shift in the law shows a clear gulf in understanding or the communication of the law by the media.

Public understanding of the law is then often a significant hurdle. This is not the fault of the general public, but this does not mean it is the fault of the law or the criminal justice system either. Both have been at pains to communicate the law clearly, from Government initiatives and campaigns highlighting key issues to accessible and plainly written judgments from the courts. This is not to say the blame for misinformation cannot be laid occasionally at the door of politicians or members of the criminal justice system[5] but the media plays a large part in misrepresenting these complicated issues.

Which protect individuals, especially children and the more vulnerable, from abuse and exploitation

Protection of the vulnerable was a central theme of the Act. Vulnerability has now become a slightly outdated term, casting victims of offences as weak and defenceless. If the Act was being conceived today vulnerability would perhaps be replaced with "exploitation" as this has become key to discussions regarding offences against those who cannot, or should not, be able to give legal consent. For example, as a result of many amendments the prostitution offences are now strongly focussed on preventing exploitation, particularly of children and trafficked women. This said, vulnerability still captures the ethos of the Act and how it has been interpreted. For example, our understanding of the threats posed to children have become heightened as numerous reports into grooming and exploitation have focussed public and political attention on how to better protect children.

At Chapter 1 we discussed the fact that the law does not operate in a vacuum. The law-making process, the exercise of the law by agencies of the state, in courtrooms, in sentencing and in the regulation of offending behaviour are all elements that come together to make our criminal justice system. Clearly steps have already been taken to improve the situation for vulnerable victims, the offences in place now capture the offending behaviour since amendments have been made to plug any identified gaps. The Sentencing Council have also provided a sentencing regime that takes into account exploitative behaviour and the police and Crown Prosecution Service have responded by improving their processes for dealing with victim reports and reaching charging decisions.

Children are often understood to be the most vulnerable in society and by sweeping away the old regime the SOA 2003 comprehensively expanded and clarified offences against children and other vulnerable parties. By establishing specific offences with more serious penalties the SOA 2003 has properly reflected the abuse against these parties. Perhaps the biggest change brought about by the Act was the introduction of the sets of offences at sections 5–9 and 9–12. Covering such a broad range of offending behaviour, the offences do protect children under the age of 16.

As part of this comprehensive regime we have a set of offences that criminalize sexual experimentation between children. The rationale for the offences at sections 9–12 being capable of being committed by children (via s13) was that there was no clear way of excluding child offenders who may be exploiting those of a similar age. This rationale is a poor one. Criminalizing consensual teenage experimentation makes a mockery of the law and carries a danger of criminalizing 'innocent' teenagers. Some other jurisdictions, for example Canada, make provision for this by allowing consent as a defence when the parties are of a similar age and no party is in a position of trust, dependency or authority over the other. Adopting this more flexible regime would not have simplified our already convoluted set of child sex offences, but it does demonstrate there is a method of targeting exploitative behaviour while protecting normal child sexual experimentation.

The current offences protecting abuse within the home, institutions and against those with a mental disorder do provide a strong regime. The offences at sections 25 and 26 are perhaps too broad, extending the meaning of "familial" to relationships most would not consider to fall under this definition and would perhaps be better placed under the abuse of a position of trust offences. Those offences at sections 16–19 are sound; the problem lies with the definition of position of trust and how prescriptive section 21 is. Post the numerous inquiries into grooming, this is now perhaps the time to revisit these offences and – very publicly – amend the meaning of a position of trust.

A robust set of sexual offences means nothing if the agencies of the criminal justice system fail to act on the claims of victims. Numerous reports have now made it clear that victims of institutional abuse have been let down not by the substantive law but by agents and agencies of the criminal justice system. In July 2015 Justice Lowell Goddard opened an independent public inquiry that will examine the way public bodies and other institutions handle their duty of care to protect children from sexual abuse. The inquiry will be wide ranging and will consider claims of a cover-up of historical child sex abuse involving public figures, including politicians. The need for accurate recording of abuse will also be part of the inquiry. As well as looking at mistakes made in the past, it will make recommendations for the future. It is not expected to report until 2020.[6]

There have been few difficulties with those offences that seek to protect individuals with mental disabilities. The numerous reports into institutional abuse that have focussed on offending against children do raise the question of how far offences against those with disabilities have gone unrecorded. It appears that for these offences, and those committed against children, the emphasis needs to be on continuing to encourage complainants to come forward and providing support for those who do.

Enable abusers to be appropriately punished

We have not had room in this textbook to fully address sentencing for sexual offences although the maximum sentences have been set out. As we have discussed in a number of chapters, any sentence handed down must reflect the harm caused by the offence and the offender's culpability and will normally be within the sentencing range established by the Sentencing Council.

Despite this you may have read about "soft sentences" given to sexual offenders. It is not uncommon for the media to pick up on sentences that appear to be wholly out of line with the severity of the crime. Sometimes these reports are based on a lack of information about the offence and its aggravating and mitigating features as media reports are rarely so detailed, nor (tabloid) journalists so well informed, that these aspects can be fully contextualized.[7] At other times their concerns are entirely justified, legally recognized and invariably taken to the appeal courts on this basis.

Suffice it to say the SOA 2003 increased the maximum sentences for many offences that had existed previously, has provided a sound sentencing regime for the offences it introduced and the Sentencing Council has kept the sentencing ranges up to date. That sexual offences often cause long-term psychological damage is now taken into account when sentencing.

As Chapter 10 has explored, punishment also extends into the community and the orders, notification requirements and general regulation of sexual offenders are punishment in the sense that they place significant restrictions on the lives of the offenders. However, they also seek to exercise control over sex offenders in the hope that this will prevent further offending in the future.

Be fair and non-discriminatory in accordance with the ECHR and Human Rights Act

Whether offences are fair and non-discriminatory is a very general statement and *Setting the Boundaries* viewed it in quite a limited sense, namely that:

> It was an important part of our task to recommend a law that was self-evidently fair to all sections of society, and which made no unnecessary distinctions on the basis of gender or sexual orientation. We saw this as a positive contribution to achieving a "safe, just and tolerant society".[8]

The homophobic offences and those offences that required male perpetrators and female victims had been largely swept away by the time of the review, although obvious disparities remained and gender neutrality has now been achieved in terms of the offences themselves. It is notable that the Act does, in many cases, delineate penetration (penile or otherwise) as a serious form of offending – both explicitly at section 1 and section 5 SOA 2003 and through the sentencing provision for offences such as section 4 and section 25. Undoubtedly a penetration offence is at the upper end of offending behaviour but the Act was very careful to make this penetration something that could be, where possible, committed by males and females. This is not to say there is not an inherently gendered bias to the Act. Section 71 has of course been subject to criticism as an offence set to criminalize homosexual men but, that said, a gender bias holds true for the majority of the offences, with men statistically more likely to be charged and convicted for any sexual offence. Gender is also being read back into the Act with the development of conditional consent suggesting gender can still be a decisive issue when considering whether consent is given freely. Gender neutrality has perhaps been better served by the advances made by the Gender Recognition Act 2004, which has recognized gender is not fixed at birth and the Marriage (Same Sex Couples) Act 2013 which has finally recognized same-sex marriage.

In terms of private sexual relations, although the jurisprudence of the European Court of Human Rights suggests our approach to regulating sexual activity between family members is not in violation of human rights, the offences themselves are out of line with the ethos of the Act. Sections 64 and 65 do not set out to protect the vulnerable. If offences are committed against a family member as a child we can hold them to account through sections 25 and 26. Equally if there is a question about whether the relationship is exploitative and consent has not been freely given then the offences at sections 1–4 should be charged. If neither party is victimized then it is difficult to justify criminalization. The same criticisms could be levelled at those offences that have the higher age of consent of 18. Although in light of the many abuses of trust that have come to light – and those that will undoubtedly be uncovered by the Goddard Inquiry – it seems likely our current approach would be viewed necessary and proportionate.

The Way Forward

Writing this textbook has been difficult: the law in this area is ever changing and detailing and reflecting on these changes has been a challenging task. Many of our criticisms of the law and the criminal justice system have been set out in the preceding chapters and below we detail how we believe the law and criminal justice system could respond to some general challenges faced. We are not reflecting on all problems that have emerged; this is a broad brush approach and you may have spotted issues that require attention or may arise as we move forward. As we have said, this area of the law is fast paced and the law cannot and should not stand still.

The law

Sexual offences often take place in private and the SOA 2003 has allowed for this by embracing internet-based offences. Thankfully the SOA 2003 was conceived when new media was well-established and as a relatively new Act the SOA 2003 has not suffered from the problems evident in older Acts such as the Protection of Children Act 1978 or the Offences Against the Person Act 1861, which were not enacted to deal with the online environment. The offences in the SOA 2003 are then largely up to date. This is not to say that technology will not overtake the Act; for example it already seems that streaming may be something the Act may not embrace (see Chapter 7). It is likely the judiciary will continue to take their expansive approach to interpretation to include emerging technologies, but ideally there needs to be a way to embrace this in the drafting of the legislation.

The substantive law is not always perfect and we have detailed some of the faults above and in the preceding chapters. Despite the myriad criticisms that can be levelled at the SOA 2003 and subsequent legislative measures, they have, in practicality, provided a workable regime. This said, criminalization is not always the answer. For example, we have taken a robust approach towards female genital mutilation. Clearly it is an evil perpetrated against, often, very young girls but this does not mean that the criminal law is the best way to tackle this problem. Sexual activity between consenting teenagers raises the same issues as something unlikely to be reported to the authorities as it is widely accepted by the wider community. Criminalizing these activities may then only make people less likely to report when they are aware of the harsh sanctions, which will often impact on those close to them. The law can be a blunt instrument and sometimes other methods may be better suited to tackling these hidden activities. Perhaps in these areas our resources are better deployed educating the relevant parties.

As pornography and prostitution occupy such a significant place in regulating sexual offending it would be useful to have a clear legislative regime – and one that is accessible to the public as these practices impinge upon everyday life for a good number of people. The law in these areas is unnecessarily complex, scattered across a number of Acts and incomprehensible to the lay person. Clarity would give individuals the opportunity to regulate their behaviour in line with the law.

The terminology in the SOA 2003 has also not been without criticism and we will not revisit here our discussions at earlier chapters. In terms of moving forward it is worth commenting on the definitions provided in the SOA 2003. Being so explicit in terminology is a new development and, in the past, terms such as "penetration" and "sexual" would have been left to the courts to interpret and including them in the Act was a nod to clarity. However these definitions have been rather ad hoc; where is the definition for "freedom" at section 74, for "underwear" at section 68 or for "sexual gratification" (at various sections)? Most of the definitions either rely on old case law (penetration) or seek to combat specific problems (the definition of sexual). Undoubtedly it was a sensible decision not to define every term as the law needs a measure of flexibility to work effectively. If offences are not going to fall rapidly out of date then they need to be amenable to social change. This is problematic as, at times, the SOA 2003 is very specific and at other points broad terms are left to the jury, which provide a measure of uncertainty in the law. In light of the case law that has been generated we cannot help feeling that terms such "underwear" and "breasts" were either ill thought out or should have been defined. In the future it would be helpful to have some commentary about why specific terms have been defined.

In many incidences the substantive law has shifted the burden to the police and CPS. By establishing unequivocal offences, such as those criminalizing sexual activity between teenagers and adult family members, it has been left to the discretion of these agencies to decide whether to proceed. This leads to uncertainty but makes the substantive law more dynamic. Unfortunately it also places a significant burden on agencies of the criminal justice system that are already under considerable pressure. It may be that this is the way forward for the law, that discretion is increasingly passed to these agencies. If that is the case then these agencies need the appropriate training and resources to enable them to properly make decisions. This is discussed further below.

The criminal justice system

One of the most significant shifts in the past ten years has been the greater focus placed on the victim by all agencies of the criminal justice system, from the 'victim-focused' approach recommended by the 2009 Rape Experience Review[9] to the changes brought about by the CPS discussed at Chapter 3.

The practice and policies informing police and CPS decision-making are constantly under review and are capable of being far more responsive to social issues than the substantive law. Although the Savile Inquiry has thrown the agencies of the criminal justice system into sharp relief, the lasting effect of the inquiry will be that the substantive law works within the existing criminal justice system and it is in this wider landscape that there is the most opportunity for change.

A number of lessons have been learnt in recent years that will inform how we proceed, including how offences are investigated. The review by Her Majesty's Inspectorate of Constabulary (HMIC) into the way allegations against Jimmy Savile were investigated identified a failure to connect different allegations made by different victims, which if they had been linked together may have resulted in appropriate action being taken.[10] Inquiries into child grooming in Rochdale and Oxford reached similar conclusions. The management of information in relation to allegations of sexual offences is therefore critical and requires a multi-agency approach.

The review by HMIC also recognized the cultural context of the time, which had a bearing on decisions made by the police. In November 2014 a further report was published, which analysed crime recording between 2012 and 2013. This showed that overall a quarter of sexual offences reported to the police were not being recorded as crimes.[11] However, the results were very mixed, with some forces showing very good recording of sexual crimes, whereas others were described as "unacceptably bad". Together with no-criming by the police and the victim credibility issues raised in earlier chapters this tells us that these gatekeepers to the criminal justice system are not always exercising their discretion appropriately. Further action needs to be taken to address this and recommendations have been made.[12]

The CPS have already taken steps to address mistakes made in prosecution policy, particularly concerning child sexual abuse, and these have been addressed at Chapter 4.

The shortcomings of the courts in providing appropriate support for victims of sexual offences, particularly rape, were addressed in the Stern Review[13] and processes have been tightened up. However there are indications that vulnerable victims may still not be receiving justice and further action is required.[14]

Society

We must not forget that the genesis of the law and how the agencies have approached this is in response to societal need. We addressed at Chapters 1 and 2 the relevance of social norms in shaping the law. The law bears a heavy burden in the area of sexual offending by looking to provide a regime that will only impinge upon behaviours that are widely accepted to be criminal or it will lose legitimacy. For example, if gross indecency or buggery were still offences in our jurisdiction the law would be widely condemned. In this respect both the SOA 2003 and the changes to law that have followed such as the Gender Recognition Act (2004) and the Marriage (Same Sex Couples) Act 2013 have kept up to date with social change.

The difficulty with the SOA 2003 is that, as statutory law, it needs be certain enough to allow individuals to regulate their behaviour but also be sufficiently flexible to take account of social change. Although *Setting the Boundaries* made clear that the Act was conceived by taking account of societal perceptions of criminal behaviour these have, and will continue to, change. For example, jury trials such as *Peacock*, *Walsh*[15] and *Lock*,[16] do provide some insight into the public mind, suggesting there may now be social acceptance of some consensual activities that are criminalized. The mainstream success of sadomasochism in films and books also tells us that this is not something the general public is adverse to. This suggests both *Brown*[17] and the criminalization of the possession of mild sadomasochistic images may now be out of date. Here perhaps we need to return to the suggestions of the Law Commission and raise the level of injury to which one can consent to grievous bodily harm to reflect current attitudes and sexual practices. These offences are of course regulated by offences outside of the SOA 2003 and the Act itself has stood up surprisingly well to social shifts.

But how can we ensure the law continues to keep up to date with social norms? In a practical sense this is the purpose of the criminal justice system where the police, CPS and the courts can refuse to either proceed or convict where the 'criminal' behaviour is socially excusable. This said the substantive law should, as far as possible, be kept under review and the Law Commission and agencies of the criminal justice system usually do a good job of this.

The relationship between the law and society is symbiotic and, while the law needs to keep up with societal change, so too does society need to keep up with the realities of offending behaviour. For example, the ready acceptance of rape myths (see Chapter 3) and a lack of recognition of female sexual offenders (see Chapter 2) demonstrate there are still barriers to justice in some areas. The SOA 2003 did an admirable job in addressing the difficult issues of consent and gender neutrality, but if these offences and offenders are not appropriately responded to then we will be stuck with our old (out-of-date) conceptions of offences and offenders.

Globalization

The law of England and Wales cannot operate in a vacuum. It is becoming increasingly evident that the law needs to address the globalization of offending, especially in relation to children and vulnerable adults. Many offences do now have an international perspective and the Modern Slavery Act 2015 is a recent attempt to deal with the world-wide issue of trafficking for the purpose of exploitation, sexual or otherwise. The controls on travel by sex offenders discussed in Chapters 9 and 10 also recognize that we have a duty to protect the vulnerable abroad and not just our own citizens. Further international cooperation between agencies in different countries will be crucial in order to address some of these issues in the future.

Conclusion

The law is constantly changing, and it needs to do so in order to keep up with modern values and our understanding of offending behaviour. It must respond to new technologies as they arise, or perhaps anticipate them. It must respond to changes in social values and shifts in morality. Not only must the substantive law be alive to these shifts but the agencies of the criminal justice system also need to be flexible and adapt to new ideas and attitudes, particularly to the growing awareness of the extent of abuse of the vulnerable in our society. New ideas of how to deal with sex offenders will no doubt be piloted and evaluated and will impact on how we manage offenders. Taking everything into account this is a colossal task and the effective management of sexual offending can only be achieved by constant vigilance on behalf of the law and all agencies of the criminal justice system.

Notes

1 Home Office, *Setting the Boundaries: Reforming the Law on Sex Offences* London: Home Office (2000).
2 Setting the Boundaries, para 0.3.
3 *CPS and Police focus on Consent at first joint National Rape Conference*, January 28, 2015, Accessible at http://www.cps.gov.uk/news/latest_news/cps_and_police_focus_on_consent_at_first_joint_national_rape_conference.
4 Among other reports; 'Men must prove a woman said Yes' *Daily Telegraph* January 29, 2015; 'Should men have to prove that a woman said yes?' *Express* January 30, 2015; 'Men must prove that women said yes to avoid rape charge' *Daily Telegraph* January 29, 2015; 'Men will have to prove they have consent under DPP's tough new rape guidelines' *Independent* January 29, 2015.
5 For example MP Ken Clarke made comments suggesting date rape was not always rape in the social sense, for which he later apologized. MP George Galloway was criticized for suggesting Julian Assange (accused at the time of sexual assault) had merely exercised "bad sexual etiquette". Comments made by the judiciary have also been considered at Chapter 3.
6 See 'Child sexual abuse inquiry could last until 2020', July 9, 2015, BBC news website, http://www.bbc.co.uk/news/uk-33442588.
7 There is significant variance in the quality of media reportage on crime stories. For further discussion see J. Rowbotham, K. Stevenson and S. Pegg *Crime News in Modern Britain* Hampshire: Palgrave Macmillan (2013).
8 *Setting the Boundaries*, para 1.1.10.
9 S. Payne 'Redefining Justice: Addressing the individual needs of victims and witnesses' London: Home Office (2009)
10 HMIC *"Mistakes Were Made", HMIC's Review into Allegations and Intelligence Material Concerning Jimmy Savile between 1964 and 2012* London: HMIC (March 2013). Accessible at http://www.justiceinspectorates.gov.uk/hmic/media/review-into-allegations-and-intelligence-material-concerning-jimmy-savile.pdf.
11 HMIC *Crime-recording: Making the Victim Count* London: HMIC (November 2014). Accessible at https://www.justiceinspectorates.gov.uk/hmic/publications/crime-recording-making-the-victim-count.
12 The post-inspection review on the child protection work by South Yorkshire Police post the Rochdale grooming case makes clear South Yorkshire Police have taken steps to improve their management and responses to child sexual exploitation but more still needs to be done. HMIC *National Child Protection Inspection Post Inspection Review South Yorkshire Police 28 April – 1 May 2015* London: HMIC (July 2015). Accessible at http://www.justiceinspectorates.gov.uk/hmic/wp-content/uploads/south-yorkshire-national-child-protection-inspection-revisit.pdf.

13 Baroness Stern *A Report by Baroness Vivien Stern CBE of an Independent Review into How Rape Complaints are Handled by Public Authorities in England and Wales* Home Office: London (2010).

14 M. Hester *From Report to Court: Rape and the Criminal Justice System in the North East* Bristol: University of Bristol (2013); O. Smith and T. Skinner 'Observing court responses to victims of rape and sexual assault' *Feminist Criminology* (2012) 7(4) pp. 298–326.

15 Both unreported (2012) but discussed in Chapter 7.

16 Unreported (2012) but discussed in Chapter 3.

17 *R. v Brown* [1993] 2 All ER 75, HL.

Index